Grant Allen

Paris

Grant Allen

Paris

ISBN/EAN: 9783337428549

Printed in Europe, USA, Canada, Australia, Japan

Cover: Foto ©ninafisch / pixelio.de

More available books at **www.hansebooks.com**

GRANT ALLEN'S HISTORICAL GUIDES

PARIS

LONDON: GRANT RICHARDS
9 HENRIETTA STREET
COVENT GARDEN
1897

INTRODUCTION

THE object and plan of these Historical Handbooks is somewhat different from that of any other guides at present before the public. They do not compete or clash with such existing works; they are rather intended to supplement than to supplant them. My purpose is not to direct the stranger through the streets and squares of an unknown town towards the buildings or sights which he may desire to visit; still less is it my design to give him practical information about hotels, cab fares, omnibuses, tramways, and other every-day material conveniences. For such details, the traveller must still have recourse to the trusty pages of his Baedeker, his Joanne, or his Murray. I desire rather to supply the tourist who wishes to use his travel as a means of culture with such historical and antiquarian information as will enable him to understand, and therefore to enjoy, the architecture, sculpture, painting, and minor arts of the towns he visits. In one word, it is my object to give the reader in a very compendious form the result of all those inquiries which have naturally suggested themselves to my own mind during thirty-five years of foreign travel, the solution of which has cost myself a good deal of research, thought, and labour, beyond the facts which I could find in the ordinary handbooks.

For several years past I have devoted myself to collecting and arranging material for a set of books to embody the idea

I had thus entertained. I earnestly hope they may meet a want on the part of tourists, especially Americans, who, so far as my experience goes, usually come to Europe with an honest and reverent desire to learn from the Old World whatever of value it has to teach them, and who are prepared to take an amount of pains in turning their trip to good account which is both rare and praiseworthy. For such readers I shall call attention at times to other sources of information.

These guide-books will deal more particularly with the Great Towns where objects of art and antiquity are numerous. In every one of them, the general plan pursued will be somewhat as follows. First will come the inquiry why a town ever gathered together at all at that particular spot—what induced the aggregation of human beings rather there than elsewhere. Next, we shall consider why that town grew to social or political importance and what were the stages by which it assumed its present shape. Thirdly, we shall ask why it gave rise to that higher form of handicraft which we know as Art, and towards what particular arts it especially gravitated. After that, we shall take in detail the various strata of its growth or development, examining the buildings and works of art which they contain in historical order, and, as far as possible, tracing the causes which led to their evolution. In particular, we shall lay stress upon the origin and meaning of each structure as an organic whole, and upon the allusions or symbols which its fabric embodies.

A single instance will show the method upon which I intend to proceed better than any amount of general description. A church, as a rule, is built over the body or relics of a particular saint, in whose special honour it was originally erected. That saint was usually one of great local importance at the moment of its erection, or was peculiarly implored against plague, foreign enemies, or some other pressing and dreaded misfortune. In dealing with such a church, then, I endeavour to show what were the circumstances which led to its erection, and what memorials of these circumstances it still retains. In other cases it may derive its origin from some special monastic body—Benedictine, Dominican, Franciscan—and may therefore be full of the peculiar symbolism and historical allusion of the order who founded it. Wherever I have to deal with such a church, I try as far as possible to exhibit the effect which its origin had upon its architecture and decoration; to trace the image of the patron saint in sculpture or stained glass throughout the fabric; and to set forth the connection of the whole design with time and place, with order and purpose. In short, instead of looking upon monuments of the sort mainly as the product of this or that architect, I look upon them rather as material embodiments of the spirit of the age—crystallizations, as it were, in stone and bronze, in form and colour, of great popular enthusiasms.

By thus concentrating attention on what is essential and important in a town, I hope to give in a comparatively short space, though with inevitable conciseness, a fuller account than is usually given of the chief architectural and monumental works of the principal art-cities. In dealing with Paris, for example, I shall have little to say about such modern constructions as the Champs Elysées or the Eiffel Tower; still less, of course, about the Morgue, the Catacombs, the waxworks of the Musée Grévin, and the celebrated Excursion in the Paris Sewers. The space thus saved from vulgar wonders I shall hope to devote to fuller explanation of Notre-Dame and the Sainte Chapelle, of the mediæval carvings or tapestries of Cluny, and of the pictures or sculptures in the galleries of the Louvre. Similarly in Florence, whatever I save from description of the Cascine and even of the beautiful Viale dei Colli (where explanation is needless and word-painting superfluous), I shall give up to the Bargello, the Uffizi, and the Pitti Palace. The passing life of the moment does not enter into my plan; I regard each town I endeavour to illustrate mainly as a museum of its own history.

For this reason, too, I shall devote most attention in every case to what is locally illustrative, and less to what is merely adventitious and foreign. In Paris, for instance, I shall have more to say about truly Parisian art and history, as embodied in St. Denis, the Île de la Cité, and the shrine of Ste. Geneviève, than about the Egyptian and Assyrian collections of the Louvre. In Florence, again, I shall deal rather with the Etruscan remains, with Giotto and Fra Angelico, with the Duomo and the Campanile, than with the admirable Memlincks and Rubenses of the Uffizi and the Pitti, or with the beautiful Van der Goes of the Hospital of Santa Maria. In Bruges and Brussels, once more, I shall be especially Flemish; in the Rhine towns, Rhenish; in Venice, Venetian. I shall assign a due amount of space, indeed, to the foreign collections, but I shall call attention chiefly to those monuments or objects which are of entirely local and typical value.

As regards the character of the information given, it will be mainly historical, antiquarian, and, above all, explanatory. I am not a connoisseur—an adept in the difficult modern science of distinguishing the handicraft of various masters, in painting or sculpture, by minute signs and delicate inferential processes. In such matters, I shall be well content to follow the lead of the most authoritative experts. Nor am I an art-critic—a student versed in the technique of the studios and the dialect of the modelling-room. In such matters, again, I shall attempt little more than to accept the general opinion of the most discriminative judges. What I aim at rather is to expound the history and meaning of each work—to put the intelligent reader in such a position that he may judge for himself of the æsthetic beauty and success of the object before him. To recognise the fact that this is a Perseus and Andromeda, that a St. Barbara enthroned, the other an obscure episode in the legend of St. Philip, is not art-criticism, but it is often an almost indispensable prelude to the formation of a right and sound judgment. We must know what the artist was trying to represent before we can feel sure what measure of success he has attained in his representation.

For the general study of Christian art, alike in architecture, sculpture, and painting, no treatises are more useful for the tourist to carry with him for constant reference than Mrs. Jameson's *Sacred and Legendary Art*, and *Legends of the Madonna* (London, Longmans). For works of Italian art, both in Italy and elsewhere, Kugler's *Italian Schools of Painting* is an invaluable *vade-mecum*. These books should be carried about by everybody everywhere. Other works of special and local importance will occasionally be noticed under each particular city, church, or museum.

I cannot venture to hope that handbooks containing such a mass of facts as these will be wholly free from errors and misstatements, above all in early editions. I can only beg those who may detect any such to point them out, without unnecessary harshness, to the author, care of the publisher, and if possible to assign reasons for any dissentient opinion.

CONTENTS

	PAGE
INTRODUCTION	3
HOW TO USE THESE GUIDE-BOOKS	10
ORIGINS OF PARIS	11
I THE ÎLE DE LA CITÉ	16
A. The Palais de Justice and the Sainte Chapelle .	17
B. Notre-Dame	22
Map of Historic Paris	33
II THE LEFT OR SOUTH BANK	34
A. The Roman Palace and the Musée de Cluny .	35
B. The Hill of Ste. Geneviève	55
III RENAISSANCE PARIS (THE LOUVRE) . . .	62
A. The Fabric	64
B. The Collections	71
I. Paintings	72
II. Sculpture	153
1. Antique Sculpture	154
2. Renaissance Sculpture . . .	168
3. Modern Sculpture	187
III. The Smaller Collections. . . .	189
IV THE NORTH BANK (RIVE DROITE) . . .	197
A. The Core of the Right Bank	198
B. The Outer Ring of Louis XIV. . . .	208
V THE FAUBOURG ST. GERMAIN	213
VI ST. DENIS	230
VII THE OUTER RING, ETC.	246

HOW TO USE THESE GUIDE-BOOKS

THE portions of this book intended to be read at leisure **at home,** *before proceeding to explore each town or monument, are enclosed in brackets* [*thus*]. *The portion relating to each* **principal object** *should be quietly read and digested* **before** *a visit, and referred to again afterwards. The portion to be read* **on the spot** *is made as brief as possible, and is printed in large legible type, so as to be easily read in the dim light of churches, chapels, and galleries. The* **key-note** *words are printed in* **bold type,** *to catch the eye. Where objects are numbered, the numbers used are always those of the latest official catalogues.*

Baedeker's Guides are so printed that each principal portion can be detached entire from the volume. The traveller who uses Baedeker is advised to carry in his pocket one such portion, referring to the place he is then visiting, together with the plan of the town, while carrying this book in his hand. These Guides do **not** *profess to supply practical information.*

Individual works of merit are distinguished by an asterisk (***); *those of very exceptional interest and merit have two asterisks.* **Nothing** *is noticed in this book which does not seem to the writer worthy of attention.*

See little at a time, and see it thoroughly. **Never** *attempt to "do" any place or any monument. By following strictly the order in which objects are noticed in this book, you will gain a conception of the* **historical evolution** *of the town which you cannot obtain if you go about looking at churches and palaces hap-hazard. The order is arranged, not quite chronologically, but on a definite* **plan,** *which greatly facilitates comprehension of the subject.*

ORIGINS OF PARIS

PARIS is **not**, like Rome, London, Lyons, **an inevitable city.** It does not owe its distinctive place, like New York, Chicago, San Francisco, Melbourne, to natural position alone. Rather does it resemble Madrid or Berlin in being in great part of artificial administrative origin. It stands, no doubt, upon an important navigable river, the Seine; but its position upon that river, though near the head of navigation, when judged by the standard of early times, is not exactly necessary or commanding. Rouen in mediæval days, Havre at the present moment, are the real ports of the Seine. The site of Paris is in itself nothing more than one among the many little groups of willow-clad alluvial islets which are frequent along the upper reaches of the river. The modern city owes its special development as a town, first to its Roman conquerors, then to its bridges, next to its mediæval counts, last of all to the series of special accidents by which those counts developed at last into kings of the nascent kingdom of France, and inheritors of the traditions of the Frankish sovereigns. It is thus in large part a royal residential town, depending mainly for prosperity upon its kings, its nobles, its courts of justice, its parliaments, its university, its clergy, and its official classes; comparatively little, till quite recent times, upon the energy and industry of its individual citizens. We say, as a rule, that Paris is the capital of France; it would be truer to say that France is the country which has grouped itself under the rulers of Paris.

The name itself points back to the antiquity of some human aggregation upon this particular spot. It is **the name of a tribe,** *not* that of their capital. The Parisii were a Celtic people of comparatively small importance, who occupied the banks of the Seine at the period of the Roman conquest. Their town or stronghold, Lutetia, called distinctively Lutetia Parisiorum (Lutetia of the Parisii), was situated, says Cæsar, "in an island of the river Sequana"—the same which is now called the Île de la Cité. Two adjacent islands of the same alluvial type have long since coalesced to form the Île St. Louis : a fourth, the Île Louviers, is at present enclosed in the mainland of the northern bank by the modern quays.

This **stockaded island village** of the Parisii was conquered by the Romans in B.C. 53. Under Roman rule, it remained at first an unimportant place, the really large towns of Gaul at that time being Arles, Nîmes, Marseilles, Bordeaux, and Lyons. In the north, Treviri was the chief Roman settlement. Towards the end of the Roman period, however, Paris seems to have increased in importance, and overflowed a little from the island to the south bank. The town owed its rapid rise, no doubt, to the two Roman bridges which here crossed the two branches of the Seine, probably on the same sites as the modern Petit-Pont and Pont Notre-Dame. The river formed its highway. Constantius Chlorus, who lived in Gaul from A.D. 292 to 306, is supposed to have built in the faubourg on the south side the palace of the Thermes, which now forms a part of the Museum of Cluny. Julian certainly inhabited that palace in 360. The town was known as Lutetia almost as long as the Roman power lasted ; but after the Frankish invasion (and even in late Roman times), the name of the tribe superseded that of the ancient fortress : Lutetia became known as Paris, the stronghold of the Parisii, just in the same way as the Turones gave their name to Tours, the Ambiani to Amiens, and the Senones to Sens.

After the occupation of Gaul by Clovis (Hlodwig), Paris sank for a time to the position of **a mere provincial town.** The Merwing (or Merovingian) kings, the successors of Clovis, resided as a rule at Orleans or Soissons. The Frankish emperors and kings of the line of Charlemagne, again (the Karlings or Carlovingians), held their court for the most part at Aix-la-Chapelle. The town by the Seine was so completely neglected under later sovereigns of the Karling line (who were practically Germans), that during the invasions of the Northmen from 841 to 885 it was left entirely to its own resources. But its count,

Eudes, defended it so bravely from the northern pirates, that he became the real founder of the French State, the first inaugurator of France as a separate country, distinct from the Empire. His provincial city grew into the kernel of a mediæval monarchy. From his time on, Paris emerges as the capital of a struggling kingdom, small in extent at first, but gradually growing till it attained the size which it now possesses. The Teutonic King of the Franks was reduced for a time to the rocky fortress of Laon; the **Count of Paris** became Duke of the French, and then **King of France** in the modern acceptation.

As the kingdom grew (absorbing by degrees Flanders, Normandy, Aquitaine, Provence, Champagne, and Burgundy), the capital grew with it; its limits at various times will be more fully described in succeeding pages. From first to last, however, Paris preserved its character as rather the official and administrative centre than the commercial emporium. Nevertheless, even under the Romans, its symbol was a ship. Its double debt to the river and the monarchy is well symbolised by its mediæval coat of arms, which consists of a vessel under full sail, surmounted by the *fleur de lis* of the French kings, and crested above by a mural crown.

So few remnants of **Roman Paris** exist at our day, that we will begin our survey with the **Île de la Cité**, the nucleus of the mediæval town, leaving the scanty earlier relics to be noted later on in their proper places. But before we proceed to this detailed description, two other facts of prime importance in the history of old Paris must be briefly mentioned, because without them the character of the most ancient buildings in the city cannot be properly understood. These two facts—even if mythical, yet facts none the less—are the histories of the two great patron saints of the early burghers. It is not too much to say that to the mediæval Parisian, Paris appeared far less as the home of the kings or the capital of the kingdom than as the **shrine of St. Denis** and the **city of Ste. Geneviève**.

Universal tradition relates that **St. Denis** was the first preacher of Christianity in Paris. He is said to have suffered martyrdom there in the year 270. As the apostle and evangelist of the town, he was deeply venerated from the earliest times; but later legend immensely increased his vogue and his sanctity. On the one hand, he was identified with Dionysius the Areopagite; on the other hand, he was said to have walked after his decapitation, bearing his head in his hand, from his place of martyrdom on the hill of Montmartre (Mons Martyrum), near the site from which the brand-new church of the Sacré Cœur now overlooks the vastly greater modern city, to a spot two miles away, where a pious lady buried him. On this spot, a chapel is said to have been erected as early as A.D. 275, within five years of his martyrdom; later, Ste. Geneviève, assisted by the people of Paris, raised a church over his remains on the same site. In the reign of King Dagobert, the sacred body was removed to the **Abbey of St. Denis** (see later), which became the last resting-place of the kings of France. It is probable that the legend of the saint having carried his head from Montmartre arose from a misunderstanding of images of the decapitated bishop, bearing his severed head in his hands as a symbol of the mode of his martyrdom; but the tale was universally accepted as true in mediæval days, and is still so accepted by devout Parisians. Images of St. Denis, in episcopal robes, carrying his mitred head in his hands, may be looked for on all the ancient buildings of the city. St. Denis thus represents the earliest patron saint of Paris—the saint of the primitive Church and of the period of persecution.

The second patron saint of the city—the saint of the Frankish conquest—is locally and artistically even more important. Like Jeanne d'Arc, she touches the strong French sentiment of patriotism. **Ste. Geneviève**, a peasant girl of Nanterre (on the outskirts of Paris), was born in 421, during the stormy times of the barbarian irruptions. When she was seven years old, St. Germain, of Auxerre (of whom more will be said under the church of St. Germain l'Auxerrois), on his way to Britain, saw *la pucellette Geneviève*, and became aware, by divine premonition, of her predestined glory. When she had grown to woman's estate, and was a shepherdess at Nanterre, a barbarian leader (identified in the legend with Attila, King of the Huns) threatened to lay siege to the little city. But Geneviève, warned of God, addressed the people, begging them not to leave their homes, and assuring them of the miraculous protection of heaven. And indeed, as it turned out, the barbarians, without any obvious reason, changed their line of march, and avoided Paris. Again, when Childeric, the father of Clovis, invested the city, the people suffered greatly from sickness and famine. Then Geneviève took command of the boats which were sent up stream to Troyes for succour, stilled by her prayers the frequent tempests, and brought the ships back laden with provisions. After the Franks had captured Paris, Ste. Geneviève carried on Roman traditions into the Frankish court; she was instrumental in converting Clovis and his wife Clotilde; and when she died, at eighty-nine, a natural death, she was buried by the side of her illustrious disciples. The history of her body will be given at length when we come to examine her church on the South Side, commonly called the Panthéon; but her image may frequently be recognised on early buildings by the figure of a devil at her side, endeavouring in vain (as was his wont) to extinguish her lighted taper—the taper, no doubt, of Roman Christianity, which she did not allow to be quenched by the Frankish invaders.

Round these two sacred personages the whole art and history of early Paris continually cluster. The beautiful figure of the simple peasant enthusiast, Ste. Geneviève, in particular, has largely coloured Parisian ideas and Parisian sympathies. Her shrine still attracts countless thousands of the faithful.

Having premised these facts, we are now in a position to commence our survey of the city. I strongly recommend the reader to visit the various objects of interest in the exact order here prescribed. Otherwise, he will not understand the various allusions to points already elucidated. But no necessary organic connection exists between the **collections of the Louvre** and the town in which they are housed. Therefore, they may be visited off and on at any time (see Introduction to the Collections in Part III). **Utilize rainy days in the Galleries of the Louvre.**

I
THE ÎLE DE LA CITÉ

THE Île de la Cité, the oldest Paris, consisted in the Middle Ages of a labyrinth of narrow and tortuous lanes, now entirely replaced by large and stately modern official buildings. In Roman and Frankish times, it comprised the whole of the town, save a small suburb extending as far as the present Museum of Cluny, on the South Side. Among its sunless alleys, however, in later mediæval days, numerous churches raised their heads, of which **Notre-Dame** and the **Sainte Chapelle** alone now remain; while others, dedicated to the oldest local saints, such as Ste. Geneviève-des-Ardents, St. Éloy, and St. Germain-le-Vieux, have been entirely destroyed. The west extremity of the island was formerly occupied by the old **Royal Palace,** parts of which still survive, included in the buildings of the modern Palais de Justice. On the east end stood the cathedral of Notre-Dame, with the episcopal palace in its rear; while, close by, rose the earliest hospital in Europe, the Hôtel-Dieu, said to have been originally founded by Clovis, and now represented by a vastly larger modern building on a different site. As the burgesses began to shift their homes to the quarters north of the Seine, in the twelfth and thirteenth centuries, the Cité was gradually given over to the clergy. The kings also removed from the Palace of the Capets to their new residences on the North Bank (Bastille, Hôtel Saint-Paul, old castle of the Louvre), and gave up their island mansion to the Parlement or Supreme Court, since which time it has been commonly known as the **Palais de Justice,** and extensively modernised. At the present day, the Cité has become the head-quarters of Law, Police, and Religion, and is almost entirely occupied by huge official structures, which cover enormous areas, and largely conceal its primitive character. It still contains, however, the most precious mediæval monuments of Paris.

At least **two days** should be devoted to the Île de la Cité; one to the Palace and the Sainte Chapelle, another to the Cathedral. Do not attempt to see them both together.]

A. THE PALAIS DE JUSTICE AND THE SAINTE CHAPELLE

Go along the Rue de Rivoli as far as the Square of the Tour St. Jacques. If driving, alight here. Turn down the Place du Châtelet to your right. In front is the pretty modern fountain of the Châtelet : right, the Théâtre du Châtelet ; left, the Opéra Comique. The bridge which faces you is the Pont-au-Change, so-called from the money-changers' and jewellers' booths which once flanked its wooden predecessor (the oldest in Paris), as they still do the Rialto at Venice, and the Ponte Vecchio at Florence.

Stand by the right-hand corner of the bridge before crossing it. In front is the Île de la Cité. The square, dome-crowned building opposite you to the left is the modern Tribunal de Commerce ; beyond it leftward lie the Marché-aux-Fleurs and the long line of the Hôtel-Dieu, above which rise the towers and spire of Notre-Dame. In front, to the right, the vast block of buildings broken by towers forms part of the Palais de Justice, the ancient **Palace of the French kings,** begun by Hugues Capet. The square tower to the left in this block is the Tour de l'Horloge. Next, to the right, come the two round towers of the Conciergerie, known respectively as the Tour de César and the Tour de Montgomery. The one beyond them, with battlements, is the Tour d'Argent. It was in the Conciergerie that Marie Antoinette, Robespierre, and many other victims of the Revolution were imprisoned.

These mediæval towers, much altered and modernized, are now almost all that remains of the old Palace, which, till after the reign of Louis IX (St. Louis), formed the residence of the Kings of France. Charles VII gave it in 1431 to the Parlement or Supreme Court. Ruined by fires and rebuilding, it now consists for the most part of masses of irregular recent edifices. The main modern façade fronts the Boulevard du Palais.

Cross the bridge. The Tour de l'Horloge on your right, at the corner of the Boulevard du Palais, contains the oldest public clock in France (1370). The figures of Justice and Piety by its side were originally designed by Germain Pilon, but are now replaced by copies. Walk round the Palais by the quay along the north branch of the Seine till you come to the Rue de Harlay. Turn there to your left, towards the handsome and imposing modern façade of this side of the Palais de Justice. The interior is unworthy a visit. The Rue de Harlay forms the westernmost end of the original Île de la Cité. The prow-shaped extremity of the modern island has been artificially produced by embanking the sites of two or three minor islets. The Place Dauphine, which occupies the greater part of this modern extension, was built in 1608; it still affords a characteristic example of the domestic Paris of the period before Baron Haussmann. Continue along the quay as far as the Pont-Neuf, so as to gain an idea of the extent of the Île de la Cité in this direction. The centre of the Pont-Neuf is occupied by an equestrian statue of Henri IV, first of the Bourbon kings. Its predecessor was erected in 1635, and was destroyed to make cannon during the great Revolution. Louis XVIII re-erected it. From this point you can gain a clear idea of the two branches of the Seine as they unite at the lower end of the Île de la Cité. To your right, looking westward, you also obtain a fine view of the Colonnade of the Old Louvre, with the south-western gallery, and the more modern buildings of the Museum behind it. (See later.)

Now, walk along the southern quay of the island, round the remainder of the Palais de Justice, as far as the Boulevard du Palais. There turn to your left, and go in at the first door of the Palace on the left (undeterred by sentries) into the court of **the Sainte Chapelle**, the only important relic now remaining of the home of Saint Louis. You may safely neglect the remainder of the building.

[The thirteenth century (age of the Crusades) was a period of profound religious enthusiasm throughout Europe. Conspicuous among its devout soldiers was Louis IX, afterwards canonized as **St. Louis.** The saintly king purchased from Baldwin, Emperor of Constantinople, the veritable **Crown of Thorns,** and a fragment of the **True Cross**—paying for these relics an immense sum of money. Having become possessed of such invaluable and sacred objects, Louis desired to have them housed with suitable magnificence. He therefore entrusted one Pierre de Montereau with the task of building a splendid chapel (within the precincts of his palace), begun in 1245, and finished three years later, immediately after which the king set out on his Crusade. The monument thus breathes throughout the ecstatic piety of the mystic king; it was consecrated in 1248, in the name of the Holy Crown and the Holy Cross, by Eudes de Châteauroux, Bishop of Tusculum and papal legate.

Three things should be noted about the Sainte Chapelle. (1) It is a **chapel,** not a church; therefore it consists (practically) of a choir alone, without nave or transepts. (2) It is the **domestic Chapel of the Royal Palace.** (3) It is, above all things, the **Shrine of the Crown of Thorns.** These three points must be constantly borne in mind in examining the building.

Erected later than Notre-Dame, it represents the pointed style of the middle of the thirteenth century, and is singularly pure and uniform throughout. Secularized at the Revolution, it fell somewhat into decay; but was judiciously restored by Viollet-le-Duc and others. The "Messe Rouge," or "Messe du St. Esprit," is still celebrated here once yearly, on the re-opening of the courts after the autumn vacation, but no other religious services take place in the building. The Crown of Thorns and the piece of the True Cross are now preserved in the Treasury at Notre Dame.

Open daily, free, except Mondays, 11 to 4 or 5. Choose **a very bright day** to visit it.]

Examine the **exterior** in detail from the court on the south side. More even than most Gothic buildings, the Sainte Chapelle is supported entirely by its massive piers, the wall being merely used for enclosure, and consisting for the most part of lofty windows. As in most French Gothic buildings, the choir terminates in a round apse, whereas English cathedrals have usually a square end. The beautiful light **flèche** or spire in the centre has been restored. Observe the graceful leaden angel, holding a cross, on the summit of the *chevet* or round apse. To see **the façade,** stand well back opposite it, when you can observe that the chapel is built in four main stories,—those, namely, of the Lower Church or crypt, of the Upper Church, of the great rose window (with later flamboyant tracery), and of the gable-end, partially masked by an open parapet studded with the royal fleurs-de-lis of France. The Crown of Thorns surrounds the two pinnacles which flank the fourth story.

The chapel consists of a lower and an upper church. The **Lower Church** is a mere crypt, which was employed for the servants of the royal family. Its portal has in its tympanum (or triangular space in the summit of the arch) the Coronation of the Virgin, and on its centre pillar a good figure of the Madonna and Child. Enter the Lower Church. It is low, and has pillars supporting the floor above. In the polychromatic decoration of the walls and pillars, notice the frequent repetition of the royal lilies of France, combined with the three castles of Castille, in honour of Blanche of Castille, the mother of St. Louis.

Mount to ****the Upper Chapel** (or Sainte Chapelle proper) by the small spiral staircase in the corner. This soaring pile was the oratory where the royal family and court attended service; its gorgeousness bespeaks its origin and nature. It glows like a jewel. First go out of the door and examine the **exterior and doorway** of the chapel. Its platform was directly approached in early times from the Palace. The centre pillar bears a fine figure of Christ. In the tympanum (as over the principal doorway of almost every important church in Paris and the district) is a relief of the Last Judgment. Below stands St. Michael with his scales, weighing the souls; on either side is depicted the Resurrection, with the Angels of the Last Trump. Above, in the second tier, is Christ, holding up His hands with the marks of the nails, as a sign of mercy to the redeemed: to R and L of Him angels display the Crown of Thorns and the True Cross, to contain which sacred relics the chapel was built.

Extreme L kneels the Blessed Virgin; extreme R, Sainte Geneviève. This scene of the Last Judgment was adapted with a few alterations from that above the central west door of Notre-Dame, the Crown of Thorns in particular being here significantly substituted for the three nails and spear. The small lozenge reliefs to R and L of the portal are also interesting. Those to the L represent in a very naïve manner God the Father creating the world, sun and moon, light, plants, animals, man, etc. Those to the R give the story of Genesis, Cain and Abel, the Flood, the Ark, Noah's Sacrifice, Noah's Vine, etc.; the subjects of all which the visitor can easily recognise, and is strongly recommended to identify for himself.

The **interior** consists almost entirely of large and lofty windows, with magnificent stained glass, in large part ancient. The piers which divide the windows and alone support the graceful vault of the roof, are provided with statues of the twelve apostles, a few of them original. Each bears his well-known symbol. Spell them out if possible. Beneath the windows, in the quatrefoils of the arcade, are enamelled glass mosaics representing the martyrdoms of the saints—followers of Christ, each wearing his own crown of thorns: a pretty conceit wholly in accord with St. Louis's ecstatic type of piety. Conspicuous among them are St. Denis carrying his head, St. Sebastian pierced with arrows, St. Stephen stoned, St. Lawrence on his gridiron, etc. Examine and identify each separately. The apse (formerly separated from the body of the building by a rood-screen, now destroyed) contains the vacant base of the high altar, behind which stands an arcaded tabernacle, now empty, in whose shrine were once preserved the Crown of Thorns, the fragment of the True Cross, and other relics. Amongst them in later times was included the skull of St. Louis himself in a golden reliquary. Two angels at the summit of the large centre arch of the arcade bear a representation of the Crown of Thorns in their hands. Above the tabernacle rises a canopy or baldacchino, approached by two spiral staircases; from its platform St. Louis and his successors, the kings of France, were in the habit of exhibiting with their own hands the actual relics themselves once a year to the faithful. The golden reliquary in which the sacred objects were contained was melted down in the

Revolution. The small window with bars to your R, as you face the high altar, was placed there by the superstitious and timid Louis XI, in order that he might behold the elevation of the Host and the sacred relics without being exposed to the danger of assassination. The visitor should also notice the inlaid stone pavement, with its frequent repetition of the fleur-de-lis and the three castles. The whole breathes the mysticism of St. Louis: the lightness of the architecture, the height of the apparently unsupported roof, and the magnificence of the decoration, render this the most perfect ecclesiastical building in Paris.

In returning from the chapel, notice on the outside, from the court to the S., the apparently empty and useless porch, supporting a small room, which is the one through whose grated window Louis XI used to watch the elevation.

I would recommend the visitor on his way home from this excursion to walk round the remainder of the Île de la Cité in the direction of Notre-Dame, so as to gain a clear idea of the extent of the island, without, however, endeavouring to examine the cathedral in detail on this occasion.

Vary your artistic investigations by afternoons in the Bois de Boulogne, Champs Elysées, etc.

B. NOTRE-DAME

[In very early times, under the Frankish monarchs, the principal church of Paris was dedicated to **St. Stephen the Protomartyr.** It stood on part of the site now covered by Notre-Dame, and was always enumerated first among the churches of the city. A smaller edifice, dedicated to the Blessed Virgin Mary, also occupied a part of the site of the existing cathedral. About the middle of the twelfth century, however, it was resolved to erect a much larger cathedral on the Île de la Cité, suitable for the capital of so important a country as France had become under Louis VI and Louis VII; and since the cult of the Blessed Virgin had then long been increasing, it was also decided to dedicate the new building to Our Lady alone, to the exclusion of St. Stephen. The two early churches were therefore cleared away by degrees, and in 1163 the work of erecting the present church was begun under Bishop Maurice de Sully, the first stone being laid by Pope Alexander III, in person. The relics of St. Stephen were reverently conveyed to a new church erected in his honour on the hill of Ste. Geneviève, south of the river (now represented by St. Etienne-du-Mont, to be described hereafter), and Our Lady was left in sole possession of the episcopal edifice. Nevertheless, it would seem that the builders feared to excite the enmity of so powerful a saint as the Protomartyr; for many **memorials of St. Stephen** remain to this day in the existing cathedral, and will be pointed out during the course of our separate survey.

Notre-Dame de Paris is an edifice in the **Early French Gothic style,** the first great church in that style to be erected in France, and the model on which many others were afterwards based. Begun in 1163, it was consecrated in 1182, but the western front was not commenced till 1218, and the nave was only finished towards the middle of the 13th century. Much desecrated in the Revolution, the cathedral has been on the whole admirably restored. It stands at present lower than it once did, owing to the gradual rise of the surrounding ground·; formerly, it was approached by thirteen steps (the regulation number, imitated from the Temple at Jerusalem). It has **two western towers,** instead of one in the centre where nave and transepts intersect, as is usual in England; so have all the cathedrals in France which imitate it. This peculiarity is due to the fact that French Gothic **aims** especially **at height,** and, the nave being raised so very high, a tower could not safely be added above it. Other differences between English and French Gothic will be pointed out in detail in the course of our survey.

Though Notre-Dame was the first great building in Paris proper, it must be borne in mind that the magnificent Basilica of St. Denis, four miles to the north, and also the Abbey Church of St. Germain-des-Prés, in the southern suburb, antedated it by several years.

Recollect three things about Notre-Dame. (1) It is **a church of Our Lady:** therefore, most of it bears reference to her cult and legends. (2) It is the **cathedral church of Paris:** therefore, it is full of memorials of local saints—St. Denis, Ste.

Geneviève, St. Marcel, Bishop of Paris, etc., amongst whom must also be classed St. Stephen. (3) It is **a royal church**: therefore it contains many reminders of the close alliance of Church and State. Thus understood, Notre-Dame becomes an epic in stone.

Open daily, all day long, free. Take your opera-glasses.]

Go along the Rue de Rivoli as far as the Square of the Tour St. Jacques. Walk through the little garden. Notice, in passing, *the tower—all that now remains of the church of St. Jacques-de-la-Boucherie—used at present as a meteorological observatory. Turn down the Rue St. Martin to the Pont Notre-Dame. In front, L, stands the Hôtel-Dieu; R, the Tribunal de Commerce; centre, the Marché-aux-Fleurs; at its back, the Préfecture de Police. Continue straight along the Rue de la Cité, passing, R, the main *façade* of the modern Palais de Justice (with a glimpse of the Ste. Chapelle) till you come to the broad and open Place Notre-Dame (generally known by its mediæval name of the Parvis). Take a seat under the horse-chestnuts on the north side of the Place, opposite the equestrian statue of Charlemagne, in order to examine the **façade** of the cathedral.

The **west front,** dating from the beginning of the 13th century (later than the rest), consists of two stories, flanked by towers of four stories. The *first* story contains the three main portals: L, the door of Our Lady; centre, of her Son; R, of her Mother. On the buttresses between them stand four statues: extreme L, St. Stephen; extreme R, St. Marcel, Bishop of Paris (a canonized holder of this very see); centre L, the Church, triumphant; centre R, the Synagogue, dejected (representing between them the Law and the Gospel). This first story is crowned and terminated by the Galerie des Rois, containing figures of the kings of Israel and Judah, ancestors of the Blessed Virgin (others say, kings of France to the date of the building), destroyed in the great Revolution, but since restored. On the parapet above it stand, R and L, Adam and Eve; centre, Our Lady and Child with two adoring angels—the Fall and the Redemption. The *second* story contains the great rose window and two side-arches with double windows. The *third* story of the towers consists of a graceful open-work screen, continued in front of the nave, so as to hide its ugly gable (which is visible from further back in the Place), thus giving the main front a fallacious appearance of having three stories. The final or *fourth* story of the towers is pierced on each side by two gigantic windows, adding lightness to their otherwise massive block. The contemplated spires have never been added. This *façade* has been copied with modifications in many other French cathedrals.

Now approach the front, to examine in detail the ****great portals**, deeply recessed, as is usual in French cathedrals, owing to the massive masonry of the towers. The left or *northern* doorway—that of **Our Lady** (by which her church is usually entered) bears on its central pier a statue of the Virgin and Child ; beneath her feet are scenes from the temptation of Eve, who brought into the world sin, and the first murderer Cain, as contrasted with her descendant, the Blessed Virgin, who brought into the world the Redeemer of mankind. Over Our Lady's head, a tabernacle, representing the relics preserved within. In the tympanum, first tier, L, three patriarchs ; R, three kings, typifying the ancestors of the Blessed Virgin. Above, second tier, the Entombment of the Virgin, placed in her sarcophagus by angels, and attended by the apostles with their familiar symbols. Higher still, third tier, the Coronation of the Virgin, in the presence of her Son, with adoring angels. The whole thus represents the Glory of Our Lady. At the sides below, life-size figures ; extreme L, Constantine, first Christian Emperor ; extreme R, Pope Silvester, to whom he is supposed to have given the patrimony of St. Peter—the two representing the union of Church and State. Next to these the great local saints : L, St. Denis, bearing his head, and guided by two angels ; R, St. John Baptist, St. Stephen, and Ste. Geneviève, with the devil endeavouring to extinguish her taper, and a sympathizing angel. The figures on the arch represent spectators of the Coronation of the Virgin. Minor subjects—signs of the Zodiac, Months, etc.—I leave to the ingenuity and skill of the reader. The * *centre* doorway (commonly called the Porte du Jugement) is that of the Redeemer, **Our Lady's Son** ; on its central pier, fine modern figure of Christ blessing ; above, in the tympanum, the usual Last Judgment. First tier (modern), the General Resurrection, with angels of the last trump, and kings, queens, bishops, knights, etc., rising from their tombs; conspicuous among them is naturally St. Stephen. Second tier, St. Michael the Archangel weighing souls, with devils and angels in waiting, the devils cheating; R, the wicked (on Christ's left) hauled in chains to hell; L, the saints (on His right) ascending to glory. On the summit, third tier, the New Jerusalem, with Christ enthroned, showing His wounds in mercy, flanked by adoring angels holding the cross, spear, and nails; L, the Blessed Virgin, patroness of this church; and R, Ste. Geneviève, patroness of Paris, interceding for their votaries. (Last figure is usually, but I think incorrectly, identified as St. John the Evangelist, who has no function on a Parisian Cathedral.) This relief, closely copied at the Ste. Chapelle, is itself imitated from one at St. Denis. On the lintels the Wise (L) and Foolish (R) Virgins; L and R on jambs, life-size figures of the Twelve Apostles, with their usual symbols. Observe the beautiful ironwork of the hinges. The third or *southern* portal, that of St. Anne—the **Mother of the Virgin**—contains older work than the other two, replaced from the earlier church on the same site. The style of the figures is therefore Romanesque, not Gothic; so is the architecture represented in them. On the centre pier, St. Marcel, Bishop of Paris. Above, tympanum, history of St. Anne; first tier, centre, the meeting of Joachim and Anna at the Golden Gate; L, Marriage of the Virgin; R, her Presentation by St. Anne in the Temple, etc. Second tier, the Nativity, and the visit of the Magi to Herod; at the summit, third tier, Madonna enthroned, with adoring angels, a king, and a bishop—Church and State once more identified. The work on this doorway much resembles that at St. Denis. Magnificent iron hinges, brought from old St. Stephen's.

Walk round the quay on the South side to examine **the body of the church.** Notice the lofty Nave, and almost equally lofty Aisles, with (later) side-chapels built out as far as the level of the Transept; also, the flying buttresses. As in most French churches, the transepts are short, and project but little from the aisles. The South Transept has a good late *façade* with two rose windows. Its portal—ill visible—is dedicated (in compensation) to the displaced St. Stephen, and contains on the pier a figure of the saint, robed, as usual, as a deacon; in the tympanum are reliefs of his preaching, martyrdom, death, and glorification. Note, to the R, a small relief of St. Martin of Tours dividing his cloak with the beggar.

Enter the little garden further east, which occupies the site of the former archevêché, in order to observe the characteristic French form of the **choir**—a lofty and narrow apse, with apsidal aisles and circular chapels added below, the whole forming what is called a *chevet*. The light flying buttresses which support the soaring and slender choir add greatly to the beauty and picturesqueness of the building. Pretty modern Gothic fountain. Quit the garden and continue round the Northern side of the Cathedral. The first (small) door at which we arrive—the Porte Rouge—admits the canons. It is a late addition, built in 1407 by Jean sans Peur, Duke of Burgundy, in expiation of his murder of the Duke of Orleans; the donor and his wife kneel on each side of the Coronation of the Virgin in the tympanum. Notice here the gargoyles and the graceful architecture of the supports to the buttresses. The second (larger) door—the Portail du Cloître, so called from the cloisters long demolished—in the North Transept contains a good statue of the Madonna on the pier; above, in the tympanum, confused figures tell obscurely the legend of the monk Theophilus, who sold his soul to the devil. Stand opposite this door, on the far pavement, to observe the architecture of the North Transept. The best point of view for the whole body of the cathedral, as distinct from the *façade*, can be obtained from the Quai de Montebello on the south side of the river.

To visit the **interior**, enter by the L, or northern door of the *façade*—that of Our Lady. The lofty nave is flanked by double aisles, all supported by powerful piers. Walk across the church and notice all five vistas. Observe the height and the delicate arches of the triforium, or pierced gallery of the second story, as well as the windows of the clerestory above it—the part of the nave which rises higher than the aisles, and opens freely to the exterior. Walk down the outer R aisle. The side-chapels, each dedicated to a separate saint, contain the altars and statues of their patrons. Notice the shortness of the Transepts, with their great rose windows; observe also the vaulting of the roof, especially at the intersection of the four main arms of the building. The entrance to the **choir** and **ambulatory** is in the R or S Transept. Close by, near the pillar, Notre-Dame de Paris, *the* wonder-working mediæval statue of Our Lady. The double aisles are continued round the choir, which is separated from them by a wall and gateways. Approach the brass grills, in order to inspect the interior of the choir, whose furniture was largely modernised and ruined by Louis XIV, in accordance with a misguided vow of his father. Chapels surround the ambulatory, many of them with good glass windows and tolerable frescoes. The chapel at the end is that of Our Lady of the Seven Sorrows.

By far the most interesting object in the interior, however, is the series of ** **high reliefs in stone,** gilt and painted (on the wall between choir and ambulatory), executed early in the 14th century by Jehan Ravy and his nephew, Jehan de Bouteillier, which, though inferior in merit to those in the same position in Amiens cathedral, are admirable examples of animated and vigorous French sculpture of their period. The series begins on the N side of the choir, at the point most remote from the grill which leads to the Transept. The remaining subjects (for some, like the Annunciation, are destroyed) comprise the Visitation; Adoration of the Shepherds; Nativity; Adoration of the Magi (note the Three Kings, representing the three ages of man; the oldest, as usual, has removed his crown, and is offering his gift); the Massacre of the Innocents; the Flight into Egypt (where a grotesque little temple, containing two odd small gods, quaintly represents the prevalence of idolatry); the Presentation in the Temple; Christ among the Doctors; the Baptism in Jordan (with attendant angel holding a towel); the Miracle at Cana; the Entry into Jerusalem (with Zacchæus in the tree, and the gate of the city); the Last Supper; the Washing of the Apostles' feet; and the Agony in the Garden. The tourist should carefully examine all these subjects, the treatment of which strikes a keynote. Similar scenes, almost identical in their figures, will be found in abundance at Cluny and elsewhere. Note, for example, the symbolical Jordan in the Baptism, with St. John pouring water from a cup, and the attendant angel, all of which we shall often recognise hereafter.

The series is continued on the other (S) side of the choir (a little later in date, with names in Latin underneath; better modelled, but neither so quaint nor so vigorous). The subjects begin by the grill of the South Transept, with the "Noli me tangere" or Apparition to Mary Magdalen (Christ as a gardener); the Apparition to the Marys; to Simon Peter; to the Disciples at Emmaus (dressed as mediæval pilgrims); to the Eleven Apostles; to the Ten and Thomas; to the Eleven by the sea of Tiberias; to the Disciples in Galilee; and on the Mount of Olives. The intervening and remaining subjects—Scourging, Crucifixion, Ascension, etc.—were ruthlessly destroyed by Louis XIV, in order to carry out his supposed improvements in accordance with the vow of his father, Louis XIII. The woodwork of the choir-stalls, executed by his order, is celebrated, and uninteresting. You may omit it. The Treasury contains little of artistic value. The Crown of Thorns still figures in its inventory.

Leave the Choir by the door by which you entered it, and seat yourself for a while at the intersection of the Nave and Transepts, in order to gain a good idea of the Apse, the Choir, and the general arrangement of the shortly cruciform building. Observe the beautiful vaulting of the roof, and the extent to which the church is borne on its piers alone, the intervening walls (pierced by windows and triforium-arches) being intended merely for purposes of enclosure. Note also the fine ancient glass of the rose windows. Quit the church by the North or Left Aisle, and come back to it often.

Those who are not afraid of a spiral staircase, mostly well lighted, should **ascend** the Left or **North Tower** (tickets fifty cents. each, at the base of the tower). Stop near the top to inspect the gallery, with the famous birds and demons. The view hence embraces from the front the Tower of St. Jacques; behind it, the hill of Montmartre, with the white turrets and cupolas of the church of the Sacré Cœur; a little to the L, St. Eustache; then the Tribunal de Commerce; St. Augustin; the Louvre; the roof of the Ste. Chapelle; the Arc de Triomphe; the twin towers of the Trocadéro; the Eiffel Tower; the gilded dome of the Invalides; St. Sulpice, etc. The Île de la Cité is well seen hence as an island. Note also the gigantic size of the open screen, which looked so small from below. Ascend to the top. Good general panorama of the town and valley. This is the best total view of Paris, far superior to that from the Eiffel Tower, being so much more central.

Return by the Pont d'Arcole (whence you get a capital notion of the bifurcation of the Seine around the Île St. Louis), and then pass the modern Hôtel-de-Ville, with St. Gervais behind it, on your way home to the Rue de Rivoli.

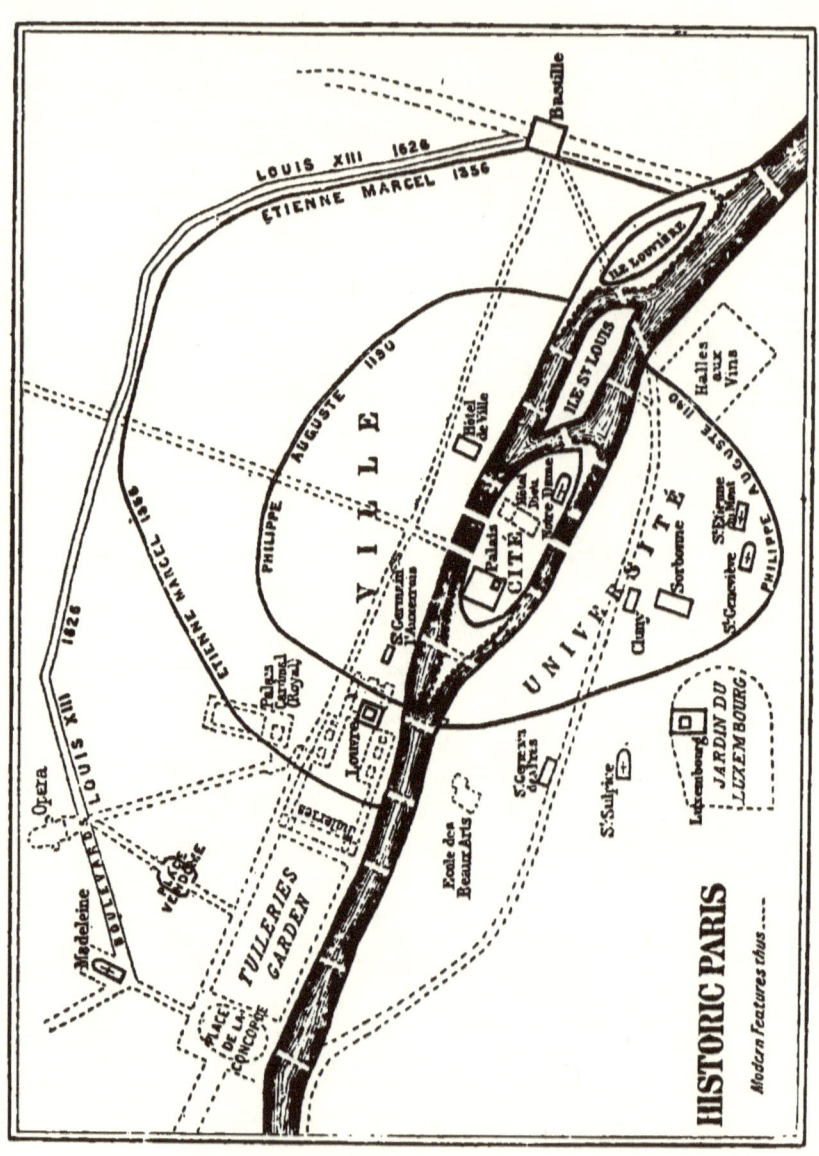

MAP OF HISTORIC PARIS.

This Map represents approximately the growth of Paris, outside the island, at different epochs. Earlier buildings are printed in black; later streets and edifices are shown by means of dotted lines. But the Map does **not** represent the aspect of Paris at any one time; it merely illustrates this Guide: thus, the original Château of the Louvre is marked in black; the later Palace is dotted; whereas the Madeleine, a much more modern building than the Louvre of François I, is again inserted in black, because it does not interfere with the site of any more ancient building. In very early times the town spread south as far only as Cluny, and north (just opposite the island) as far as the Rue de Rivoli. The subsequent **walls** are marked approximately on the Map, with the chief edifices enclosed by them. The fortifications of Louis XIII were demolished by Louis XIV, who substituted for them the broad streets still known as the **Boulevards** This Map shows, roughly speaking, the extent of Paris under Louis XIV; by comparing it with Baedeker's Map of Modern Paris, the small relative size of the 17th-century town will be at once appreciated. Nevertheless, the inner nucleus here mapped out contains almost everything worthy of note in the existing city.

II

THE LEFT OR SOUTH BANK

THE earliest **overflow** of Paris was from the Île de la Cité to the **Left** or **South Bank** (*Rive Gauche*).
The reason for this overflow is clear. The city was situated on a small island, near the head of navigation; it guarded the passage of the Seine by the double bridge. Naturally, however, at a time when all civilization lay to the south, as the town began to grow, it spread southward, towards Rome, Lyons, Marseilles, Bordeaux, Toulouse, Arles, Nîmes, and the Roman culture. To the north at that time lay nothing but comparative barbarism—the Britons and the Germans; or later, the English, the Normans, and the Teutonic hordes. Hence, from a very early date, Paris first **ran southward** along the road to Rome. Already in Roman times, here stood the palace of Constantius Chlorus and Julian, now the Thermes—the fortress which formed the *tête du pont* for the city. Later, the southern suburb became the seat of learning and law; it was known by the name which it still in part retains of the Université, but is oftener now called the *Quartier Latin*. At first, however, only a small portion of the Left Bank was built over. But gradually the area of the new town spread from the immediate neighbourhood of the old Hôtel-Dieu, with its church or chapel of St. Julien-le-Pauvre, to the modern limit of the Boulevard St. Germain; and thence again, by the time of Louis Quatorze, to the further Boulevards just south of the Luxembourg. It is interesting to note, too, that all this southern side, long known as the Université, still retains its position as the learned district. Not only does it include the students' region—the Quartier Latin—with many of the chief artistic studios, but it embraces in particular the Sorbonne, or

University, the Institute of France, with its various branches (Académie Française, Académie des Inscriptions et Belles-Lettres, Académie des Sciences, des Beaux-Arts, etc.), the École des Beaux-Arts, the École de Médicine, the Collège de France, the Lycées St. Louis, Louis-le-Grand, and Henri IV, the École Polytechnique, the École des Mines, the Bibliothèque Ste. Geneviève, the Jardin des Plantes, and the Luxembourg Museum of Modern Paintings. In short, the Left Bank represents literary, scientific, artistic, and educational Paris—the students in law, arts, and medicine, with their own subventioned theatre, the Odéon, and their libraries, schools, laboratories, and *cafés*. It is further noticeable that these institutions cluster thickest round the older part of the southern suburb, just opposite the Cité, while almost all of them lie within the limits of the outer boulevards of Louis XIV.

The **Quartier Latin** surrounds the Sorbonne, and is traversed by the modern Boulevard St. Michel. The **Faubourg St. Germain,** immediately to the west of it (surrounding the old Abbey of St. Germain-des-Prés) is of rather later date; it owes its origin in large part to the Renaissance spirit, and especially to Marie de Médicis' palace of the Luxembourg. It is still the residence of many of the old nobility, and is regarded as the distinctively aristocratic quarter of Paris, in the restricted sense, while the district lying around the Champs Élysées is rather plutocratic and modern than noble in the older signification of the word.

The visitor will therefore bear in mind distinctly that the **South Side is the Paris of the Students.**]

A. THE ROMAN PALACE AND THE MUSÉE DE CLUNY

[The primitive nucleus of the suburb on the South Side consists of the **Roman fortress palace,** the *tête au pont* of the Left Bank, now known as the Thermes, owing to the fact that its principal existing remains include only the ruins of the baths or *thermæ*. This colossal building, probably erected by Constantius Chlorus, the father of Constantine, covered an enormous area south of the river. After the Frankish conquest, it still remained the residence of the Merwing and Karling kings on the rare occasions when they visited Paris; and it does not seem to have fallen into utter decay till a comparatively late date in the Middle Ages. With the Norman irruptions, however, and the rise of the real French monarchs under Eudes and the Capets, the new sovereigns found it safest to transfer their seat to the Palace on the Island (now the Palais de Justice), and the Roman fortress was gradually dismantled. In 1340 the gigantic ruins came into the hands of the powerful Benedictine Abbey of Cluny, near Mâcon, in Burgundy; and about 1480, the abbots began to erect on the spot **a town mansion** for themselves, which still bears the name of the **Hôtel de Cluny.** The letter K, the mark of Charles VIII (1483-1498), occurs on many parts of the existing building, and fixes its epoch. The house was mostly built by Jacques d'Amboise, abbot, in 1490. The style is late Gothic, with Renaissance features. The abbots, however, seldom visited Paris, and they frequently placed their town house accordingly at the disposition of the kings of France. Mary of England, sister of Henry VIII, and widow of Louis XII, occupied it thus in 1515, soon after its completion. It was usual for the queens of France to wear white as mourning; hence her apartment is still known as the *Chambre de la reine blanche.*

At the Revolution, when the property of the monasteries was confiscated, the Hôtel de Cluny was sold, and passed at last, in 1833, into the hands of M. du Sommerard, a zealous antiquary, who began the priceless collection of works of art which it contains. He died in 1842, and the Government then bought the house and museum, and united it with the Roman ruin at its back under the title of *Musée des Thermes et de l'Hôtel de Cluny.* Since that time many further objects have been added to the collection.

At Cluny the actual building forms one of the most interesting parts of the sight, and is in itself a museum. It is a charming specimen of a late mediæval French mansion; and the works of art it contains are of the highest artistic value. I am able briefly to describe only what seem to me the most important out of its many thousands of beautiful exhibits. At least two whole days should be devoted to Cluny—one to the lower and one to the upper floor. Much more, if possible.]

Go to the Place du Châtelet; cross the bridge, and the Île de la Cité; also, the Pont St. Michel to the South Side. Good view of Notre-Dame to L. In front lies the modern Boulevard St. Michel, with the Fontaine St. Michel in the foreground (statue by Duret). Continue along the Boulevard till you reach the Boulevard St. Germain, another great modern thoroughfare which cuts right through the streets of the old

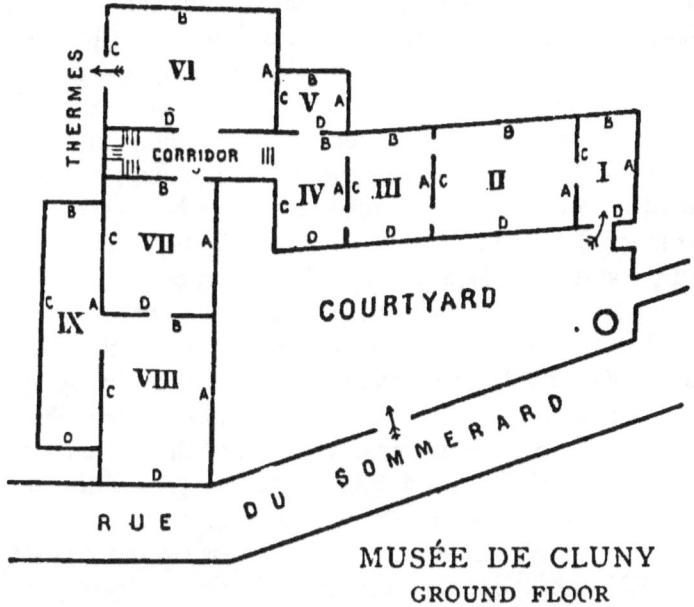

MUSÉE DE CLUNY
GROUND FLOOR

Faubourg and the narrow alleys of the Latin Quarter. The Garden at the corner contains all that remains of the Roman Palace. Notice its solid masonry as you pass. Then, take the first turn to the L, the Rue du Sommerard, which leads you at once to the door of the **Museum.**

Notice the late semi-Gothic **Gateway,** resembling that of an Oxford college. Pass through the flat-arched gate into the handsome courtyard. To the L is a late Gothic *loggia*, containing a few antiques. In front stands the main building, with square windows and high dormers, bearing the staff and pilgrim's scallop, the symbol of St. James, with the cardinal's hat and scutcheons and devices of the family D'Amboise, thus indicating the name of Jacques d'Amboise, the abbot who built it. Entrance to the R. Open free, daily, 11 to 4 or 5, except Mondays.

The first suite of rooms which we enter form some of the apartments of the original building. Observe the fine timbered **ceilings.**

ROOM I.—Panels, etc., in wood-carving.

ROOM II.—*Fine French chimney-piece, by Hugues Lallement, dated 1562, representing Christ and the Woman of Samaria at the well, brought from a house at Châlons-sur-Marne. R and L of entrance (**wall A** on plan), wooden seats, with canopy, holding good Gothic wood-carvings. Notice L of door, a Deposition in the Tomb; (801) Madonna and Child; then, Birth of the Virgin, with St. Anne in a bed; and below, head of a Saint, hollow, intended to contain her skull or relics. Near it (762), decapitation of St. John Baptist, German, 16th century; and (789) Death of the Virgin. R of doorway, three reliquary heads, and (783 and 784) two groups of the Education of the Virgin. Above, several representations of the Circumcision. **Wall B,** between the windows, (745) quaint reliquary head of St. Mabile, one of St. Ursula's 11,000 virgins, the hair gilt, Italian, 15th century; near it, Angel of the Annunciation; Madonna and Child; and Flight into Egypt. Fine wooden chests. In the **cases,** collections of **shoes,** uninteresting.

ROOM III.—Wood-carvings, more or less Gothic. **Wall A,** (788) Madonna supporting the dead Christ, under a canopy, 16th century; (816) Holy Women, with small figure of the donor, kneeling. (709) large carved altar-piece, end of 15th century; in the centre, Crucifixion, with quaintly brutal Roman soldiers, fainting Madonna, and Holy Women in fantastic head-dresses of the period; below, Nativity, and Adoration of the Magi; L side, above, Flagellation, with grotesquely cruel soldiers; beneath it, angels displaying the napkin of St. Veronica; R side, above, Deposition in the Tomb; beneath it, angels supporting the instruments of the Passion—a splendid piece of Flemish carving. Above, two statues of St. George. Further on (712), votive triptych against the plague, Flemish, carved, with painted flaps on the doors; L, St. Sebastian, with arrows of the pestilence; R, St. Roch exhibiting his plague-spot, with angel who consoled him and dog who fed him (see the legend in Mrs. Jameson); centre, Adoration of the Magi; the Three Kings represent (as usual) the three ages of man, and also the three old continents, Europe, Asia, Africa; hence the youngest king is represented as a Moor. Other episodes (Flight into Egypt, Return of Magi, etc.), in the background—late 15th century. **Wall B,** first window, stained glass, German panes, 15th century, Annunciation, in two panels (1960 and 1957). Beyond it (830), in woodwork, 16th century, Coronation of the Virgin by Christ and God the Father—a somewhat unusual treatment. Above (758), Stem of Jesse, representing the descent of Christ; notice David with his harp and other kings of Israel; late 15th century. Second window (1958 and 1959), St. Hubert and St. Lambert, companions to the Annunciation; (721) dainty little Crucifixion (16th century), in coloured German wood-carving; (1686) Flemish painting. school of Van Eyck, Crucifixion. **Wall D,** windows (1961 and 1962), St. Peter and St. George; (1963 and 1964) St. Hubert, and St. Antony Abbot (with his pig, staff, and bell). **Wall C,** altar-piece, unnumbered; subjects much as opposite; centre, Crucifixion; beneath it, Nativity, Adoration of Magi. L, Way to Calvary (with grotesquely brutal soldiers); beneath it, Annunciation (notice the *prie-dieu*, book, and bed in the background), and Visitation; R, Descent from the Cross, with St. John and the Marys; beneath it, Circumcision, and Presentation in the Temple. (710) Deposition from the Cross, very good, with painted wings from the Passion. All the wood-carvings in this room deserve careful attention. Inspect them all, and, as far as possible, discover their subjects.

ROOM IV.—Fine Renaissance chimney-piece, by Hugues Lallement, 16th century, representing Actæon transformed into a stag by Diana, whom he has surprised in the act of bathing. (Subjects from the myth of Diana are favourites with the French Renaissance artists, owing to the influence of Diane de Poitiers.) From Châlons-sur-Marne, same house as that in Room II. **Wall A** (1779 and 1778), Renaissance classical paintings, part of a large series continued elsewhere; (1428) fine

Renaissance carved cabinet (Diana and Chimæras); contrast this and neighbouring Renaissance work with the mediæval carvings in adjacent rooms. **Wall B** (6329), quaint old Flemish tapestry, representing the Angels appearing to the Shepherds; the Nativity; the Adoration of the Magi; and the Agony in the Garden. Study the arrangement of all these figures, which are conventional, and will reappear in many other examples of various arts. **Wall C,** R and L of fireplace, good Renaissance wood-carving. **Wall D,** fine cabinets. In the cases, medals.

ROOM V, to the side. **Debased Italian and Spanish work** of the 17th and 18th centuries. **Centre,** Adoration of the Magi, a meretricious Neapolitan group of the 17th century, intended to place in a church as a Christmas *berceau*. The costumes of the Three Kings, representing the three continents, the ruined temple in which the action takes place, and the antique statue in the background of the Madonna and St. Joseph, should all be noticed. Contemptible as a work of art, this florid composition of dolls is interesting and valuable for its spirited arrangement, and for the light it casts on the conception of the subject. The room also contains other similar church furniture of the 17th and 18th centuries. Observe their theatrical tinsel style and their affected pietism, as contrasted with the simplicity, naïveté, and truth of earlier periods. Take, as an extreme example of this tendency, the relief of the Annunciation on **Wall D,** to the R of the entrance door, and compare it with examples of the same subject in other rooms of the collection. **Wall B,** facing the entrance, good case of miscellaneous woodwork containing excellent Spanish art of this bad period—a Last Supper, a St. Francis receiving the Stigmata, a Massacre of the Innocents, the Faint of St. Catherine, St. Antony the Abbot, St. Antony of Padua carrying the infant Christ, and other figures. A large gilt tabernacle, on **Wall C,** also contains a debased figure of St. Anthony of Padua, from an altar dedicated to the Saint. Identify as many of these saints as possible, and remember their symbols.

We now quit the older suite of apartments, and enter a large central glass-covered court—ROOM VI, entirely modern. The **Corridor** is occupied by early altar paintings, for the most part of little value. Notice on the L, by the staircase (1701) a Giottesque Madonna and Child—Florentine, 15th century. Near it (1666), two oval panels, representing the Annunciation, divided (as frequently happens with this subject) into two distinct portions, and probably flanking a doorway in their original position—Italian, 14th century. All the paintings on this wall, mostly unsatisfactory as works of art, are valuable for their symbolism and the light they throw on the evolution of their subjects. For example : (1676), between the Annunciation pictures, represents the distribution of holy wine which has touched the relics (I think) of St. Hubert. Further on, we have a group of six Apostles ; beginning from the R, St. Peter with the keys, St. John Evangelist with the cup and serpent, St. Andrew with his cross, St. Bartholomew with his knife, St. James the Greater with the pilgrim's staff and scallop, and St. James the Less with a crosier and book. R of the staircase is a stone figure of St. Denis bearing his head, French, 15th century ; also, a good statue of the Madonna, a little later. Above the doorway, R, are portions of a large Spanish altar-piece ; in the centre, the Crucifixion ; extreme R, Assumption of the Virgin, etc. Beyond it comes the continuation of the tabernacle already noticed, containing the six remaining Apostles, with the symbols of their martyrdom. Next, a fine Spanish altar-piece of the 15th century, from a church of St. Martin ; in the centre, St. Martin dividing his cloak with the beggar ; round it various other subjects, among them St. Antony with his pig, St. Stephen, in deacon's robes, with the stones of his martyrdom, St. Jerome in the desert beating his bosom with a flint before the crucifix, St. Francis displaying the stigmata or five wounds of Christ, St. Paul the hermit with his lion, etc. R, towards the courtyard, a fine figure of Adam from St. Denis, a splendid example of the best French nude sculpture of the 14th century.

We now enter the **covered courtyard** or ROOM VI proper, filled with fine examples of French mediæval sculpture. Several of the objects bear labels sufficiently descriptive. I will therefore only call attention to a few among them. **Wall D**, two wooden Flemish statues (Our Lady and St. John at Calvary), R and L of the doorway ; (417) carved marble monument of the 10th or 11th century ; very fine workmanship, with distinct reminiscences of the antique. **Wall A**, *Magnificent stone frieze or reredos, originally gilt and coloured, representing the History of St. Benedict, from St. Denis ; in the centre, Baptism in Jordan (compare the relief of the same subject in Notre-Dame) ; R and L., preaching and miracles of St. Benedict (overthrow of idols, cure of a dying woman). Middle of wall (6328), fine Italian tapestry, 16th century, representing the Adoration of the Magi; observe the attitude of the kings, together with the ox and ass in the background, invariable concomitants of the Nativity in art. Beneath (728), early wooden Madonna (13th century, Auvergne), with Byzantine aspect. Beautiful Romanesque capitals—Creation of Eve, etc. **Wall B** *(237), exquisite stone frieze or reredos from the church of St. Germer, about 1259, much mutilated, but originally one of the most perfect specimens of French 13th century carving ; it still betrays traces of colour. In the centre, Crucifixion, with Virgin and St. John : on either side (as at Notre-Dame), the Church, with cross and chalice, and the Synagogue, with eyes blinded : then, R and L of cross, St. Peter and St. Paul : beyond them, Annunciation and Visitation : finally, L, St. Ouen, uncle of St. Germer, cures a wounded warrior ; R, St. Germer asks leave of King Dagobert to found the Abbey from which this came. Above it (509), exquisitely grotesque relief of the Resurrection with sleeping Roman soldiers, one of a set in alabaster, French 14th century (500 to 512), all of which deserve to be inspected ; meanings of all are obvious except (501) St. Ursula. Still higher, fragment of the original Last Judgment on the central west door of Notre-Dame, Paris, before the restoration—interesting as showing the grounds on which Viollet-le-Duc proceeded ; (6322), tapestry, Arras, 15th century, various scriptural subjects, confused, but decipherable. Beneath it, L, *beautiful stone relief (reredos) of the legend of St. Eustace, from the church of St. Denis—a fine French work of the 14th century. In the centre, Crucifixion ; extreme L, St. Eustace, hunting, is converted by the apparition of the Christ between the horns of the stag he is pursuing ; further R, his baptism, nude, in a font, as in all early representations ; still further R, his trials and history; while he crosses a river with one of his children, a wolf seizes one, while a lion devours the other ; last of all, reunited miraculously with his family, he and they are burned alive as martyrs by the

Emperor Trajan, in a brazen bull. Observe naif boy with bellows. The whole most delicately and gracefully sculptured. Next, coloured stone relief of the Passion—French 14th century; subjects, from R to L: the kiss of Judas (observe Peter drawing the sword); Flagellation; Bearing of the Cross, with Simon of Cyrene; Deposition in the Tomb; Resurrection; and Christ in Hades, delivering Adam and Eve from the jaws of death, realistically represented here and elsewhere as the mouth of a monster; notice in this work the colour and the Gothic architecture and decoration of the background, which help one to understand features that are missing in many other of these reredoses. Then, stone relief of the Annunciation, Visitation, and Nativity, very simply treated: notice the usual ox and ass in the manger. Above it, *(4763), good mosaic of the Madonna and Child with adoring angels, by Davide Ghirlandajo, of Florence, placed by the President Jean de Ganay (as the inscription attests) in the church of St. Merri at Paris. **Wall C** (513-518), interesting alabaster reliefs of the Passion, French, 14th century. Between them, Coronation of the Virgin, French, 15th century. (725) Good wooden figure of St. Louis, covered with fleur-de-lis in gold, from the Sainte Chapelle. [Here is the door which leads to the Musée des Thermes. Pass it by for the present.] Beyond it, continuation of the alabaster reliefs (514 and 517), etc.: examine them closely. Between them (435), Circumcision, in marble, early 15th century, French, full of character. Beneath it (429, etc.), admirable figures of mourners, from the tomb of Philippe le Hardi, at Dijon, 14th century. **Wall D**, again (1291), terra-cotta, coloured: Madonna and St. Joseph, with angels, adoring the Child (child missing), ox and ass in background; R, Adoration of Magi; notice once more the conventional arrangement: L, Marriage of the Virgin, a high priest joining her hand to Joseph's, all under Gothic canopies, 15th century, from the chapel of St. Eloy, near Bernay, Eure. I omit many works of high merit.

The **centre** of this room is occupied by several good statues. Examine each; the descriptive labels are usually sufficient. (A noble *St. Catherine; St. Barbara with her tower; St. Sebastian, pierced with the holes where the arrows have been; a beautiful long-haired wooden Madonna; a fine [Pisan] Angel of the Annunciation, in wood, etc.) Also, several excellent figures of Our Lady. The large part played by the Madonna in this Room, indeed, is typical of her importance in France, and especially in Paris, from the 13th century onward. The church of Notre-Dame is partly a result, partly a cause, of this special cult of the Blessed Virgin.

Room VII (beyond the corridor, a modern covered courtyard).—**Tapestries and textile fabrics,** interesting chiefly to ladies. On **Wall A,** and others, Flemish tapestry, representing the History of Bathsheba, much admired and very ugly; compare it with the tapestry of the Lady and the Unicorn, to be visited later in Room III, upstairs, contrasting them as models of what such work should and should not be. **Wall B,** admirable Renaissance relief of the Cardinal Virtues. Above it, a good Madonna, and figures of Grammar and Astronomy. **Wall C,** Caryatid of inferior art, French, 16th century. **(448), Admirable group of the Three Fates, attributed to Germain Pilon, the great French sculptor of the 16th century, whom we shall meet again at the Louvre—a fine specimen of the plastic art of the Renaissance, said to represent Diane de Poitiers and her daughters. Below **(447), exquisite Renaissance bas-relief of the huntress Diana, of the School of Jean Goujon, again in allusion to Diane de Poitiers. (478) Good mask of the same epoch. (251) Virgin and Child, meretricious; in the decadent style of the 16th century; very French in type, foreshadowing the Louis XV spirit—the Madonna resembles a little-reputable court lady. **Wall D** (463, etc.), Judgment of Solomon, Solomon and the Queen of Sheba, Annunciation, and other reliefs in the florid and least pleasing French style of the 16th and 17th centuries. Table by the doorway **(449), exquisite small marble statue of the Deserted Ariadne (perhaps Diane de Poitiers), in the best Renaissance manner, probably by Germain Pilon: found in the Loire, near Diane's *château* of Chaumont. Beside it, three sleeping Venuses, one of which is also said to be Diane de Poitiers, the goddess of the Renaissance in Paris. L of doorway (457), singular marble relief of Christ and the Magdalen after the Resurrection (Noli me tangere); the Saviour strangely represented (as often) in a gardener's hat and with a spade; in the background, angels by the empty sepulchre; Flemish, florid style of the 16th century. Beside it (467 and 468), two exquisite Renaissance reliefs of Venus. In front of it, on the table *(479), Entombment, with the body of Christ placed in the sarcophagus by Joseph of Arimathea and Nicodemus—portraits, I think, of the donors.

Room VIII —Textile fabrics and ecclesiastical robes. **Wall B**, L. of door (487), pretty but meretricious little group of Venus and Cupids, with grapes, French style of the 17th century; the national taste still more distinctly showing itself. R of door (459), in two separate figures, a quaint Annunciation—French, 16th century, frankly anachronistic. Close by (464), the Judgment of Solomon, same school and period. Above (563), clever small alabaster group of the Rape of the Sabines, after Giovanni da Bologna. These all stand on a handsome French carved chest of the 16th century. **Wall C**, greatly worn altar-relief of the Adoration of the Magi, from the chapel of the Château d'Anet, French Renaissance, 16th century. Above it (446), Mary Magdalen, kneeling, with long hair and the alabaster box of ointment —her symbol in art—15th century, curious. At the back, gilt and painted figures of the Holy Trinity, from the demolished church of St. Marcel at Paris, 17th century. Similar representations of the Trinity, showing the three Persons thus, are common in Italian art. Further on (493), good figure of a shepherd, French, 16th century. **Wall A** (266), curious altar back, Herod ordering the Massacre of the Innocents. (267) St. Eustace crossing the river (see Room VI) with the lion and the wolf seizing his children. A very different treatment from the previous one. (291) A lintel of a chimney, Flemish, dated 1555; centre, a river god; L and R, pelican and eagle; between the figures, Faith, Hope, Charity and Prudence. (273) Madonna and Child (Notre-Dame de l'Espérance, throned on an anchor). On the wall, far L, interesting piece of French 14th century tapestry, with a legend of St. Marcel and St. John Evangelist, most naïvely represented.

Room IX.—State coaches and Sedan chairs of the 17th century, as ugly as can be imagined. They need not detain you.

The **staircase** to the FIRST FLOOR is in the Corridor to Room

VI. Observe the staircase itself, in carved wood, bearing the arms of France and Navarre, and also the crowned initials of Henri IV and Marie de Médicis. It was formerly in the old Chambre des Comptes of Paris, and was re-erected here at the installation of the Museum.

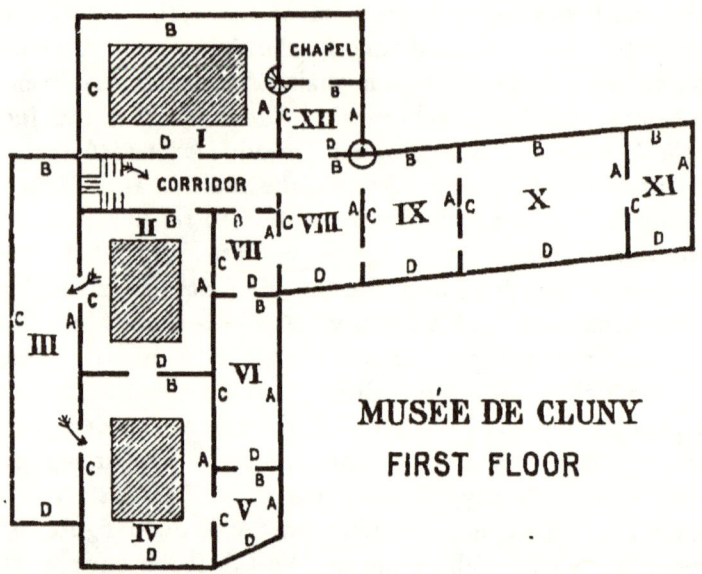

MUSÉE DE CLUNY
FIRST FLOOR

The **corridor** above contains arms and armour. At the head of the staircase (742), very quaint Magdalen in wood with the box of ointment; German in style, 15th century; observe her long hair, here twisted and plaited with German neatness. (1466 and 1468) Renaissance cabinets in ebony.

ROOM I.—Gallery, looking down on the courtyard of Room VI, below. **Wall D,** by which you enter; tiles, French Renaissance. **Wall C:** first case, blue Flemish stoneware. Fine wrought-iron gates, gilt. In front of them, female Satyr, French, 18th century, very characteristic of the national taste; opposite it, male Satyr, the same. Second case: Palissy ware, French 16th and 17th centuries. This fine ware is full of Renaissance feeling. Notice particularly (3140), a Sacrifice of Abraham; (3145) the Baptism in Jordan, conventional treatment; (3139) Judith and Holofernes, with several other scriptural scenes in the older spirit; intermingled with these are classical and mythological scenes, displaying the growing love for the nude; observe particularly (3119), a Venus with Cupids; and another dish below it, unnumbered, same subject; also, a Creation of Eve; (3131) Susanna and the Elders, and other scenes of similar character. Observe that while the early work is purely scriptural or sacred, the Renaissance introduces classical subjects. Note too the frequent scenes of the Baptism in the same connection. Centre (3102), beautiful vase with lid, of the period of Henri II. Study all the Palissy ware. **Wall B,** French pottery of the 18th century, exhibiting the rapid decline in taste under Louis XIV and XV, especially as regards colour. The most satisfactory pieces are the blue and white dishes with royal monograms, arms, etc. Second case: Rouen ware of the 18th century, far superior in style and tone to the preceding. Good nude figure of Venus. **Wall A,** Nevers pottery, delicate blue and white; (3338) figure of a page, to support a lamp. Last case: Dutch pottery, Delft, 18th century, exhibiting the strong domestic Dutch tendency.

ROOM II.—Also galleries, surrounding a courtyard. Exquisite Italian Renaissance pottery. **Wall B, R** of entrance, beautiful Italian specimens of Faenza ware, 15th and 16th centuries (whence the word *faïence*); these should be closely studied in detail. (2811) Quaint dish with Diana as archer; beside it, portraits. (2824 and 2825) Decorative plaques with heads of women. (3949) St. George and the Dragon in green pottery. Behind it, plate with admirable portrait. In the same case, Judith receiving the head of Holofernes; (3024) Hercules playing the lyre to entice Auge. **Wall C,** first case, Deruta and Chaffagiolo ware of the 16th century. Exquisite decorative dishes and plaques; (2814) Actæon changed to a stag by Diana. (2849) Susanna and the Elders. (2887) St. Jerome in the desert, with his lion. (2895) The doubting Thomas. (2823) Another Actæon. Observe frequent repetition of certain scenes. Fine plates with arms of Medici Popes, etc. Second case: Deruta ware, still more splendid specimens, many of them with remarkable lustre. (2894) Madonna and Child, with infant St. John of Florence. Other plates with Mercury, a sphinx, a lion, the huntress Diana, a Moor's head, portraits and decorative designs. Examine in detail. **Wall D,** first case, Casteldurante and Gubbio ware, 16th century (3007) Manius Curtius leaping into the Forum. (3015) Crucifixion, with the sun and the moon darkened. (3004) Dædalus and the Minotaur. (3008) Fine conventional design. Other plates have heads of St. Paul and mythological persons. (2802) a quaint Temptation of St. Antony. (2818) Leda and the Swan, etc. Second case : Urbino ware, 17th century. Head of Raphael, and delicate Raphaelesque scenes, instinct with the later Renaissance feeling. (2961) Perseus and Andromeda. (3064) Expulsion from Paradise ; on either side, Temptation, and Adam eating the fruit. (2872) a Baptism in Jordan. Notice again the mixture of religious and mythological scenes, with a preference for those where the nude is permissible— Judith and Holofernes, Orpheus, etc. **Wall A,** fine Florentine terra-cotta bust of the young St. John, patron saint of the city. More Urbino ware, to be carefully examined. The greater part of this wall, however, is occupied by ****Della Robbia** ware, glazed Florentine majolica of the 15th and 16th centuries. (2794) Fine figure of St. Michael. (2799) Martyrdom of St. Catherine, the wheels of her torture broken by angels. Above it, Madonna adoring the Child ; observe in this and many other cases the beautiful setting of fruit and flowers, characteristic of the Della Robbias. Beneath, no number, the Beheading of St. Catherine ; in the background, angels conveying her soul to Heaven. (2795) The Infant St. John, patron Saint of Florence. (2793) Temperance, with flagon and patera. Then, more Urbino ware, very fine examples of the end of the 16th century ; above them, touching Madonna and Child, Della Robbia. **Wall B,** again, Castello ware, and Venetian pottery, 15th, 16th and 17th centuries. Apothecary's jars, plaques, etc., extremely beautiful.

ROOM III.—A long corridor. **Wall A,** is entirely occupied by the **magnificent suite of six early French tapestries, known as " The Lady and the Unicorn " (symbol of chastity), the finest work of its sort ever executed. They come from the Château de Boussac, and belong to the second half of the 15th century. The Lady is represented engaged in various domestic pursuits of a woman of rank of her time, always accompanied by the beast of chastity. The colour is inexpressibly lovely. Above it, similar tapestry representing the History of St. Stephen, and the Discovery of his Relics. Along **Wall A**, R of entrance door (774), crowned wooden figure of St. Catherine, holding the sword of her martyrdom, her broken wheel at her feet, and trampling upon the tyrant, Maximian. L of door, good early Madonna and Child; another St. Catherine; and (760) Magdalen, described (erroneously, I think) as Pandora. **Wall B** is mostly occupied by a handsome French Renaissance chimney-piece (16th century), brought here from a house at Rouen, and representing the history of the Casa Santa at Loreto,—its transport over the sea by angels, its reception by the Faithful, and worship in front of it. The ceiling above also comes from the same room. **Wall C**, small stained-glass windows of various ages. Examine them separately. **Wall D**, large enamelled plaques brought from François Premier's Château of Madrid, in the Bois de Boulogne, stated to be the largest enamels in existence. Beneath them, fine wooden statue of the Virgin and infant Christ, German 15th century, very characteristic in its flat features, as well as in the dress, and treatment of the hair, of the German style of the period. Compare it with French Madonnas below. The **screens** towards **Wall A** contain specimens of fine Renaissance wood-carving. Contrast the finish and style of these with their Gothic predecessors. Notice, near the chimney-piece (828), an Annunciation, with God the Father, wearing a triple crown (like the Pope), and the Holy Spirit descending upon the Madonna. Next screen, various classical scenes in the taste of the Renaissance—Judgment of Paris, Venuses and Cupids, etc. Much fine nude Renaissance detail. **Centre case**, old glass; notice, in particular (4763), fine 13th century Arab mosque-lamp. Further on, more Renaissance woodcarving—Leda and the Swan in very high relief: low reliefs of classical subjects and decorative panels. All these works should be closely studied as typically illustrative of Renaissance feeling. **Cases by the window (wall C)**, Limoges and other enamels, too numerous to treat in full detail, but many of them, at least, should be closely inspected and comprehended by the visitor. Case **next** the chimney-piece, old raised enamels (12th and 13th centuries), enamelled gold reliquaries for containing bones of Saints; fine crucifix, etc. Notice on 4497, the Flight into Egypt, Peter walking on the Sea, the Adoration of the Magi, and the Presentation in the Temple; on 4498, the Crucifixion, and the Twelve Apostles; beneath, 4514, enamelled book-cover; near it, Crucifixion, Adoration of the Magi, and other figures. Identify as many of these as possible, and observe their archaic striving after effects too high for the artist. Second case: Limoges enamels, more modern in type (15th century): Madonna holding the dead Christ, Crucifixion, Bearing of the Cross, and other scenes. Notice particularly (4575), little triptych with a Nativity, Adoration of the Magi, and Circumcision, in all of which observe the conventional treatment. Third case: Limoges enamels of the High Renaissance (16th and 17th centuries), Raphaelesque in spirit, better in execution, but far less interesting; good portraits in frames; a fine Flagellation, and other scenes from the Passion; above, delicate Tazzas. Observe in particular (4628), the Descent into Hell, Christ rescuing Adam and Eve and the other dead from Hades, typically Renaissance. On the far side of the case, remote from window, a good series of the Gospel history,—Marriage of the Virgin, Annunciation, Birth of the Virgin (incorrectly labelled Nativity), etc. Last cases: more recent enamels. Among the best are, in the last case of all, the Expulsion from Paradise, and a series of the Gospel History; observe particularly (4650), Christ and the Magdalen, with the usual curious disguise as a gardener. I recommend to those who can spare the time, most attentive detailed study of the subjects and treatment in all these enamels, many of which throw much light on similar themes treated by other arts in the same collection. Several hours should, if possible, be devoted to them.

Room IV contains various ** **Mohammedan potteries**, exquisitely decorative, but (owing to the general absence of figure subjects, prohibited by Islam) requiring comparatively little explanation. Occasional animal forms, however, occur in the midst of the usually decorative arabesque patterns. **Wall C**, L of entrance, charming Rhodian pottery (made by Persian workmen), in prevailing tones of blue and green, with the wonderful Persian feeling for colour. **Wall B,** Hispano-Moorish lustre ware, the most exquisitely beautiful ever manufactured. The second case contains several lovely specimens. **Wall A,** Rhodian ware again. **Wall D,** Persian. The reader must examine these minutely for himself. It is impossible to do more than point out their beauty.

Room V.—**Jewish** works of art of the Middle Ages, interesting as showing the wealth and artistic taste of the mediæval Hebrews—phylacteries, seven-branched candlesticks, goldsmiths' work, etc. (188) Chimney-piece (Christian) from an old house at Le Mans. The groups represent the three ages of life: right and left, the two sexes—man, armed; woman, with a ball of wool.

Room VI.—**Wall C,** opposite windows, carved chest (1360), French, 17th century, with figures in high relief of the Twelve Apostles. The paintings above it (1704, 1707, 1714), etc., are the fronts of similar chests, Florentine, 15th century. Such boxes were commonly given to a bride to contain her trousseau and household linen. For instance, one (1710) contains the mythical history of a betrothal and wedding (Æneas and Lavinia). The others have in many cases similar appropriate subjects from classical story. (1455) Florentine mosaic cabinet, in the worst taste. Beyond it, other cabinets and fronts of wedding chests. This room also contains musical instruments, interesting as illustrating the evolution of modern forms. Also, florid Italian inlaid tables, in the bad expensive taste of the 17th century. In the windows, stained glass.

Room VII.—Carved oak cabinets. (1435) Good Flemish work of the 17th century.

Room VIII.—(189) Carved chimney-piece, similar to that in the Jewish room, and from the same house; marriage scene, allegorical. Carved wooden cabinets and portals, all interesting, but requiring little description. (1431) Again the favourite Renaissance device of Actæon and Diana. Carved oak bed, of age of François Ier, with hangings of the same period. (1509) Good panel of a chair, with the Presentation of the Virgin in the Temple by Saints Joachim and Anna; above, Nativity; then Adoration of the Magi, and Flight into Egypt; on the front, patron saints of the owners.

ROOM IX.—**Magnificent collection of ivories and ebonies, all of which the spectator should examine in detail. Nothing in this museum is more interesting. Notice, for example, the beautiful triptych** (1081) in the centre of the **first case** by the window of **Wall D;** lower tier, Annunciation ; Shepherds ; Joseph and the Madonna, with the babe in the manger ; and Adoration of the Magi ; upper tier, Kiss of Judas, Crucifixion, and Christ and the Magdalen in the Garden ; beautiful Italian work of the 14th century. L of it **(1088), exquisite coloured triptych with Madonna and Child ; L, St. Paul (with his sword) and St. Catherine ; R, St. Peter and the Magdalen ; notice their symbols. Several small ivories in the same case should be observed carefully. Below the large triptych, for example, are scenes from the Passion (*not* chronologically arranged in their existing order), namely, from L to R, Crown of Thorns, Scourging, Resurrection, Ascension, Disciples at Emmaus, Apparition to the three Marys, Peter on the Sea, and Christ with the Magdalen ; very naïve French work of the 15th century. (718) Exquisite little wood-carving of the Crucifixion, with scenes from the Passion ; Spanish, 16th century. Above it (7227), comb, with Adoration of the Magi ; 14th century, very curious. The **next case** contains still earlier and more interesting work. In the centre, a triptych ; lower tier, Adoration of the Magi, Madonna with angels, Presentation in the Temple ; upper tier, Bearing the Cross, Crucifixion, and Descent from the Cross ; exquisite French work, in high relief, of the 14th century. L of it (1082), Scenes from the Passion, Last Supper, Agony in the Garden, Kiss of Judas (with Peter cutting off Malchus's ear), Flagellation, etc. Each compartment here consists of two subjects, which identify ; charming French work of the 14th century. Above it (1085 and 1086), secular scenes, life in a garden—14th century. R of the triptych (1065, 1063, 1066, 1064), legends of saints ; St. Denis beheaded and bearing his head ; Flagellation of an unknown Martyr, who takes it most comfortably ; St. Peter, crucified, head downward ; and other episodes—charming French 14th century work. Examine all the pieces in this case carefully. In the first case, towards the **centre of the room,** early ivory carvings, a *consular diptych of the 5th or 6th century, very interesting ; and other works still displaying classical influence. (1035) Byzantine, Christ and Saints. (1049) Death of the Virgin; fine work showing Byzantine influence; 12th century. (1054) Extremely rude Northern 11th century ivory, representing scriptural scenes, mingled with decorative animals treated in withy-band fashion. (1038) Fine Italo-Byzantine plaque with Crucifixion and Saints, the name of each inscribed beside him. **Central case:** Ivory statuettes, all deserving close attention. (1032) Antique Roman goddess. (1037) Fine early French Madonna; 10th century. Behind her (1052), beautiful ivory reliquary, French, 12th century, with figures of Saints; L, the personages of the Adoration (*i.e.*, the Three Kings) bearing their gifts, and with their names inscribed above them; R, the personages of the Presentation—Madonna, Joseph, Simeon. Further side (1060), beautiful coloured ivory coffer, 14th century, with numerous scriptural scenes, easily recognisable; identify them. Inspect also the **ebony cabinets,** of which 1458, time of Henri IV, with classical scenes, is a magnificent Renaissance example. By **Wall A,** more ebony cabinets and carvings, and exquisite ivory statuettes, of later date, among which notice particularly (1141) a Portuguese Madonna; (1163) a Spanish St. Peter; (1164) Spanish St. Antony of Padua; and (1167) a very curious Peruvian Good Shepherd, showing distinct traces of native art, influenced by introduced Spanish feeling. Further to the R, good classical figures of the later Renaissance. I have only indicated a few of the most interesting among these exquisite carvings; but many hours may be devoted to this room, by those who can afford the time, with great advantage.

Room X.—Bronzes and Renaissance metal work, mostly self-explanatory. (193) Chimney-piece from a house in Troyes—French, 16th century; Plenty, surrounded by Fauns and trophies. Good collection of keys, knives, etc.

Room XI.—**Goldsmith's work** and objects in the precious metals. **Wall A** (4988), gold altar-piece of the Emperor Henry II, of Germany, with Christ, and figures of Saints, bearing their names above them, given by the Emperor to Bâle Cathedral in the beginning of the 11th century. Central case, **the Guerrazar find:** votive offerings of crowns of the early Gothic kings of Spain, the largest one being that of Reccesvinthus (died 672), discovered near Toledo. The crowns are rude Byzantine work of the 7th century, inlaid with precious stones. The names inscribed below them were probably added when they were made into votive offerings. Uninteresting as works of art, these curious relics possess great value as specimens of the decadent workmanship of their period. Most of the other objects in this room derive their importance more from the material of which they are composed than from artistic beauty, or even relative antiquarian importance. Of these (4994), in the case near **Wall D,** represents the Last Supper, with the fish which in very early Christian work is a symbol of Christ. Near it, quaint figures of the four Evangelists, writing, with their symbols. Other symbols of the Evangelists in the same case. Quaint Nuremberg figure of St. Anne, holding on her knee the crowned Madonna, and a little box to contain a relic. (5008) Reliquary foot of a Saint, to enclose his bones; it bears his name—Alard. (4995) Curious figure of the Madonna, Limoges work, very Byzantine in aspect. Other cases contain crucifixes, monstrances, and similar articles of church furniture in the precious metals, mostly of early date. The case by **Wall B** has Gallic torques and Merovingian jewellery.

Return to Room VIII, and enter ROOM XII to the R. It contains bed furniture and book-bindings. (782) Fine Renaissance Flagellation, after Sebastiano del Piombo.

From this room we enter

The Chapel,

a small apartment, with roof sustained by a single pillar. Good niches, now destitute of their saints; church furniture of the Middle Ages, much of which deserves close attention. (708) Fine wooden altar-piece, Flemish, 15th century: centre, the Mass of St. Gregory, with Christ appearing bodily in the Holy Sacrament; beneath it, adoring angels; L wing, Abraham and Melchisedek, frankly mediæval; R wing, the Last Supper; an excellent specimen. Other objects are: (726) Stiff early wooden Madonna. (723) Crucifix, Auvergne, 12th century. (727) St. John. End wall, Annunciation, with the Madonna separated, as often, from the Angel Gabriel by a vase of lilies.

The staircase in the corner leads out to the **Garden,** where are several fragments of stone decoration. Pass through the door, and traverse Room VI ; the opposite door leads to.

Les Thermes,

the remains of the old Roman palace. The scanty remnant, as its name indicates, consists entirely of the baths attached to the building. The masonry is massive. Fragments of Roman altars and other remains found in Paris are arranged round the room. The descriptive labels are sufficient for purposes of identification.

If this brief survey of Cluny has succeeded in interesting you in mediæval art, buy the official catalogue, come here often, and study it in detail.

B. THE HILL OF STE. GENEVIÈVE

(Panthéon, St. Étienne-du-Mont.)

[" High places" are always the first cemeteries and holy sites —as at Montmartre and elsewhere. But the nearest rising ground to Old Paris is the slight elevation just S. of Cluny, now crowned by the colossal dome of the Panthéon. In Frankish times, this hill lay quite outside the city ; but on its summit (just behind his Palace of Les Thermes), Clovis, after his conversion by Ste. Geneviève, is said to have erected a church to St. Peter and St. Paul. Here **Ste. Geneviève** herself was buried in 512 ; and the chapel raised over her tomb grew into a church—the favourite place of pilgrimage for the inhabitants of Paris. The actual body of the patron saint was enclosed, in 550, in a magnificent shrine, executed by St. Éloy, the holy blacksmith. Throughout the Middle Ages this church and tomb of Ste. Geneviève, which occupied the site of the existing Panthéon, nearly, were the objects of the greatest devotion. St. Denis was the saint of the kings and nobles ; but Ste. Geneviève was, and still remains, the saint of the people, and especially of the women. Miracles were constantly performed at her shrine, and her aid was implored at all moments of national danger or misfortune. A great (Augustin) abbey grew up in time behind the church, and was dedicated in honour of the holy shepherdess. The wall of Philippe Auguste bent abruptly southward in order to include her shrine and this powerful abbey.

In the twelfth century, when the old church of St. Stephen (in French, St. Étienne), on the site of Notre-Dame, was pulled down in order to make room for the existing cathedral, the relics of St. Stephen contained in it were transferred to a new edifice—**St. Étienne-du-Mont**—which was erected by the monks, close to the Abbey of Ste. Geneviève, as a parish church for their servants and dependents. In the sixteenth century this second church of St. Stephen was pulled down, with the exception of its tower, which is still standing. The existing church of St. Étienne was then begun on the same site in the Gothic style, and slowly completed with extensive Rennaissance alterations.

Later still, the mediæval church of Ste. Geneviève, hard by, having fallen into decay in the middle of the eighteenth century, Louis XV determined to replace it by a sumptuous domed edifice in the style of the period. This building, designed by Soufflot, was not completed till the Revolution, when it was immediately secularised as the **Panthéon,** under circumstances to be mentioned later. The remains of Ste. Geneviève, which had lain temporarily meanwhile in a sumptuous chapel at St. Étienne-du-Mont (the subsidiary church of the monastery) were then taken out by the Revolutionists; the mediæval shrine, or reliquary (which replaced St. Éloy's), was ruthlessly broken up; and the body of the patroness and preserver of Paris was publicly burned in the Place de Grève. This, however, strange to say, was not quite the end of Ste. Geneviève. A few of her relics were said to have been preserved : some bones, together with a lock of the holy shepherdess's hair, were afterwards recovered, and replaced in the sarcophagus they had once occupied. Such at least is the official story ; and these relics, now once more enclosed in a costly shrine, still attract thousands of votaries to the chapel of the saint in St. Étienne-du-Mont.

The Panthéon, standing in front of the original church, is now a secular burial-place for the great men of France. The remains of Ste. Geneviève still repose at St. Étienne. Thus it is impossible to dissociate the two buildings, which should be visited together; and thus too it happens that the patroness of Paris has now no church in her own city. Local saints are always the most important; this hill and Montmartre are still the holiest places in Paris.]

Proceed, as far as the garden of the Thermes, as on the excursion to Cluny. Then continue straight up the Boulevard St. Michel. The large edifice visible on the R of the Rue des Écoles to your L, is the new building of the Sorbonne, or University. Further up, at the Place du Sorbonne, the domed church of the same name stands before you. It is the University church, and is noticeable as the earliest true dome erected in Paris. The next corner shows one, R, the Luxembourg garden, and L, the Rue Soufflot, leading up to the **Panthéon**.

The colossal domed temple which replaces the ancient church of Ste. Geneviève was begun by Soufflot, under Louis XV, in imitation of St. Peter's, at Rome. Like all architects of his time, Soufflot sought merely to produce an effect of pagan or "classical" grandeur, peculiarly out of place in the shrine of the shepherdess of Nanterre. Secularised almost immediately on its completion, during the Revolution, the building was destined as the national monument to the great men of France, and the inscription, "Aux Grands Hommes la Patrie Reconnaissante," which it still bears, was then first placed under the sculptures of the pediment. Restored to worship by the Restoration, it was again secularised under the Third Republic in order to admit of the burial of Victor Hugo. The building itself, a vast bare barn of the pseudo-classical type, very cold and formal, is worthy of notice merely on account of its immense size and its historic position; but it may be visited to this day with pleasure, not only for some noble modern paintings, but also for the sake of the reminiscences of Ste. Geneviève which it still contains. Open daily, free, from 10 to 4, Mondays excepted.

The **tympanum** has a group by David d'Angers, representing France distributing wreaths to soldiers, politicians, men of letters, men of science, and artists.

The **interior** is in the shape of a Greek cross (with equal arms). Follow round the walls, beginning from the R. In the R Aisle are paintings (modern) looking like frescoes, and representing the preaching of St. Denis, by Galand; and *the history of Ste. Geneviève—her childhood, recognition by St. Germain l'Auxerrois, miracles, etc., delicate and elusive works, by Puvis de Chavannes. The paintings of the South Transept represent episodes in the early history of France. Chronologically speaking, they begin from the E. central corner. Choir, Death of Ste. Geneviève, by Laurens, and Miracles before her Shrine. Apse of the tribune, fine modern (archaic) mosaic, by Hébert, representing Christ with the Guardian Angel of France, tne Madonna, Jeanne d'Arc, and Ste. Geneviève. Stand under the dome to observe the proportions of the huge, bare, unimpressive building. L, or Northern Transept, E. side, the history of Jeanne d'Arc; she hears the voices; leads the assault at Orleans; assists at the coronation of Charles VII at Rheims; and is burnt at Rouen. W. side, St. Louis as a child instructed by Blanche of Castille; administering justice in the Palace; and a captive among the Saracens. N. aisle, history of Ste. Geneviève and St. Denis (suite). The building is thus at once the apotheosis of patriotism, and the lasting memorial of the part borne by Christianity in French, and especially Parisian, history.

As you descend the steps of the Panthéon, the building that faces you to the L is the Mairie of the 5th Arrondissement; that to the R, the École de Droit. Turn to the R, along the N. side of the Panthéon. The long, low building which faces you is the Bibliothèque Ste. Geneviève. Nothing now remains of the Abbey of Ste. Geneviève except the tall early Gothic tower seen to the R, near the end of the Panthéon, and rising above the modern buildings of the Lycée Henri IV. The singularly picturesque and strangely-mingled church across the little square is **St. Étienne-du-Mont,** which we now proceed to visit.

Stand in the left-hand corner of the Place to examine the *façade.* The church was begun (1517) as late Gothic; but before it was finished, the Renaissance style had come into fashion, and the architects accordingly jumbled the two in the most charming manner. The incongruity here only adds to the beauty. The quaintly original Renaissance portal bears a dedication to St. Stephen the Protomartyr, beneath which is a relief of his martyrdom, with a Latin inscription, "Stone destroyed the temple of the Lord," *i.e.*, Stephen, "Stone rebuilds it." R and L of the portal are statues of Sts. Stephen and Geneviève, whose monograms also appear on the doors. In the pediment is the usual representation of the Resurrection and Last Judgment. Above it, the rose window, on either side of which, in accordance with Italian rather than with French custom (showing Italian Renaissance influence) are the Angel of the Annunciation and the Madonna receiving his message. In the third story, a gable-end. Singular tower to the L, with an additional round turret, a relic of the earlier Gothic building. The whole *façade* (17th century), represents rather late Renaissance than transitional architecture.

The **interior** is the most singular, and in some ways the most picturesque, in Paris—a Gothic church, tricked out in Renaissance finery. The nave is flanked by aisles, which are divided from it by round pillars, capped by a singular balustrade or gallery with low, flat arches, simulating a triforium. The upper arches are round, and the decorations Renaissance; but the vaulting, both of nave and aisles, with its pendant keystones, recalls the Gothic style, as do also most of the windows. Stand near the entrance, in the centre of the nave, and look up the church. The most striking feature is the beautiful Renaissance *jubé* or ****rood-loft** (the only one now left in Paris) which divides the Choir from the body of the building. This rood-loft still bears a crucifix, for the reception of which it was originally intended. On the arch below are two charmingly sculptured Renaissance angels. The rood-loft is flanked by two spiral staircases, which are wholly unique architectural features. Notice also the exquisite pendentive of the roof at the point of intersection of the nave and short false transepts.

Now walk up the Right Aisle. The first chapel is the Baptistery, containing the font and a modern statue of the boy Baptist. Third chapel, St. Antony of Padua. The fourth chapel contains a curious Holy Sepulchre, with quaint life-size terra-cotta figures of the 16th century. Fifth chapel, a gilt *châsse*. Notice the transepts, reduced to short arms, scarcely, if at all, projecting beyond the chapels. From this point examine the exquisite Renaissance tracery of the rood-screen and staircases. Then pass under the fine Renaissance door, with lovely decorative work, into the **ambulatory**. The Choir is in large part Gothic, with late flamboyant tracery. The apparent triforium is continued round the ambulatory. The splendid gilded shrine in the second choir-chapel contains the **remains of Ste. Geneviève,** or what is left of them. Candles burn perpetually around it. Hundreds of votaries here pay their devotions daily to the Patroness of Paris. The shrine, containing what is alleged to be the original sarcophagus of the Saint (more probably of the 13th century) stands under a richly-gilt Gothic tabernacle, adorned with figures legibly named on their pedestals. The stained-glass window behind it has a representation of a processional function with the body of the Saint, showing this church, together with a view of the original church of Ste. Geneviève, the remaining tower, and adjacent houses, historically most interesting. The window beyond the shrine also contains the history of Ste. Geneviève—her childhood, first communion, miracles, distribution of bread during the siege of Paris, conversion of Clovis, death, etc. Indeed the long sojourn of the body of Ste. Geneviève in this church has almost overshadowed its dedication to St. Stephen, several memorials of whom may, however, be recognised by the attentive visitor—amongst them, a picture of his martyrdom (by Abel de Pujol) near the entrance to the choir. The Protomartyr also stands, with his deacon's robe and palm, in a niche near the door of the sacristy, where L and R are frescoes of his Disputation with the Doctors, and his Martyrdom. The chapel immediately behind the high altar is, as usual, the Lady Chapel. The next contains a good modern window of the Marriage of the Virgin. Examine in detail all the windows; one of the mystic wine-press is very interesting. Votive offerings of the city of Paris to Ste. Geneviève also exist in the ambulatory. Curious frescoes of the martyrdom of the 10,000 Christians on Mount Ararat on the N side. The best view of the choir is obtained from the N. side of the ambulatory, opposite the shrine of Ste. Geneviève. In the north aisle notice St. Louis with the Crown of Thorns. Stand again in the centre of the nave, near the entrance, and observe the curious inclination of the choir and high altar to one side—here particularly noticeable, and said in every case to represent the droop of the Redeemer's head on the cross.

Go out again. As you emerge from the door, observe the cold and bare side of the Panthéon, contrasted with the internal richness of St. Étienne. Curious view of the late Gothic portion of the church from the little Place on the N. side. Return by the Rue Cujas and Rue St. Jacques, passing the Lycée Ste. Barbe, Lycée Louis-le-Grand, University, and other scholastic buildings, which give a good idea of the character of the quarter.

III

RENAISSANCE PÁRIS (THE LOUVRE)

PARIS, which spread rapidly Southward at first, was somewhat slower in its **Northward** development. Nevertheless, by the time of Philippe Auguste, the Town (**La Ville**)—the commercial portion N. of the river—more than equalled the learned district on the S. side. This central northern region, however, containing the Hôtel de Ville, St. Eustache, and some other important buildings, I purposely postpone to the consideration of **the Louvre** and its neighbourhood, which, though later in date, form the heart and core of Renaissance Paris—the Paris of François Ier and his splendour-loving successors.

Most of the buildings we have hitherto considered are mediæval and Gothic. The Louvre introduces us at once to a new world—the world of the **Renaissance**. The transition is abrupt. In Italy, and especially in Florence, the Renaissance was *a natural growth*; in France it was *a fashion*. It came in, full-fledged, without history or antecedents. To trace its evolution, one must follow it out in detail in Florence and Venice. There, it grows of itself, organically, by gradual stages. But in France, Gothic churches and mediæval *châteaux* give place at once, with a bound, to developed Renaissance temples and palaces. The reason for this fact is, that the French kings, from Charles VIII onward to Henri IV, were thoroughly Italianate. They fought, travelled, and married in Italy, to parts of which they laid claim; and being closely allied with the Medici and other Italian families,—husbands of Medici wives, sons of Medici mothers,—they introduced at once into France the developed products of the Italian Renaissance. At the same time the increased and centralized power of the Crown enabled them to build magnificent palaces, like the Louvre and Fontainebleau; and to this artificial impulse is mainly due the sudden outburst of art in France under François Ier and his immediate successors.

It is impossible to characterize the **Renaissance** in a few short sentences. In one aspect, it was a return from **Gothicism** to **Classical usage**, somewhat altered by the new conditions of life. At first you will probably only notice that in architecture it substituted round arches for pointed, and introduced square doors and windows; while in other arts it replaced sacred and Christian subjects and treatment by mythological and secular. But, in contrast with mediævalism, it will reveal itself to you by degrees as essentially **the dawn of the modern spirit.**

The **Louvre** is the noblest monument of the **French Renaissance.** From the time of St. Louis onward, the French kings began to live more and more in the northern suburb, the town of the merchants, which now assumed the name of La Ville, in contradistinction to the Cité and the Université. Two of their chief residences here were the Bastille and the Hôtel St. Paul, both now demolished—one, on the Place so called, the other, between the Rue St. Antoine and the Quai des Célestins. But from a very early period they also possessed a *château* on the site of the Louvre, and known by the same name, which guarded the point where the wall of Philippe Auguste abutted on the river. François Ier decided to pull down this picturesque turreted mediæval castle, erected by Philippe Auguste and altered by Charles V. He began the construction in its place of a magnificent Renaissance palace, which has ever since been in course of erection. Its subsequent growth, however, is best explained opposite the building itself, where attention can be duly called to the succession of its salient features. But a visit to the exterior fabric of the Louvre should be preceded by one to **St. Germain l'Auxerrois,** the parish church, and practically the chapel, of the old Louvre, to which it stood in somewhat the same relation as the Ste. Chapelle to the home of St. Louis. Note, however, that the church was situated just within the ancient wall, while the *château* lay outside it. The visitor will doubtless be tolerably familiar by this time with some parts at least of the exterior of the Louvre; but he will do well to visit it now **systematically**, in the order here suggested, so as to gain a clear general idea of its history and meaning.]

A. THE FABRIC

Go along the Rue de Rivoli, past the Palais Royal, till you reach the Rue du Louvre. Turn down it, with the Louvre on your right. To your left stands a curious composite building, with a detached belfry in the centre, and two wings, as it seems, one on either side. The southernmost wing is the old **church of St. Germain l'Auxerrois,** the sole remnant of the earliest Louvre; the northernmost wing is the modern Mairie of the 1st Arrondissement, unhappily intended to "harmonize" with it. The real result is, that the modern building kills the old one. The belfry was designed to fill up the gap between the two. Its effect is disastrous.

The church is older than the oldest Louvre. St. Germanus, Bishop of Auxerre (d. 430), was almost one of the first generation of Gallic saints, celebrated for his visit to Britain, where he assisted in gaining the Hallelujah victory over the heathen invaders. A church on this site is said to have been erected in his honour as early as the days of Chilperic. Sacked by the Normans, it was re-erected in something like its present form in the 12th century, but received many subsequent additions.

The beautiful **porch,** which we first examine, is of much later date, having been added in 1431 by Jean Gaussel, at a time when the old *château* of the Louvre had become one of the principal residences of the French kings, in order to give greater dignity, and to afford a covered approach for the royal worshippers to what was practically their own chapel. It therefore contains (restored) statues, in niches, relating especially to the **royal and local Saints of Paris,** whose names are beneath them:—St. Cloud, the Princess Ste. Clotilde, Ste. Radégonde of France, St. Denis, St. Marcel, St. Germain himself, St. Landry, Ste. Isabelle, Ste. Bathilde, St. Jean de Valois, and others. The saints of the royal house are distinguished by crowns or coronets. Two of these statues are old: St. Francis, at the south end, and St. Mary of Egypt, nude, with her long hair, and the three loaves which sustained her in the desert, on the second north pillar. The modern frescoes, destroyed, are by Mottez.

Observe the congruity of all these saints to the church and the *château*. St. Landry or Landeric, an early Frankish bishop of Paris, was buried within, and his shrine was a place of pilgrimage. St. Marcel was also a bishop of Paris. St. Cloud was a holy anchorite whose cell was in the wood which occupied the site of the palace (now destroyed) that bears his name. All these saints are therefore closely bound up with the town of Paris and the royal family. You must never forget this near alliance in France between the church and the crown: it colours all the architecture of the early period.

Within the porch, we come to the **main façade**, of the 13th century. R and L, two sainted bishops of Auxerre, successors of St. Germain. Central portal, a queen, a king (probably Childebert and Ultrogothe, the original Frankish founders), St. Vincent; then St. Germain himself, and Ste. Geneviève, with the usual devil and candle, and her attendant angel, etc. On the pier, Madonna and Child, under a canopy. The tympanum had formerly the usual relief of the Last Supper, now destroyed, and replaced by a fresco. Reminiscences of its subject still remain in the quaint figures to R and L on the arch, at its base, representing respectively, with childish realism, the Jaws of Hell and Abraham's Bosom, to which the wicked and the just were consigned in the centre.

In this church, and in that of St. Germain-des-Prés (see later), **St. Vincent** ranks as a local Parisian saint, because his tunic was preserved in the great abbey church of the other St. Germain beyond the river. He bears a martyr's palm and is habited as a deacon; whence he is often hard to distinguish from his brother deacon, St. Stephen: both are often put together in Parisian churches. It is probable that St. Germain of Paris consecrated this church to his older name-sake and St. Vincent—for his connection with whom you had better wait till you visit St. Germain-des-Prés.

The **interior** is low, but impressive. The R aisle is entirely railed off as a separate church or Lady Chapel. It contains an interesting 14th-century Root of Jesse, seldom accessible. Pretty modern font, by Jouffroy, after Mme. de Lamartine, in the South Transept. Walk round the Ambulatory (behind the Choir), and observe the stained glass and other details, which the reader may now be trusted to discover unaided. A mass of the detail is well worthy of notice. The Gothic pillars of the Choir were converted in the 18th century into fluted columns. Over the Sacristy, in the South Ambulatory, is a modern fresco of St. Germain and St. Vincent. Note many other memorials of the latter. When you leave, walk to the south side of the church to inspect the exterior and the **square tower,** from which, as parish church of the Louvre, the bell rang for the massacre of St. Bartholomew, to be answered by that in the Palace on the island.

On emerging from the church, contrast its Gothic quaintness and richness of detail with the cold, classical *façade* of that part of the **Louvre** which fronts you. This *façade*, known as Perrault's Colonnade, with its classical pediment and Corinthian columns, was erected by Claude Perrault for Louis XIV, whose LL and crown appear on every part of it. Nothing could better illustrate the profound difference between Gothic and Classical architecture than this abrupt contrast.

The portion of the palace that faces you is the real **front door** of the Louvre. Notice the smaller barred windows on the ground floor, and the upper story converted into a *loggia*. Now pass in through the **gateway,** under the Chariot of the Sun—an Apotheosis of Louis—into the First Court, known distinctively as the **Cour du Louvre.** For all that follows, consult the excellent coloured map in Baedeker, page 86. I advise you to cut it out, and carry it round in your hand during this excursion.

Begin by understanding distinctly that this court (le vieux Louvre) is the real and **original Louvre:** the rest is mere excrescence, intended to unite the main building with the Tuileries, which lay some hundreds of yards to the west of it. Notice, first, that the Palace as a whole, seen from the point where you now stand, is constructed on the old principle of relatively blank external walls, like a castle, with an interior courtyard, on which all the apartments open, and almost all the decoration is lavished. Reminiscences of defence lurk about the Louvre. It can best be understood by comparison with such ornate, yet fortress-like, Italian palaces as the Strozzi at Florence. Notice the four opposite portals, facing the cardinal points, which can be readily shut by means of great doors; while the actual doorways of the various suites of apartments open only into the protected courtyard. This is the origin of the familiar French *porte-cochère*.

Again, the portion of the building that **directly faces you** as you enter the court from St. Germain is the **oldest part**, and represents the early Renaissance spirit. It is the most primitive Louvre. Note in particular the central elevated portion, known as a *Pavillon*, and graced with elegant Caryatides. These *Pavillons* are lingering reminiscences of the mediæval towers. You will find them in the corners and centres of other blocks in the Louvre. They form a peculiarly French Renaissance characteristic. The Palace is here growing out of the Castle. The other three sides of the square are, on the whole, more classical and later.

Now cross the square directly to the **Pavillon de l'Horloge**, as it is called, from the clock which adorns it. To your L, on the floor of the court, are two circular **white lines**, enclosed in a square. These mark the site of the original *Château* of the Louvre, with its Keep, or *donjon*. François Ier, who began the existing building, originally intended that his palace should cover the same area. It was he who erected the L wing, which now faces you, marked by the crowned H on its central round gable, placed there by his successor, Henri II, under whom it was completed. To the same king are also due the monograms of H and D (for Diane de Poitiers, his mistress), between the columns of the ground floor. The whole of the Pavillon de l'Horloge, and of this west wing, should be **carefully examined in detail** as the finest remaining specimen of highly decorated French Renaissance architecture. (But the upper story of the Pavillon, with the Caryatides, is an age later.) Observe even the decoration lavished on the beautiful chimneys. Pierre Lescot was the architect of this earliest wing; the exquisite sculpture is by Jean Goujon, a Frenchman, and the Italian, Paolo Ponzio. Examine much of it. The crossed K's of certain panels stand for Catherine de Médicis.

The R wing, beyond the *Pavillon*, was added, in the same

style, under Louis XIII, who decided to double the plan of his predecessors, and form the existing Cour du Louvre.

The other three sides, in a more classic style, with pediments replacing the Pavillons, and square porticoes instead of rounded gables, are for the most part later. The S. side, however, as far as the central door, is also by Pierre Lescot. It forms one of the two fronts of the original square first contemplated. The attic story of these three sides was added under Louis XIV, to whom in the main is due this Cour du Louvre. A considerable part of Louis XIV's decorations bear reference to his representation as *le roi soleil*.

Now, pass through the Pavillon de l'Horloge (called on its W. side Pavillon Sully) into the **second** of the three courts of the Louvre. To understand this portion of the building, again, you must remember that shortly after the erection of the Old Louvre, Catherine de Médicis began to build her palace of the **Tuileries**, now destroyed, to the W. of it. She (and subsequent rulers) designed to unite the Old Louvre with the Tuileries by a **gallery** which should run along the bank of the river. Of that gallery, Catherine de Médicis herself erected a considerable portion, to be described later, and Henri IV almost completed it. Later on, Napoleon I conceived the idea of extending a similar gallery along his new Rue de Rivoli, on the N. side, so as to enclose the whole space between the Louvre and the Tuileries in one gigantic double courtyard. Napoleon III carried out his idea. The **second court** in which you now stand is entirely flanked by buildings of this epoch—the Second Empire. Examine it cursorily as far as the modern statue of Gambetta.

Stand or take a seat by the railing of the garden opposite the Pavillon Sully. The part that now faces you forms a portion of the building of François Ier and Louis XIII, redecorated in part by Napoleon I. The portions to your R and L (consult Baedeker's map) are entirely of the age of Napoleon III, built so as to conceal the want of parallelism of the outer portions. Observe their characteristic Pavillons, each bearing its own name inscribed upon it. This recent square, though quite modern in the character of its sculpture and decoration, is Renaissance in its general architecture, and, when looked back upon from the gardens of the Tuileries, affords a most excellent idea of that stately style, as developed in France under François Ier. The whole of this splendid plan, however, has been rendered futile by the destruction of the Tuileries, without which the enclosure becomes wholly meaningless.

Now, continue **westward**, pass the Monument of Gambetta, and take a seat on the steps at the base, near the fine nude figure of Truth. In front of you opens the **third square** of the Louvre, known as the **Place du Carrousel**, and formerly enclosed on its W. side by the Palace of the Tuileries, which was unfortunately burnt down in 1871, during the conflict between the Municipal and National authorities. Its place is now occupied by a garden terrace, the view from which in all directions is magnificent. Fronting you, as you sit, is the **Arc de Triomphe du Carrousel,** erected under Napoleon I, by Percier and Fontaine, in imitation of the Arch of Septimius Severus at Rome, and once crowned by the famous bronze Roman horses from St. Mark's at Venice. The arch, designed as an approach to the Tuileries during the period of the classical mania, is too small for its present surroundings, since the removal of the Palace. The **N. wing,** visible to your R, is purely modern, of the age of the First and Second Empire and the Third Republic. The meretricious character of the reliefs in its extreme W. portion, erected under the Emperor Napoleon III, and restored after the Commune, is redolent of the spirit of that gaudy period. The **S. wing**, to your L, forms part of the **connecting gallery** erected by Henri IV, but its architecture is largely obscured by considerable alterations under Napoleon III. Its W. pavillon—known as the Pavillon de Flore—is well worth notice.

Having thus gained a first idea of the **courtyard fronts** of the building, continue your walk, still westward, along the S. wing as far as the Pavillon de Flore, a remaining portion of the corner edifice which ran into one line with the Palace of the Tuileries (again consult Baedeker's map). Turn round the corner of the Pavillon to examine the S., or **River Front** of the connecting gallery—one of the finest parts of the whole building, but far less known to ordinary visitors than the cold and uninteresting Northern line along the Rue de Rivoli. The first portion, as far as the gateways, belongs originally to the age of Henri IV; but it was entirely reconstructed under Napoleon III, whose obtrusive N appears in many places on the gateways and elsewhere. Nevertheless, it still preserves, on the whole, some reminiscence of its graceful Renaissance architecture. Beyond the main gateway (with modern bronze Charioteer of the Sun), flanked by the Pavillons de la Trémoille and de Lesdiguières, we come upon the long **Southern Gallery** erected by Catherine de Médicis, which still preserves almost intact its splendid early French Renaissance decoration. This is one of the noblest portions of the entire building. The N here gives place to H's, and the Renaissance scroll-work and reliefs almost equal those in that portion of the old Louvre which was erected under François Ier. Sit on a seat on the Quay and examine the sculpture. Notice particularly the splendid Porte Jean Goujon, conspicuous from afar by its gilded balcony. Its crowned H's and coats-of-arms are specially interesting examples of the decorative work of the period. Note also the skill with which this almost flat range is relieved by sculpture and decoration so as to make us oblivious of the want of that variety usually given by jutting portions. The end of this long gallery is formed by two handsome windows with balconies. We there come to the connecting **Galérie d' Apollon**, of which these windows are the termination, and finally reach once more a portion of Perrault's façade, with its double LL's, erected under Louis XIV, and closely resembling the interior *façade* of the Cour du Louvre.

(The N. side you can examine any day as you pass along the Rue de Rivoli. You will now have no difficulty in distinguishing its various factors—first, on the E., a part of Perrault's *façade* of the Old Louvre; then, where it begins to bend outward, a portion of Napoleon the Third's connecting link; finally, beyond the main carriage way, westward, a part reconstructed under the Third Republic.)

Sit awhile on the adjacent Pont des Arts to gain a general conception of the relations of the Louvre, the Île de la Cité, the Hôtel de Ville and other surrounding buildings.

This first rough idea of the Louvre should be filled in later by detailed study. The Renaissance portions, in particular, you should look at again and again, every time you enter, piecing out your conceptions at a later stage by visiting the Renaissance Sculpture Gallery in the Cour du Louvre, and comparing the works inside it and outside it. Thus only can you gain a connected idea of Renaissance Paris, to be further supplemented by frequent visits to St. Etienne-du-Mont, St. Eustache, and Fontainebleau.

B. THE COLLECTIONS

[The Collections in the Louvre have no such necessary organic connection with Paris itself as Notre-Dame and the Sainte-Chapelle, or even those in the rooms at Cluny. They may, therefore, be examined by the visitor at *any* period of his visit that he chooses. I would advise him, however, whenever he takes them up, to begin with the paintings, *in the order here enumerated*, and then to go on to the Classical and Renaissance Sculpture. The last-named, at least, he should only examine in connection with the rest of Renaissance Paris. Also, while it is unimportant whether he takes first Painting or Sculpture, it is very important that he should take each separately in the **chronological order** here enumerated. He should not skip from room to room, hap-hazard, but see what he sees systematically.

At least **six days**—far more, if possible—should be devoted to the Louvre Collections—by far the most important objects to be seen in Paris. Of these, **four** should be assigned to the Paintings, and one each to the Classical and Renaissance Sculpture. If this is impossible, do not try to see all; see **a little thoroughly.** Confine yourself, for Painting, to the Salon Carré and the Salle des Primitifs, and for Sculpture, to a hasty walk through the Classical Gallery and to the three Western rooms of the Renaissance collection.

The object of the hints which follow is *not to describe* the Collections in the Louvre; it is to put the reader **on the right track** for understanding and enjoying them. It is impossible to make people admire beautiful things; but if you begin by trying to comprehend them, you will find admiration and sympathy grow with comprehension. **Religious symbolism is the native language of early art,** and you cannot expect to understand the art if you do not take the trouble to learn the language in which it is written. Therefore, do not walk listlessly through the galleries, with a glance, right or left, at what happens to catch your eye; begin at the beginning, work systematically through what parts you choose, and endeavour to grasp the sequence and evolution of each group separately. Stand or sit long before every work, till you feel you know it; and return frequently. Remember, too, that I do not point out always what is most worthy of notice, but rather suggest a mode of arriving at facts which might otherwise escape you. Many beautiful objects explain themselves, or fall so naturally into their proper place in a series that you will readily discover their meaning and importance without external aid. With others, you may need a little help, to suggest a point of view, and that is all that these brief notes aim at. Do not be surprised if I pass by many beautiful and interesting things; if you find them out for yourself, there is no need to enlarge upon them. Should these hints succeed in interesting you in the succession and development of art, get Mrs. Jameson and Kugler, and read up at leisure in your rooms all questions suggested to you by your visits to the galleries. My notes are intended to be looked at **before the objects themselves,** and merely to open a door to their right comprehension.

The galleries are open, free, daily, except Mondays. Painting from 9, Sculpture from 11. For details, see Baedeker.]

I. PAINTINGS.

Take Baedeker's Plan of the Galleries (1st Floor) with you. Enter by the door in the Pavillon Denon. (Sticks and umbrellas left here; tip optional.) Turn to L and traverse long hall with reproductions of famous antiques in bronze (Laocoon, Medici Venus, Apollo Belvedere, etc.), which those who do not intend to visit Rome and Florence will do well to examine. Observe, in passing, in the centre of the hall, a fine antique sarcophagus, with figures in high relief, representing the story of Achilles. Begin on the furthest side of the sarcophagus: (1) Achilles, disguised as a woman, among the daughters of Lycomedes, in order to avoid the Trojan war; (2) is discovered by Ulysses as a pedlar, through his choice of arms instead of trinkets; (3) arming himself for the combat; and (4, modern) Priam redeeming the body of Hector. (The work originally stood against a wall, and had therefore three decorative sides only.) Further on, fine sarcophagus from Salonica, Roman period, with Combat of Amazons, representing on the lid husband and wife, couched, somewhat after the Etruscan fashion.

Mount the staircase (Escalier Daru). Near the top is the famous Nikè of Samothrace, a much-mutilated winged figure of Victory, standing like a figure-head on the prow of a trireme. It was erected by Demetrius Poliorcetes, in commemoration of a naval engagement in B.C. 305. Attitude and drapery stamp the work as one of the finest products of Hellenic art. Victory alights on the vessel of the conqueror.

Turn to your L just before reaching the last flight, and pass several Etruscan sarcophagi and sarcophagus-shaped funereal urns, many with the deceased and his wife on the lid, accompanied in some cases by protecting genii. The early Etruscans buried; the later often burned their dead, but continued to enclose the ashes in miniature sarcophagi. At the top, on the L, a fresco by *Fra Angelico*, the Dominican painter, St. Dominic embracing the Cross, with the Madonna and St. John Evangelist: not a first-rate example of the master. End wall, R of door, a fresco by *Botticelli*, Giovanni Tornabuoni receiving the Muses. Opposite it, L of door, another by the same, Giovanna his wife receiving the Graces, and accompanied by Cupid. These two frescoes stood in the hall of the owner's villa, and gracefully typify the husband entertaining Literature, Science, and Art, while the wife extends hospitality to Love, Youth, and Beauty. Descend one flight of staircase again, passing yet other Etruscan sarcophagi (which examine), and, mounting opposite stairs, pass the Nikè and turn to your R. Traverse the photograph-room and the Salle Duchâtel beyond it, as well as the Salon Carré. Enter the Long Gallery, and, taking the first door to your R, you arrive at once in Room I (Baedeker's VII), the

SALLE DES PRIMITIFS.

The pictures in this room consist for the most part of those by early followers of Giotto, and by members of the schools which sprang from him, till the moment of the Renaissance.

As these earliest pictures strike the key-note of types, continued and developed later, it is absolutely necessary to examine them *all* very closely. In most cases, subject and treatment were rigorously prescribed by custom; scenes recur again and again, almost identically. Where saints are grouped round the Madonna, they were *ordered* by the purchaser, and oftenest represent his own patrons. In order to obtain a chronological view, begin at the centre of the end wall. Most of these pictures are altar-pieces. I follow the **small numbers below,** the only ones for which a detailed catalogue is yet published.

* 153, *Cimabue* (the point of departure for Tuscan art); Madonna and Child with six angels. Almost a replica of the great picture in Santa Maria Novella at Florence; gold ground; the Madonna's face still strongly Byzantine in type, with almond-shaped eyes; the Child, draped, after the earlier fashion. Later, he is represented nude. Observe, however, the greater artistic freedom in the treatment of the attendant angels, where Cimabue was slightly less hampered by conventional precedents. Do not despise this picture because of its stiffness and its archaic style. It is an immense advance upon the extremely wooden Byzantine models which preceded it: and in the angels it really approaches correctness of drawing.

225. (Skied) *Don Lorenzo Monaco.* A Tabernacle for an altar of St. Lawrence; centre, St. Lawrence, enthroned on his gridiron; L, St. Agnes with her lamb; R, St. Margaret with her dragon, all on gold grounds. A poor example. This Saint is usually represented in deacon's robes. The other saints are probably those who shared the chapel with him. See the much later St. Margaret by Raphael as an example of Renaissance treatment of the same figure.

*192. *Giotto.* St. Francis receiving the Stigmata. A genuine picture, painted for the saint's own church of San Francesco at Pisa; one of the earliest representations of this subject, often afterwards copied. Christ, as a six-winged seraph, red-feathered, appears in heaven to the Saint; rays proceed from his five wounds to the hands, feet, and side of St. Francis, which they impress with similar marks. A mountain represents La Vernia; two tiny buildings, the monastery. Compare with this subject two smaller treatments in the same room, both on the lowest tier: one, to the L as you go towards the door, 431, of the school of Perugino, where an attendant Brother (Leo) is seen astonished at the vision; the second on the R, 287, attributed to Pesello, and closely similar in treatment. Careful comparison of these pictures will serve to show the close way in which early painters imitated, or almost copied one another. The base (or predella) of the Giotto also contains three other subjects: Innocent III, asleep, is shown by St. Peter the falling church sustained by St. Francis; he confirms the Franciscan order; St. Francis preaches to the birds. All very spirited. Notice these little pictures for comparison later with others painted in the Dominican interest by Fra Angelico.

Continuing along L wall are some small pictures of the Sienese school, which should be carefully examined. (Do not suppose that because I do not call attention to a picture it is necessarily unworthy of notice.) Most of these little works breathe the pure piety and ecstatic feeling of the School of Siena.

**426. *Perugino.* Tondo, or round picture; the Madonna Enthroned; L, St. Rose with her roses; R, St. Catherine with her palm of martyrdom; behind, adoring angels. An exquisite example of the affected tenderness, delicate grace, and brilliant colouring of the Umbrian master, from whose school Raphael proceeded. An early specimen. Observe the dainty painting of the feet and hands, which is highly characteristic.

Beneath it, 1701, *Gentile da Fabriano.* Presentation in the Temple. Look closely into it. A delicate little example of the Umbrian rival of Fra Angelico. The arrangement will explain many later ones. Every one of the figures and their attitudes are conventional.

427. *Perugino.* Madonna and Child, with St. John Baptist and St. Catherine. The introduction of St. John shows the picture to have been probably painted for a Florentine patron. Not a pleasing example.

Beneath it, *Vittore Pisano,* characteristic portrait of an Este princess, in the hard, dry, accurate manner of this Veronese medallist, who borrowed from his earlier art the habit of painting profiles in strong low relief, with a plastic effect.

Perugino. St. Sebastian. One of the loveliest examples of the Umbrian master's later manner. Contrasted with the Madonna and St. Rose, it shows the distance covered by art during the painter's lifetime. Observe its greater freedom and knowledge of anatomy. St. Sebastian, bound as usual to a pillar in a ruined temple, is pierced through with arrows. Face, figure, and expression are unusually fine for Perugino. Sebastian was the great saint for protection against the plague, and pictures containing him are almost always votive offerings under fear of that pestilence. Many in this gallery. The face here is finer than in any other presentation I know, except Sodoma's in the Uffizi at Florence.

258. *Lombard or Piedmontese School.* Annunciation. An unusual treatment; the Madonna, as always, kneels at a *prie-dieu*, and starts away, alarmed and timid, at the apparition of the angel Gabriel. The action, as usual, takes place in a *loggia*, but the angel is represented as descending *in flight* through the air, an extremely uncommon mode of depicting him. He bears the white lily of the Annunciation. The other details are conventional. Contrast with this subsequent Annunciations in this Gallery. L, are St. Augustin and St. Jerome; R, St. Stephen, bearing on his head, as often, the stones of his martyrdom, accompanied by St. Peter Martyr the Dominican, with the knife in his head. Both saints carry palms of martyrdom. A good picture in a hard, dry, local manner.

Now cross over to the **opposite side** of the room, beginning at the bottom, in order to preserve the chronological sequence.

196. *School of Giotto.* Madonna in Glory, with angels. Compare this treatment carefully with Cimabue's great picture close by, in order to notice the advance in art made in the interval. The subject and general arrangement are the same, but observe the irregularity in the placing of the angels, and the increased knowledge of anatomy and expression.

Close by are several other **Giottesque pictures**, all of which should be closely examined; especially 425, *Vanni*, the same subject, for comparison. The little Giottesque Death of St. Bernard, in particular, is a characteristic example or type of a group which deals in the same manner with saintly obsequies. All of them will suggest explanations of later pictures. In all these cases, the saint lies on a bier in the foreground, surrounded by mourning monks and ecclesiastics. The key-note was struck by Giotto's fresco of the Death of St. Francis at Santa Croce in Florence.

187. *Agnolo Gaddi.* Annunciation; a characteristic example. Note the loggia, and the angel with the lily; the introduction of a second angel, however, is a rare variation from the type. In the corner is the Father despatching the Holy Spirit. Attitude of the Madonna characteristic; study carefully. No subject sheds more light on the methods of early art than the Annunciation. It always takes place in an arcade : the Madonna is almost always to the right of the picture : and *prie-dieu*, book, and bed are frequent accessories.

666. Quaint little Florentine picture of St. Nicolas, throwing three purses of gold as a dowry inside the house of a poor and starving nobleman.

Next to it, unnumbered, Gregory the Great sees the Angel of the Plague sheathing his sword on the Castle of St. Angelo, so called from this vision.

494. St. Jerome in the Desert; lion, skull, crucifix, rocks, cardinal's hat, all characteristic of the subject. In the foreground, a Florentine lily; in the background, Christ and the infant Baptist, patron of Florence; background L, St. Augustine and the angel who tries to empty the sea into a hole made with a bucket—a well-known allegory of the attempt of the finite to comprehend the Infinite. Look out elsewhere for such minor episodes.

Fra Angelico. Martyrdom of Sts. Cosmo and Damian, the holy physicians and (therefore) patron saints of the Medici family; a characteristic example of the saintly friar's colouring in small subjects. These two Medici saints· are naturally frequent in Florentine art.

662. *Fra Angelico.* Story of the death of St. John Baptist. Three successive episodes represented in the same picture. The lithe figure of the daughter of Herodias, dancing, is very characteristic.

166. Battle scene, by *Paolo Uccello*. Showing vigorous efforts at mastery of perspective and foreshortening, as yet but partially successful. The wooden character of the horses is

conspicuous. Paolo Uccello was one of the group of early scientific artists, who endeavoured to improve their knowledge of optics and of the sciences ancillary to painting.

199. *Benozzo Gozzoli*. Glory of St. Thomas Aquinas, the great **Dominican** teacher. This is an apotheosis of scholasticism, in the person of its chief representative. R and L stand Aristotle and Plato, the heathen philosophers, in deferential attitudes, recognising their master. Beneath his feet is Guillaume de St. Amour, a vanquished heretic. Below, the entire Church—pope, cardinals, doctors—receiving instruction from St. Thomas. Above, the Eternal Father signifying His approval in a Latin inscription, surrounded by the Evangelists with their symbols—angel, winged lion, bull, eagle. The inscription imports, "Thomas has well spoken of Me." The style is archaic: the council is supposed to be that of Agnani, presided over by Pope Alexander IV. Among the celestial personages, notice St. Paul, Moses, and others. Pictures of this double sort, embracing scenes in heaven and on earth, are common in Italy.

Beneath it (287), part 2. *Pesello*. St. Cosmo and St. Damian affixing the leg of a dead Moor to a wounded Christian, on whom they have been compelled to practise amputation. The costumes are the conventional ones for these saints. Remember them. This astounding miracle is often represented at Florence: the dead man's leg grew on the living one.

182. *Fra Angelico*. A Coronation of the Virgin, painted for a **Dominican church at Fiesole. In the foreground, St. Louis of France, with a crown of fleur-de-lis; St. Zenobius, Bishop of Florence, with the lamb of the Baptist on his crosier (indicating his see); St. Mary Magdalen, in red, with long yellow hair (so almost always), and (her symbol) the box of ointment; St. Catherine with her wheel; St. Agnes with her lamb, and others. Above St. Louis stands St. Dominic, founder of Fra Angelico's order, recognisable by his robes, with his red star and white lily (the usual attributes); beneath him, a little to the R, St. Thomas Aquinas, with a book sending forth rays of light, to signify his teaching function. Near him, St. Francis. Other Saints, such as St. Lawrence with his gridiron, and St. Peter Martyr, the Dominican, with his wounded head, must be left to the spectator. In the background, choirs of angels. Beneath, in the **predella**, the history of **St. Dominic** (marked by a red star); Pope Innocent in a dream sees him sustaining the falling Church (a Dominican variant of the story of St. Francis in the Giotto, at the end): he receives his commission from St. Peter and St. Paul; he restores to life the young man Napoleon, killed by a fall from a horse (seen to left); he converts heretics and burns their books; he is fed with his brethren by angels in his convent at Rome; and his death and apotheosis. This picture deserves most careful study—say two hours. It is one of Fra Angelico's finest easel paintings (his best are frescoes), and it is full of interest for its glorification of the Dominicans. Compare the St. Thomas Aquinas with Benozzo Gozzoli's: and remember in studying the predella that St. Dominic founded the Inquisition. The tender painting of this lovely work needs no commendation.

222. *School of Filippo Lippi.* Madonna and angels, characteristic of the type of this painter and his followers.

Above it, *Neri di Bicci.* Madonna, very wooden. He was a belated Giottesque, who turned out such antiquated types by hundreds in the 15th century.

School of Benozzo Gozzoli. Madonna and Child. L, St. Cosmo and St. Damian, with pens and surgeons' boxes; St. Jerome, with stone, lion, and cardinal's hat; his pen and book denote him as translator of the Vulgate. R, St. John Baptist (representing Florence); St. Francis with the Stigmata; St. Lawrence. The combination of Saints shows the picture to have been painted in compliment to Lorenzo de' Medici. Minor subjects around it are worthy of study.

Now **cross over the room** again. You come at once upon four pictures of nearly the same size, painted for the Court of the Gonzaga family at Mantua. Allegorical subjects, intended for the decoration of a hall or boudoir. Most of those pictures we have hitherto examined have been sacred: we now get an indication of the nascent Renaissance taste for myth and allegory.

429. *Perugino.* Combat of Love and Chastity. A frequent subject for such situations, showing Perugino at his worst. Compare it with the other three of the series.

253. *Mantegna.* Wisdom conquering the Vices. A characteristic but unpleasing example of this great Paduan painter. Admirable in anatomy, drawing, and perspective: poor in effect. Observe the festoons in the background, which are favourites with the artist and his school.

*252. *Mantegna.* The amours of Mars and Venus discovered by (her husband) Vulcan. A beautiful composition. The guilty pair, with a couch, stand on a mountain, representing Parnassus, accompanied by Cupid. Below, exquisite group of the Nine Muses dancing (afterwards imitated by Guido). To the L, Apollo with his lyre, as musician. R, Mercury and Pegasus. In the background, the injured Vulcan discovering the lovers. This splendid specimen of early Renaissance art is one of Mantegna's finest. Study it in detail, and compare with the other three which it accompanies. Observe the life and movement in the dancing Muses: also, the growing Renaissance love for the nude, exemplified in the Venus.

154. *Costa.* The Court of Isabella d'Este. The meaning of the figures is now undecipherable, but the general character indicates peace, and devotion to literature, science and art. A fine example of the Ferrarese master.

Between these four, **Mantegna*; (251), Madonna della Vittoria, a most characteristic picture, painted for Giovanni Francesco Gonzaga, Marquis of Mantua, to commemorate his victory over Charles VIII of France. The Madonna is enthroned under a most characteristic canopy of fruit and flowers, with pendents of coral and other decorative adjuncts. L, Gonzaga himself, kneeling in gratitude—a ruffianly face, well-painted. R, St. Elizabeth, mother of the Baptist, with St. John Baptist himself, representing the Marquis's wife. Behind, the patron Saints of Mantua, who assisted in the victory: St. Michael the Archangel (the warrior saint—a most noble figure), St. Andrew (Mantegna's name-Saint), St. Longinus, who pierced the side of Christ, and St. George. The whole is exquisitely beautiful. The detail deserves long and attentive study. The reliefs on the pedestal are characteristic. From the church of the same name, erected in commemoration of the victory (of the Taro). I will return hereafter at greater length to this lovely picture.

Above, to the L (*418), *Cosimo Tura.* Pietà, or body of Christ wept over by the Madonna and angels. In drawing and colouring, a characteristic example of this harsh, but very original and powerful, Ferrarese master. You will come hereafter on many Pietàs. Compare them all, and note the attitude and functions of the angels.

Cross over again to the opposite side. (183), *Botticelli*. Round Madonna and angels, very characteristic as to the drawing, but inferior in technique to most of his works.

221. *Filippo Lippi.* Madonna in Glory, with angels. The roundness of the faces, especially in the child angels, is very characteristic. At her feet, two Florentine patron saints. The absence of symbols makes them difficult to identify, but I think they represent St. Zenobius and St. Antonine. Very fine.

184. *Botticelli.* Madonna and Child, with St. John of Florence. The wistful expressions strike the key-note of this painter. Compare with nameless Florentine Madonna of the same school above it.

220. *Fra Filippo Lippi.* Nativity. Worthy of careful study, especially for the accessories : St. Joseph, the stall and bottle, the saddle, ox and ass, and wattles, ruined temple, etc., which reappear in many similar pictures. Not a favourable example of the master. Beneath it, little fragments with St. Peter Martyr, Visitation, Christ and Magdalen, meeting of Francis and Dominic, and St. Paul the Hermit. An odd conglomeration, whose meaning cannot now be deciphered. The ruined temple, frequently seen in Nativities and Adorations of the Magi, typifies the downfall of Paganism before the advance of Christianity.

Beside it, *Ghirlandajo*. Portrait of bottle-nosed man and child. Admirable and characteristic.

** 202. *Ghirlandajo.* Visitation. Probably the master's finest easel picture. Splendid colour. Attitudes of the Madonna and St. Elizabeth characteristic of the type. The scene habitually takes place in front of a portal, as here, with the heads of the main actors more or less silhouetted against the arch in the background. At the sides, Mary Salome, and "the other Mary." Such saints are introduced merely as spectators : they need not even be contemporary : they are included in purely ideal groupings. At Florence, in a similar scene, the as yet unborn St. John the Baptist stands by as an assessor.

F

185. Venus and Cupid, of the school of *Botticelli.* Very pleasing.

347. *Cosimo Rosselli.* Madonna in an almond-shaped glory (Mandorla) of red and blue cherubs. L, the Magdalen; R, St. Bernard, to whom she appeared, writing down his vision; about, adoring angels. A characteristic example of this harsh Florentine painter.

156. We come at once upon the High Renaissance in *Lorenzo di Credi's* beautiful Virgin and Child, flanked by St. Julian and St. Nicholas. Observe the three balls of gold in the corner by the latter's feet, representative of the three purses thrown to the nobleman's daughters. Notice also the Renaissance architecture and decorations. In pictures of this class, the saints to accompany the Madonna were *ordered* by the person giving the commission; the artist could only exercise his discretion as to the grouping. Notice how this varies with the advance of the Renaissance: at first stiffly placed in pairs, the saints finally form a group with characteristic action. The execution of this lovely work shows Lorenzo as one of the finest artists of his period.

70. *Bianchi,* a rare Ferrarese master. Madonna enthroned, with Saints. The angel on the step is characteristically Ferrarese, as are also the reliefs and architecture.

467. Ascetic figure of San Giovanni di Capistrano.

435. *School of Perugino.* Little Madonna, in an almond-shaped glory of cherubs. The shape belongs to Christ, or saints, ascending into glory.

Next it, front of a chest, containing the story of Europa and the Bull. Several episodes are combined in a single picture. To the extreme L, the transformed lover, like the prince in a fairy tale. Most gracefully treated.

61. *Bellini.* Madonna and Child, between St. Peter and St. Sebastian; a plague picture. These half-length Madonnas are very characteristic of Venetian art of the period. The Madonna's face and strong neck also very Venetian. Observe them as the type on which Titian's are modelled. Look long at this soft and melting picture. The gentle noble face, the dainty dress, the beautiful painting of the nude in the St. Sebastian, are all redolent of the finest age of Venetian painting.

Above it, a good *Tura.* Compare with previous one.

60. *School of Gentile Bellini.* Venetian ambassador received at Cairo. Oriental tinge frequent at Venice. This gate can still be recognised at Cairo. The figures are all portraits, and the painter probably accompanied the ambassador, Domenico Trevisano.

Beneath it (59), two fine portraits by *Gentile Bellini.*

664. Characteristic little *Montagna*; angels at the base of a Madonna now destroyed. Compare the Bianchi almost opposite. Such angels are frequent in the school of Bellini.

152. Attributed to *Cima.* Madonna Enthroned, with St. John Baptist and the Magdalen. These lofty thrones and landscape backgrounds of the Friuli country are frequent with Cima and Venetian painters of his period.

113. *Carpaccio.* Preaching of St. Stephen. One of a series of the Life of St. Stephen, now scattered. The saint is in deacon's robes, as usual; oriental costumes mark the intercourse of Venice with the East. Observe the architecture, a graceful compound of Venetian and oriental.

Over the doorway, Fresco of God the Father, in an almond-shaped glory, from the Villa Magliana. Purchased as a Raphael, probably by *Lo Spagna.*

Return frequently to this room, and study it deeply. It will give you the key to all the others.

Now traverse the Salon Carré and enter the

SALLE DUCHÂTEL.

On the R wall are two exquisite frescoes by *Luini*, removed entire from walls in Milan. To the L, the Adoration of the Magi, exquisitely tender and graceful; study it closely as an example both of painter and subject, noting the ages and attitudes of the Three Kings, the youngest (as usual) a Moor, and the exquisite face and form of the Madonna. To the R, a Nativity, equally characteristic. Look long at them. Between, Christ blessing, not quite so beautiful; and Genii with grapes, an antique motive. Above are three other frescoes of the school of Luini, not so fine. Centre, Annunciation, the Madonna separated (as often) from the angel by a lily. The Madonna never approaches the angel, and is usually divided by a wall or barrier.

On the screen by door, good portraits by *Antonio Moro*.

Other side of door (680), Madonna and Child, with the donors of the picture, by *Hans Memling*. This beautiful **Flemish** picture well represents the characteristics of Flemish as opposed to Italian art. Notice the want of ideality in the Virgin and Child, contrasted with the admirable portraiture of the donors, the chief of whom is introduced by his namesake, St. James, recognisable by his staff and scallop-shell. The female donors, several of whom are Dominican nuns, are similarly introduced by their founder, St. Dominic, whose black-and-white robes and star-like halo serve to identify him. Observe the exquisite finish of the hair and all the details. Study this work for the Flemish spirit.

At the far end of the room are two pictures by *Ingres*, marking the interval covered by French art during the lifetime of that great painter. L, Œdipus and the Sphinx, produced in the classical period of the master's youth, while he was still under the malign influence of David. R, La Source, perhaps the most exquisitely virginal delineation of the nude ever achieved in painting.

After having traversed these two rooms the spectator will probably be able to attack the

SALON CARRÉ,

which contains what are considered by the authorities as the gems of the collection, irrespective of period or country (a very regrettable jumble). Almost all of them, therefore, deserve attention. I shall direct notice here chiefly to those which require some **explanation.** Begin to the L of the door which leads from the Salle Duchâtel.

Close to the door, Apollo and Marsyas: a delicate little *Perugino*, attributed to Raphael. Good treatment of the nude, and painted like a miniature. Renaissance feeling. Compare it with the St. Sebastian in the Salle des Primitifs.

Above it, *Jehan de Paris*. Madonna and Child, with the donors; a characteristic and exceptionally beautiful example of **the early French school.** Contrast its character with the Italian and Flemish. Extremely regal and fond of tinsel ornament.

20. *Correggio.* Jupiter and Antiope, a good example of his Correggiosity and marvellous arrangement of light and shade. Very late Renaissance. Perfection of art ; very little feeling.

*446. *Titian.* Entombment. A fine but faded example of the colour and treatment of the prince of the Venetian Renaissance.

231. *Luini.* Virgin and Child. Not a pleasing example.

*419 and **417. Two admirable portraits by *Rembrandt.*

**250. *Mantegna.* Crucifixion, predella or base of the great picture in San Zeno at Verona. Notice the admirable antique character of the soldiers casting lots for Christ's raiment. The rocks are very Mantegnesque in treatment. One of the artist's finest pictures. Spend some time before it. We will return again to this fine painting.

381. *Andrea del Sarto.* Holy Family. Showing well the character of this master's tender and melting colour : also, the altered Renaissance treatment of the subject.

Beyond the doorway, two dainty little *Memlings.* Marriage of St. Catherine (the Alexandrian princess) to the Infant Christ ; and, the Donor with St. John Baptist and his lamb. When a saint places his hand on a votary's shoulder, it usually indicates the patron whose name the votary bears.

Near it, graceful little St. Sebastian of the Umbrian school. Compare with others. This plague-saint is one of the few to whom mediæval piety permitted nudity.

*370. *Raphael.* The great St. Michael, painted for François Ier. Admirable in its instantaneous dramatic action. This picture may be taken, in its spirit and vigour, as marking the culminating point of the Italian Renaissance as here represented.

Near it, *Titian.* The Man with the Glove : a fine portrait.

**19. *Correggio.* The Marriage of St. Catherine. This is a characteristic treatment, by the great painter of Parma, of this mystical subject. St. Catherine is treated as an Italian princess of his own time, on whose finger the infant Christ playfully places a ring. The action has absolutely no mystic solemnity. Behind, stands St. Sebastian, with his arrows to mark him (without them you would not know him from a classical figure), looking on with amused attention. His smile is lovely. In the background, episodes of the martyrdom of

St. Sebastian, proving this to be probably a plague picture. But the whole work, though admirable as art, has in it nothing of religion, and may be aptly compared as to tone with the Education of Cupid by the same artist in the National Gallery. Nothing could surpass the beauty of the light and shade, and the exquisite colouring. Study it as a type of the last word of the humanist Renaissance against mediæval spirituality. Compare it with the Memling close by: and, if you have been at Milan, with the exquisitely dainty Luini in the Poldi-Pezzoli Museum.

Above it, a Holy Family by *Murillo*. Spanish and theatrical.

The greater part of this wall is taken up by an enormous canvas (95), by *Paolo Veronese*, representing the Marriage at Cana of Galilee, from the refectory (or dining-hall) of San Giorgio Maggiore at Venice. Pictures of this subject, or of the Last Supper, or of the Feast in the House of Levi, were constantly placed as appropriate decorations to fill the end wall of monastic refectories (like the famous Lionardo at Milan), and were often therefore gigantic in size. This monstrous and very effective composition (proudly pointed out by the guides as "the largest oil-painting in the world") contains nothing of sacred, and merely reflects with admirable skill the lordly character of the Italian Renaissance. In the centre of the table, one barely notices the figures of the Christ and the Madonna. Attention is distracted both from them and from the miracle of the wine by the splendid architecture of the background, the loggias, the accessories, and the gorgeous guests, many of them representing contemporary sovereigns (among them François Ier, Eleanor of Austria, Charles V, and Sultan Soliman). The group of musicians in the centre foreground is also composed of portraits—this time of contemporary painters (Titian, Tintoretto, etc.). As a whole, a most characteristic picture both of the painter and his epoch, worth some study, and full of good detail.

**39. *Giorgione.* Pastoral scene, with nude figures. One of the few undoubted pictures by this master, whose genuineness is admitted by Morelli, though much repainted. Should be studied as an example of the full flush of the Venetian Renaissance, and of the great master who so deeply affected it.

Notice the admirable painting of the nude, and the fine landscape in the background. Contrast with the Bellinis in the Salle des Primitifs, in order to mark time and show the advance in technique and spirit. Giorgione set a fashion, followed later by Titian and others. Compare this work with Titian's Jupiter and Antiope in the Long Gallery.

Above it (*427) *Rubens.* Adoration of the Magi. A splendid picture. Interesting also as showing how far Rubens transformed the conceptions of the earlier masters. Compare it with the Luini in the Salle Duchâtel, and other Adorations in this gallery. Full of gorgeousness, dash, and certainty of execution.

37. *Antonello da Messina.* Characteristic hard-faced portrait by this excellent Sicilian artist.

**459. *Lionardo.* St. Anne and the Virgin. This great artist can be better studied in the Louvre than anywhere else in the world. This picture, not perhaps entirely by his own hand, is noticeable for the beautiful and very Lionardesque face of St. Anne, the playful figure of the infant Christ, and the admirable blue-toned landscape in the background. The smiles are also thoroughly Lionardesque. Notice the excellent drawing of the feet. The curious composition—the Virgin sitting on St. Anne's lap—is traditional. Two or three examples of it occur in the National Gallery. Lionardo transformed it. He is the great scientific artist of the Florentine Renaissance.

208. *Hans Holbein,* the younger. Admirable portrait of Erasmus. Full of character. Note carefully. The hands alone are worth much study. How soft they are, and how absolutely the hands of a scholar immersed in his reading and writing.

108. *Clouet.* Elizabeth of Austria. A fine example of the early French school, marking well its hard manner and literal accuracy. It shows the style in vogue in Paris before the School of Fontainebleau (Italian artists introduced by François Ier) had brought in Renaissance methods.

**162. *Van Eyck.* Madonna and Child, with the Chancellor Rollin in adoration. Perhaps Van Eyck's masterpiece. Notice the comparatively wooden Flemish Madonna and Child, contrasted with the indubitable vitality and character in the face of the Chancellor. This picture is a splendid example of the highest evolution of that type in which a votary is exhibited adoring the Madonna—the primitive form of portrait : " paint me in the corner, as giving the picture." Every detail of this finished work deserves long and close inspection. Notice the elaboration of the ornaments, and the delicious glimpse of landscape through the arcade in the background. Compare with the Memlings ; also, with contemporary Italian work in the Salle des Primitifs.

**362. *Raphael.* Madonna and Child, with infant St. John, known as *La Belle Jardinière.* To the familiar group of the Madonna and Child, Florentine painters and sculptors early added the infant Baptist, as patron of their city, thus forming a graceful pyramidal composition. This exquisite picture, by far the most beautiful Raphael in the Louvre, belongs to the great painter's Florentine period. It should be compared with the very similar Madonna del Cardellino in the Uffizi at Florence. For simplicity of treatment and beauty of colouring this seems to me the loveliest of Raphael's Madonnas, with the exception of the Granduca. Look at it long, for colour, design, and tender feeling. Then go back to the St. Michael, and see how, as Raphael gains in dramatic vigour, he loses in charm.

407. *Rembrandt.* Christ and the Disciples at Emmaus. A fine study in light and shade, and full of art, but not a sacred picture. Compare with other pictures of the scene in this gallery. The feeling is merely domestic.

433. *Rubens.* Tomyris, Queen of the Scythians, with the head of Cyrus. A fine, vigorous painting, with the action frankly transferred to the court of Henri IV. Dash and colour and all the Rubens attributes.

365. *Raphael.* Small Holy Family.

364. *Raphael.* Holy Family, known as the "Sainte Famille de François Ier" : Joseph, Madonna, infant Christ, St. Elizabeth and the Baptist, and adoring angels. Belongs to Raphael's Roman period, and already vaguely heralds the decadence. Admirable in composition and painting, but lacking the simplicity and delicacy of colour of his earlier work. Compare it with the Belle Jardinière. It marks the distance traversed in art during his lifetime. The knowledge is far greater, the feeling less.

III.] RENAISSANCE PARIS (THE LOUVRE)   89

**142. *Van Dyck.* Charles I. A famous and splendid portrait, with all the courtly grace of this stately painter.

**462. *Lionardo.* Portrait of Mona Lisa. Most undoubted work of the master in existence. Has lost much of its flesh tints by darkening, but is still subtly beautiful. Compare with any of the portraits in the Salle des Primitifs, in order to understand the increase in science which made Lionardo the prince and leader of the Renaissance. The sweet and sphinx-like smile is particularly characteristic. Observe the exquisite modelling of the hands, and the dainty landscape background. Do not hurry away from it.

363. *Raphael.* Madonna with the infant St. John, known as "La Vierge au Voile." A work of his early Roman period, intermediate in style between the Belle Jardinière and the François Ier. Compare them carefully.

Above it (379) *Andrea del Sarto.* Charity. A fine example of Andrea's soft and tender colouring.

*523. Portrait of a young man. Long attributed to Raphael. More probably *Franciabigio.* Pensive and dignified.

452. *Titian.* Alphonso of Ferrara and his Mistress. A fine portrait, with its colour largely faded.

Above it, 154. Good portrait by *Van Dyck.*

539. *Murillo.* The Immaculate Conception. Luminous and pretty, in an affected showy Spanish manner. Foreshadows the modern religious art of the people. An immense favourite with the inartistic public.

**121. *Gerard Dou.* The Dropsical Woman. A triumph of Dutch painting of light and shade and detail. Faces like miniatures. The lamp and curtain like nature. Illuminated on the darkest day. Examine it attentively.

293. *Metsu.* Officer and Lady. Another masterpiece of Dutch minuteness, but far less fine in execution.

526. *Ter Borch.* Similar subject treated with coarse directness.

**551. *Velasquez.* The Infanta Marguerite — a famous portrait.

A little above it (229), *Sebastiano del Piombo.* Visitation. Compare with the Ghirlandajo in the Salle des Primitifs. A very favourable example of this Venetian master, painted in rivalry with Raphael. It well exhibits the height often attained, even by minor masters, at the culminating point of the Renaissance.

Above, occupying a large part of the wall, *Paolo Veronese. Christ and the Magdalen, at the supper in the house of Levi. Another refectory picture, treated in Veronese's large and brilliant manner, essentially as a scene of lordly Venetian life. The Pharisee facing Christ is a fine figure. Notice the intrusion of animals and casual spectators, habitual with this artist. The sense of air and space is fine. The whole picture is instinct with Venetian feeling of the period ; scenic, not sacred. A lordly treatment. Earlier painters set their scene in smaller buildings : the Venetians of this gorgeous age chose rather the Piazza of some mighty Renaissance Italian city. Here, the architecture recalls the style of Sansovino.

This room also contains many good works of the 17th century, justly skied. Examine them by contrast with the paintings of the best ages of art beneath them. Return to them later, after you have examined the works of the French artists in later rooms of this Gallery.

Now proceed into the

Long Gallery

which contains in its **First Compartment** works of the High Renaissance masters, transitional from the conventionality of the 15th, to the freedom of the 16th, and the theatrical tendency of the 17th centuries. Begin on the L, and follow that wall as far as the **first archway.**

Francia. Crucifixion, with Madonna and St. John, and Job extended at the feet of the cross, probably indicating a votive plague offering. A tolerable example of the great Bolognese painter, from the church of San Giobbe, patriarch and plague-saint, at Bologna.

Ansuino (?) Adoration of the Magi. Note coincidences with others.

308. *Francia.* Madonna. A fair example.

168. *Dosso.* St. Jerome in the Desert. Interesting as showing a later treatment of this familiar subject.

230. *Luini.* Holy Family. A good specimen of Luini's easel work. Compare with the frescoes in the Salle Duchâtel.

The hair is characteristic, also the oval face and cast of features.

Near it, two works by *Marco da Oggiono*, a pupil of Lionardo. His work and Luini's should be compared with that of the founder of the school. The differences and agreements should be observed. Notice also the survivals from earlier treatment.

354. *Sacchi.* The Four Doctors of the Church, attended by the Symbols of the Four Evangelists. This is a composition which frequently recurs in early art. L, St. Augustine, holding his book "De Civitate Dei," with the Eagle of St. John. Next, St. Gregory, inspired by the Holy Spirit as a dove, and accompanied by the Bull of St. Luke. Then, St. Jerome, in his Cardinal's hat, with the Angel of St. Matthew. Lastly, St. Ambrose with his scourge (alluding to his action in closing the doors of the church at Milan on the Emperor Theodosius after the mascacre of Thessalonica), accompanied by the winged Lion of St. Mark. An interesting symbolical composition, deserving close study.

232. *Luini.* The daughter of Herodias with the head of St. John Baptist. A favourite subject with the artist, who often repeated it. Compare it with his other works in this gallery, till you feel you begin to understand Luini.

Above it, *Borgognone.* Presentation in the Temple. In the pallid colouring peculiar to this charming Lombard master. Observe the positions of the High Priest and other personages.

85. *Borgognone.* St. Peter Martyr introducing or commending a Lady Donor to the Madonna. One panel of a triptych; the rest of it is wanting. Look out for similar figures of saints introducing votaries. St. Peter Martyr has usually a wound or a knife in his head, to indicate the mode of his martyrdom.

Beneath, a quaint little Lionardesque Annunciation.

Solario. Calvary, characteristic of the School of Lionardo.

Beneath it, 394, *Solario. Madonna with the Green Cushion. His masterpiece, a graceful and tender work, exhibiting the growing taste of the Renaissance.

458. Attributed to *Lionardo.* The young St. John Baptist. Hair, smile and treatment characteristic; but possibly a copy. You will meet with many similar St. Johns in Florentine sculpture below hereafter.

465. School of *Lionardo*. Holy Family. St. Michael the Archangel oddly introduced in order to permit the Child Christ to play with the scales in which he weighs souls—a curious Renaissance conception, wholly out of keeping with earlier reverential feeling.

*460. *Lionardo*. " La Vierge aux Rochers." A replica of the picture in the National Gallery in London. Much faded, but probably genuine. Examine closely the rocks, the Madonna, and the Angel.

395. *Solario*. Good portrait of Charles d'Amboise, a member of the great French family who will frequently crop up in connection with the Renaissance.

461. Attributed to *Lionardo*, more probably *Bernardino de' Conti*. Portrait of a Lady. Compare with the Mona Lisa, as exhibiting well the real advance in portraiture made by Lionardo.

463. Attributed to *Lionardo*, but probably spurious; Bacchus, a fine youthful figure, begun as a St. John Baptist, and afterwards altered. Compare with the other St. John Baptist near it.

Beltraffio. The Madonna of the Casio family. A characteristic Lionardesque virgin, attended by St. John Baptist and the bleeding St. Sebastian. (A votive picture.) By her side kneel two members of the Casio family, one the poet of that name, crowned with laurel. Intermediate Renaissance treatment of the Madonna and donors.

78 and 79. Good Franciscan saints, by *Moretto*.

Between them, 298. Charming *Girolamo dai Libri*.

We now come upon a magnificent series of works by **Titian**, in whom the Venetian School, ill-represented in its origin in the Salle des Primitifs, finds its culminating point.

440. *Titian*. The Madonna with the Rabbit. This is one of a group of Titian's Madonnas (several examples here) in which he endeavours to transform Bellini's type (see the specimen in the Salle des Primitifs) into an ideal of the 16th century. The Madonna is here attended by St. Catherine of Alexandria, marked as a princess by her coronet and pearls. The child, bursting from her arms, plays with the rabbit. Once more a notion far-removed] from primitive piety. Notice the background of Titian's own country. **Landscape is now beginning to struggle for recognition. Earlier art was all figures, first sacred, then also mythological.

445. *Titian.* The Crown of Thorns. A powerful but very painful painting. The artist is chiefly occupied with anatomy and the presentation of writhing emotion. The spiritual is lost in muscular action.

**443. *Titian.* The Disciples at Emmaus. Treated in the contemporary Venetian manner. This is again a subject whose variations can be well traced in this gallery.

451. *Titian.* Allegory of a husband who leaves for a campaign, commending his wife to Love and Chastity. Finely painted.

450. *Titian.* Portrait of François Ier. Famous as having been painted without a sitting—the artist had never even seen the king. He took the face from a medal.

448. *Titian.* Council of Trent. Very much to order.

Above it, **Titian.* Jupiter and Antiope. Charming Giorgionesque treatment of the pastoral nude. Compare with the Giorgione in the Salon Carré, in order to understand how deeply that great painter influenced his contemporaries.

453. *Titian.* Fine portrait.

439. *Titian.* Madonna with St. Stephen, St. Ambrose, and St. Maurice the soldier. Observe the divergence from the older method of painting the accompanying saints. Originally grouped on either side the Madonna, they are here transformed into the natural group called in Italian, a "santa conversazione." Look at the stages of this process in the Salle des Primitifs and this Long Gallery.

442. *Titian.* Another Holy Family. Interesting from the free mode of its treatment, in contrast with Bellini and earlier artists.

**455. *Titian.* Magnificent portrait.

Above these are several excellent Bassanos, worthy of study. Compare together all these Venetian works (Bonifazio etc.), lordly products of a great aristocratic mercantile community; and with them, the Veroneses of the Salon Carré, where the type attains a characteristic development.

Now return to the door by the Salon Carré and examine the **R Wall**.

Poor *Pinturicchio*, and two inferior *Peruginos*.

403. *Lo Spagna.* Nativity. Characteristic example of this scholar of Perugino and fellow-pupil of Raphael. Notice its Peruginesque treatment. Examine in detail and compare with the two other painters. As a Nativity, it is full of the conventional elements.

189. *Raffaellino del Garbo.* Coronation of the Virgin, beheld from below by four attendant saints of, or connected with, the Vallombrosan order—St. Benedict, Saint Salvi, San Giovanni Gualberto, and San Bernardo degli Uberti. These were the patrons of Vallombrosa; and the picture comes from the Church of St. Salvi, at Florence.

246. *Manni.* Baptism in Jordan. Observe, as usual, the attendant angels, though the simplicity of early treatment has wholly disappeared. The head-dresses are characteristic of the School of Perugino. Compare with Lo Spagna's Nativity.

Above it (496) Florentine Madonna, with St. Augustine, St. John Baptist, St. Antony and St. Francis. Observe their symbols. I do not always now call attention to these; but the more you observe them, the better you will understand each picture as you come to it.

390. *Luca Signorelli.* Adoration of the Magi. A fine example of the mode of treatment of this excellent anatomical painter, the forerunner of Michael Angelo. It needs long looking into.

289. *Piero di Cosimo.* Coronation of the Virgin, with St. Jerome, St. Francis, St. Louis of Toulouse and St. Bonaventura. Compare with Raffaelino del Garbo, close by, for the double scene, on earth and in heaven. Notice the crown which Louis refused, in order to embrace the monastic profession. This is a Franciscan picture; you will find it casts much light on assemblages of saints if you know for what order each picture was painted. The grouping *always* means *something*.

16. *Albertinelli.* Madonna on a pedestal, with St. Jerome and St. Zenobius. Scenes from their legends in the background. A characteristic example of the Florentine Renaissance. The

grouping is in the style then fast becoming fashionable. Compare with Lorenzo di Credi in the Salle des Primitifs.

144. *Pontormo.* Visitation. Showing the older Renaissance tendencies. Compare with the Ghirlandajo, and note persistence of the arch in the background.

*57. *Fra Bartolommeo.* Marriage of St. Catherine of Siena. This is a variant on the legend of the other St. Catherine—of Alexandria. The infant Christ is placing a ring on the holy nun's finger. Around are attendant saints—Peter, Vincent, Stephen, etc. The composition is highly characteristic of the painter and his school.

380. *Andrea del Sarto.* Holy Family. Exquisitely soft in outline and colour.

372. Doubtful. Attributed to *Raphael.* Charming portrait of a young man.

Beyond it,* two most delicate little pictures of St. George (a man) and St. Michael (an angel, winged) of *Raphael's* very early period. Note the princess in the St. George; you will come upon her again. Simple and charming. Trace Raphael's progress in this gallery, by means of Kugler.

Beyond them, again, two portraits by *Raphael*, of which 373 is of doubtful authenticity.

*366. *Raphael.* The Young St. John: a noble figure.

**367. *Raphael.* St. Margaret: issuing triumphant from the dragon which has swallowed her. A figure full of feeling and movement, and instinct with his later science. It was painted for François Ier, out of compliment to his sister, Queen Margaret of Navarre.

All these Raphaels should be carefully studied. The great painter began with a certain Peruginesque stiffness, through which nevertheless his own native grace makes itself felt at once; he progressed rapidly in knowledge and skill at Florence and Rome, but showed a tendency in his last works towards the incipient faults of the later Renaissance. By following him here, in conjunction with Florence and Rome, you can gain an idea of the course of his development.

The **Second Compartment** of the Long Gallery, which we now enter, though containing several works by Titian and other masters of the best period, is mainly devoted to painters of the later 16th and 17th century, when the decline in taste was rapid and progressive. Notice throughout the substitution of rhetorical gesture and affected composition for the simplicity of the early masters, or the dignity and truth of the High Renaissance. Begin again on the L wall, containing finer pictures than that opposite.

441. *Titian.* Another Holy Family, with St. Catherine. Both women here are Venetian ladies of high rank and of his own period. Observe, however, the persistence of the Madonna's white head-covering. Also, the playfulness introduced in the treatment of St. Catherine's palm of martyrdom, and the childish St. John with his lamb. These attributes would have been treated by earlier painters with reverence and solemnity. Titian transfers them into mere pretty accessories. Characteristic landscape background. (The female saint in this work is usually described as St. Agnes, because of the lamb : I think erroneously. The lamb is St. John's, and the St. Catherine merely plays with it.)

88. *Calcar.* Fine portrait of a young man.

38. Attributed (very doubtfully) to *Giorgione.* Holy Family, with St. Sebastian, St. Catherine, and the donor, kneeling. A good example of the intermediate treatment of saints in groups of this character.

Above it (92) *Paolo Veronese.* Esther and Ahasuerus. Treated in the lordly fashion of a Venetian pageant. Try now to understand this Venetian ideal in style and colour.

91. *Paolo Veronese.* Similar treatment of Susanna and the Elders, a traditional religious theme, here distorted into a mere excuse for the nude, in which the Renaissance delighted.

**274. *Palma Vecchio.* Adoration of the Shepherds. A noble example of this great Venetian painter. Observe how he transforms the traditional accessories in the background, and employs them in the thorough Venetian spirit.

Beyond it, several small Venetian pictures. Self-explanatory, but worthy of close attention ; especially 94, a delicate *Paolo Veronese*, on a most unusual scale—a Venetian Dominican nun presented by her patroness, St. Catherine, and St. Joseph to the Madonna. Also, 93, by the same artist, St. George and St. Catherine presenting a Venetian gentleman to the Madonna and Child. These two saints were the male and female patrons of the Venetian territory; hence their frequency in Venetian pictures.

99. The Disciples at Emmaus. Another characteristic transformation by *Veronese* of a traditional scene. The pretence of sacredness is very thin.

98. *Paolo Veronese.* Calvary. Similarly treated.

*335. *Tintoretto.* Susanna at the Bath. Admirable example of this artist's bold and effective method. In him the Venetian School attains its last possible point before the decadence.

Beneath it, two good Venetian portraits.

336. *Tintoretto.* A characteristic Paradise (sketch for the great picture in the Doge's Palace at Venice), whose various circles of saints and angels should be carefully studied. Gloomy glory.

Above it, 17. A Venetian gentleman introduced to the Madonna by St. Francis and a sainted bishop, with St. Sebastian in the background. Doubtless, a votive picture in gratitude for the noble donor's escape from the plague.

Beyond these, we come chiefly upon Venetian pictures of the Decadence, among which the most noticeable are the Venetian views by Canaletto and Guardi, showing familiar aspects of the Salute, the Doge's Palace, San Zaccaria, and other buildings.

Further on, this compartment contains **Spanish pictures,**—an artificial arrangement not without some real justification, since in the 16th and 17th centuries, Spain, enriched by her American possessions, became, for a short period, the material and artistic inheritor of Italy, and accepted in full the mature fruits of the Italian Renaissance. At the same time, she imbued the developed arts she received from Italy with Spanish showiness and love of mere display, to the exclusion of deeper spiritual feeling. The most famous among the few Spanish pictures of the Louvre are:—

552. ***Velasquez.* Philip IV of Spain.

Beneath it, *Murillo.* One of his favourite Boy Beggars, killing fleas. A curious subject, excellently rendered.

548. *Ribera.* Adoration of the Shepherds.

540. *Murillo.* Birth of the Virgin, where the transformation

of the traditional element is even more marked than in the Italian Renaissance. The colouring splendid. St. Anne is always seen in bed; other points you could notice in the enamels at Cluny. With Murillo, they become mere excuses for display of art-faculty.

Further on, *Murillo*. The occupants of a poor monastery in Spain miraculously fed by angels, known as "La Cuisine des Anges."

I do not recommend more than a cursory examination of these fine Spanish works, which can only be properly understood by those who have visited Madrid and Seville. It will suffice to note their general characteristics, and the way in which they render traditional subjects. The best point of view for the "Cuisine des Anges," is obtained from the seat nearly opposite, beneath the archway, when the splendid luminous qualities of this theatrical picture can be better appreciated. From this point also, many of the other Spanish pictures are well seen with an opera-glass. They are not intended for close examination.

(The **columns** which separate these compartments have an interesting history. They first belonged to a classical temple in North Africa. They were brought thence by Louis XIV to support a baldacchino at St. Germain-des-Prés. Finally, the Revolution transferred them to the Louvre.)

Return again, now, to the last archway, and begin once more on the **R side,** which contains for the most part tawdry works of the Baroque period, which should, however, be studied to some extent in illustration of the decadence of art in the later 16th century, and also as examples of further transformation of the traditional motives.

53. *Barocci.* Madonna in Glory, with St. Antony and St. Lucy. A good example of the insipid style which took its name from this master.

Below it, 309. *Bagnacavallo.* Circumcision, with twisted pillars, showing the decline in architectural taste. The crowded composition may be instructively compared with earlier and simpler examples of this subject; also, with Fra Bartolommeo, whose fine but complex arrangements rapidly resulted in such confused grouping.

52. *Barocci.* Same scene. The tradition now entirely ignored, and an unpleasantly realistic, yet theatrical and mannered treatment, introduced.

304. After *Primaticcio.* Mythological concert, exhibiting the taste of the **School of Fontainebleau** (the Italian artists of Raphael's group, scholars of Giulio Romano, introduced into France by François Ier).

349. *Rosselli.* Triumphant David, with the head of Goliath. Marking the advance of the histrionic tendency.

A very cursory examination of the rest of the works on this wall will probably be sufficient. Look them over in an hour. The most celebrated are two by Salvator Rosa: 318, *Guido Reni's* Ecce Homo, full of tawdry false sentiment; and *Domenichino's* St. Cecilia (often copied), with the angel reduced to the futile decorative winged boy of the period. 324, *Guido's* St. Sebastian, may be well compared with Perugino's, as marking the decline which art had suffered. It is on works like these that the Spanish School largely based itself.

This completes the **Italian collection** of the Louvre, to which the visitor should return again and again, until he feels he has entered somewhat into the spirit and tone of its various ages.

Between the next two archways, we come to a small collection of works of the **Early French School,** too few of which unfortunately remain to us.

Left Wall. Two portraits of François Ier, may be well compared with the Titian of the same king, as indicating the gulf which still separated France from the art-world of Italy. The hard, dry, wooden manner of these French works is strongly contrasted with the finished art of the Italian Renaissance. Recollect that these seemingly archaic portraits are painted by contemporaries of Raphael and Titian.

Between them, good miniatures, by Nicolas Froment, of King René and his Queen.

Above, 650. Admirable Dead Christ, with the Madonna, Magdalen, Joseph of Arimathea, etc. In the best style of the French School of the 15th century. Observe the action of the various personages: all are conventional.

Beyond it, several good small pictures of the early French Renaissance which should be carefully examined. Fouquet's portrait of Charles VII is a capital example of the older method.

Above them, 875, characteristic 15th century Crucifixion, with Last Communion and Martyrdom of St. Denis. The executioner's face is French all over. (Scenes from the Passion have often in French art such side-scenes from lives of saints. Several at Cluny.) This picture has been employed as a basis for the restoration of the reliefs in the portals at St. Denis.

Beyond again, portraits of the early Renaissance, exhibiting considerable advance in many cases.

On the **R wall** are some works more distinctly characteristic of the **school of art** which grew up round Primaticcio and his scholars at **Fontainebleau.** Among them are a Diana hunting (D. de Poitiers again), and a Continence of Scipio. They reflect the style of Giulio Romano. Beneath the first, two good portraits, with patron saints (John and Peter). All the works in this compartment should be examined carefully, as showing the raw material upon which subsequent French art was developed.

Beyond the next archway, we come to the pictures of the **Flemish School,** which deserve almost equal attention with the Italian, as individual works, but which, as of less interest in the general history of art, I shall treat more briefly. Begin here on the **R side**, for chronological order.

Among the most noticeable pictures are Adam and Eve, unnumbered, good specimens of the frank, unidealised northern nude.

595. An exquisite early Annunciation, the spirit of which should be compared with the early Italians. Notice the general similarity of accessories, combined with the divergence in spirit, the dwelling on detail, the Flemish love for effects of light and shade on brass-work, fabrics, glasses, etc. Notice that this charming picture gives us the early stage in the evolution of that type of art which culminates in the Gerard Dou in the Salon Carré.

Beside it, an exquisitely tender Dead Christ. Remarkable for the finish in the background.

The *Quentin Matsys* is not a worthy representative of the master.

Beside it, a quaint and striking group of Votaries, listening to a sermon. Probably a mere excuse for portrait-painting. The character in the faces is essentially Flemish.

Fine portrait of a young man with a pink, in a red cap.

Triptych, with the Madonna and Child (who may be well compared with those of the Memling in the Salle Duchâtel). On the flaps, the donor and his wife, introduced by their patrons, St. John and St. Christopher.

Now cross over to the **L side.**

*698. *Rogier Van der Weyden.* Excellent Deposition, with a touching St. John, and a very emaciated Dead Christ. These scenes of death are extremely common in Flemish and German art, and resulted in a great effort to express poignant emotion, as contrasted with the calmer ecstatic character of Italian art.

**279. *Quentin Matsys.* Banker and his wife. An admirable and celebrated picture, with marvellous detail, of which there are variants elsewhere. Notice the crystal vase, mirror, leaves of book, and objects on shelves in background. The fur is exquisitely painted.

*288 and 289. Two beautiful little *Memlings.*

588. Most characteristic and finished Holy Family.

699. *Memling.* St. Sebastian, Resurrection, Ascension. Compare the first with Italian examples. Notice the extraordinarily minute work in the armour and accessories, contrasted with the blank and meaningless face of the Risen Saviour. Flemish art, perfect in execution, seldom attains high ideals.

277 and 278. *Mabuse.* Virgin and donor. Excellent.

**596. *Gerard David.* Marriage at Cana. A splendid specimen of this great and insufficiently recognised painter. Background of buildings at Bruges. Every face and every portion of the decorative work, including the jars in the foreground, should be closely noticed. The kneeling donor is an admirable portrait. As a whole, what a contrast to the Paolo Veronese! The pretty, innocent face of the bride, with her air of mute wonder, is excellently rendered. I believe the donor in this work is a younger portrait of the Canon who appears in the glorious Gerard David in the National Gallery.

Skied above all these pictures on either side are several works by *Van Veen*, *Jan Matsys*, *Snyders* and others, mostly worthy of notice. Among them, 136, *Van Dyck*, good Madonna with the Magdalen and other saints.

We now come to the ** great series by **Rubens** narrating the **History of Marie de Médicis,** in the inflated allegorical style of the period. To understand them, the spectator should first read an account of her life in any good French history. These great decorative canvasses were painted hurriedly, with even more than Rubens's usual dash and freedom, to Marie's order, after her return from exile, for the decoration of her rooms at the Luxembourg (see Part V) which she had just erected. Though designed by Rubens, they were largely executed by the hands of pupils ; and while possessing all the master's exuberant artistic qualities in composition, they are not favourable specimens of his art, as regards execution and technique. It is to be regretted that most Englishmen and Frenchmen form their impressions of the painter from these vigorous but rapid pictures, rather than from his far nobler works at Antwerp, Munich, and Vienna. I give briefly the meaning of the series.

1. The Three Fates spin Marie's destiny. A small panel for the side of a door.

2. Birth of Marie at Florence. Lucina, goddess of birth, with her torch, attends the mother. Genii scatter flowers ; others hold her future crown. In the foreground, the River God of the Arno, with his stream issuing from an urn, and accompanied by the Florentine lion, as well as by boys holding the Florentine lily. This curious mixture of allegorical personages and realities is continued throughout the series.

3. Her Education, presided over by Minerva, with the aid of Mercury (to indicate her rapidity in learning), and Apollo, as teacher of the arts. Close by are the Graces, admirable nude figures. Among the accessories, bust of Socrates, painting materials, etc.

4. The Genius of France in attendance upon Henri IV, while Love shows him Marie's portrait. The attitude of the

king expresses delight and astonishment. In the clouds, Jupiter and Juno smile compliance. Below, little Loves steal the king's shield and helmet.

5. Marriage of Marie by proxy. The Grand Duke Ferdinand represents the king. Hymen holds the torch.

6. Marie lands at Marseilles, and is received by France, while Tritons and Nereids give easy passage to her vessel. Above, her Fame. On the vessel, the balls or *palli* of the Medici family.

7. Consummation of the Marriage at Lyons. The town itself is seen in the background. In the foreground, the (personified) city, crowned with a mural coronet, and designated by her lions. Above, the King, as Jupiter, with his eagle, and the Queen, as Juno, with her peacocks.

8. Birth of her son, afterwards Louis XIII, at Fontainebleau. Health receives the infant. Fortune attends the Queen.

9. The King, setting out to his war against Germany, makes Marie Regent—allegorically represented by passing her the ball of empire—and confides to her their son.

Larger pictures: No. 10, the Coronation of the Queen, and No. 11, the Apotheosis of Henri, the painful scene of his death being avoided. He is represented as raised to the sky by Jupiter on one side, and Death with his sickle on the other. Beneath, the assassin, as a serpent, wounded with an arrow. Victory and Bellona mourning. Beyond, the allegorical figure of France presenting the regency to Marie, with the acclamation of the nobility and people.

12. The Queen's government approved of by Jupiter, Juno, and the heavenly powers. In the foreground Apollo, Mars, and Minerva (the first copied from the antique statue known as the Belvedere), representing courage, art, and literature, dispel calumny and the powers of darkness.

Continue on the **opposite side**, crossing over **directly**.

13. Civil discord arises. Marie starts for Anjou, attended by Victory. Military preparations in the background.

14. The exchange of Princesses between allegorical figures of France and Austria—each intended to marry the heir of the other empire.

15. The Happiness of the Regency. The Queen bears the

scales of justice. Plenty prevails. Literature, science, art, and beauty predominate over evil, slander, and baseness.

16. Louis XIII attains his Majority (at 14) and mans the ship of State in person, still attended by the counsels of his mother. The Virtues row it.

17. Calumny overcomes the Queen. By the advice of her counsellors, she takes refuge at Blois, escorted by Wisdom.

18. Mercury, as messenger, brings an olive branch to Marie, as a token of reconciliation from her son, through the intermediation of Richelieu and the Church party.

19. Marie enters the Temple of Peace, escorted by Mercury and Truth with her torch, while blind Rage and the evil powers stand baffled behind her.

20. Apotheosis of Marie and Louis: their reconciliation and happiness. Final overthrow of the demons of discord.

21. Time brings Truth to light. Louis recognises the good influence of his mother.

The history, as given in these pictures, is of course envisaged from the point of view of a courtier, who desires to flatter and please his patroness.

Beneath this great series of Rubens are a number of **Dutch and Flemish Pictures,** mostly admirable and well worthy of attention, but, so to speak, self-explanatory. They belong entirely to modern feeling. Dutch and Flemish art, in its later form, is the domestic development of that intense love of minute detail and accessories already conspicuous in Van Eyck, Memling, and Gerard David. Sacred subjects almost disappear; the wealthy burghers ask for portraits of themselves, their wives and families, or landscapes for their households. I would call special notice to the following among many which should be closely examined to show the progress of art :—512, *Teniers*; 691, *Rubens*; 518, *Teniers*; 238 and 239, *Van Huysum*; *425, a charming *Rubens*, in his smaller and more delicate style; 147, admirable portrait by *Van Dyck*; 513, an excellent *Teniers*; *461, a good portrait by *Rubens*; 125, exquisite, luminous *Gerard Dou*; next it ***Van der Helst's* Four Judges of the Guild of Cross-bow-men deciding on the prizes, one of the most perfect specimens of this great portrait painter.

Notice the wonderful life-like expressions. Then 123, another exquisite luminous *Dou*; 542, *Van de Velde*; 41, splendid portrait by *Bol*; 130, *Gerard Dou* by himself; ****404**, *Rembrandt*, Raphael leaving the house of Tobias, a master-piece of the artist's weird and murky luminosity—strangely contrasted with Italian examples; 205, a good *Hobbema*; 133, fine portrait by *Duchâtel*; 369, excellent family group by *Van Ostade*; next it, 126, a delicious little *Dou*. But, indeed, every one of these Dutch paintings should be examined separately, in order to understand the characteristic Dutch virtues of delicate handling, exquisite detail, and domestic portraiture. They are the artistic outcome of a nation of housewives.

On the **opposite side** the series is continued with admirable flower-pieces, landscapes by Van der Veldt and Karel du Jardin, and several noteworthy portraits, among which notice the famous *Van Dyck (143) of the children of Charles I., most daintily treated. Beyond the Rubenses, again, on this side, 144, two noble portraits by *Van Dyck*, and several excellent examples of Philippe de Champaigne, a Flemish artist who deeply influenced painting in France, where he settled. **151, *Van Dyck's* Duke of Richmond, perhaps his most splendid achievement in portraiture, deserves careful study. I do not further enlarge upon these subjects because the names and dates of the painters, with the descriptions given on the frames, will sufficiently enable the judicious spectator to form his own conceptions. Devote at least a day to Dutch and Flemish art here, and then go back to the Salon Carré, to see how the Rembrandts, Dous, and Metsus, there unfortunately separated from their compeers, fall into the general scheme of Dutch development.

Good view out of either window as you pass the next archway. Look out for these views in all parts of the Louvre. They often give you glimpses of the minor courtyards, to which the general public are not admitted.

The **next two compartments** contain further Dutch and Flemish pictures of high merit—portraits, still-life, landscape, and other subjects. The scenes of village life are highly characteristic. Notice in this connection the growing taste for **landscape**, at first with a pretence of figures and animals, but gradually asserting its right to be heard on its own account. In Italy, under somewhat similar commercial conditions, we saw this taste arise in the Venetian School, with Cima, Giorgione, and Titian ; in Holland, after the Reformation put sacred art at a discount, it became almost supreme. And note at the same time how the Reformation in commercial countries has wholly altered the **type** of northern art, focussing it on trivial domestic incidents.

Among the many beautiful pictures in these compartments the spectator should at least not miss, on the L, the very charming ** Portrait by *Rubens* (not quite finished) of his second wife and two children, scarcely inferior to the lovely specimen at Munich. Near it, an admirable Crucifixion with the Madonna, St. John, and Magdalen, more reminiscent than is usual with Rubens of earlier compositions. On the R side, notice a portrait of Elizabeth of France (459), by *Rubens*, in his other, stiffer, and more courtly manner. We may well put down this peculiarity to the wishes of the sitter. His *Kermesse, near it, is an essay in the style afterwards popularized by Teniers, in which the great artist permits his Flemish blood to overcome him, and produces a clever but most unpleasant picture. The numerous admirable fruit and flower pieces, works in still life, etc., which these compartments contain, must be studied for himself by the attentive visitor. In Rubens' great canvas of the Triumph of Religion, painted for a Spanish commission, observe his curious external imitation of Spanish tendencies.

After having completed his examination of the Long Gallery, the visitor may next proceed to the five small rooms—IX, X, XI, XII, and XIII on Baedeker's map—devoted to

THE GERMAN, ENGLISH AND EARLY FRENCH SCHOOLS.

Among the **early German works** in the 2nd of these rooms, the visitor may particularly notice (*22), *Hans Holbein's* portrait of Southwell, full of character. Above it, a quaint Venus by *Cranach*, instinct with the northern conception of the crude nude. Next, two good portraits by *Holbein*. In the centre of this wall, * a Descent from the Cross, of the School of Cologne, which should be compared with similar pictures of the Italian and

Flemish Schools. The somewhat exaggerated expression of grief on all the faces is strongly characteristic of German tendencies. The figure of the Magdalen, to the R, strikes the German keynote; so does Joseph of Arimathea receiving the Crown of Thorns. Study this well, for coincidences with and differences from Italian treatment. Beyond it, two fine *Holbeins*, of the astronomer Kratzer, and *Warham, Archbishop of Canterbury, the latter a marvellous piece of painting. The opposite wall also contains good portraits and sacred pieces, among which an altarpiece by the " Master of the Death of the Virgin," deserves careful study. (Most early German masters are unknown to us by name, and are thus identified by their most famous pictures.) The Last Supper in this work, below, is largely borrowed from Lionardo. Compare with the copy of Lionardo's fresco at Milan in the Long Gallery, probably by Marco da Oggionno, which hangs near the Vierge aux Rochers. The Adoration of the Magi (597), should also be compared with the Italian examples; notice in particular the burgher character of the Three Kings, which is essentially German. The other works in this room can be sufficiently studied (for casual observers) by the aid of the labels.

The **English Room** contains a few examples of English masters of the last and present century, none of them first-rate. The most famous is the frequently reproduced Little Girl with Cherries by the pastellist *John Russel*. It is a pleasing work, but not good in colour.

The next room, with an admirable view from the window, begins the **Modern French School** (in the wide sense), and contains Le Sueur's History of the Life of St. Bruno, painted for a Carthusian monastery near the Luxembourg—of which order the saint was the founder. They are characteristic examples of the French work of the early 17th century, and they exhibit the beginnings of the national tendencies in art. The legends are partially explained on the frames, and more fully in Mrs. Jameson's "Monastic Orders." On a cursory inspection, the observer will notice the marked French tendency in the 9th, 7th, 21st, and 22nd of the series. Cold and lifeless in design and colour, these feeble works have now little more than a historical interest.

Before proceeding to the succeeding rooms of the

FRENCH SCHOOL,

you had better form some conception of the circumstances and conditions under which that school arose. The artists whom François Ier invited to Fontainebleau had little influence on French art, except in sculpture (where we shall see their spirit abundantly at work when we come to examine the Renaissance sculpture in this collection). Primaticcio and his followers, however, left behind them in France, as regards painting, scarcely more than the sense of a need for improvement. Succeeding French artists took up the Italian Renaissance in the stage represented by the later decadents and the eclectic Caracci. Nicolas Poussin (1594–1665) is the first Frenchman to attain distinction in this line; he throws something of French sentimentality into the affected mythological scenes of contemporary Italy. Claude of Lorraine, again, is almost an Italian by training and style; his artificial landscapes, not copied direct from nature, but built up by arbitrary and often impossible conjunctions, represent the prevailing tendencies of Italian art in the 17th century. On the other hand, the influence of Rubens, many of whose greatest works were painted for French kings, or came early to France, and still more of Philippe de Champaigne, a Brussels master who settled in Paris and painted much for Richelieu and Marie de Médicis, introduced into France a strain of Flemish influence. On these two schools—decadent Italian and later Flemish—then, modern French art at first based itself; the final outcome is a resultant of the two, transmuted and moulded in spirit and form by the innate, though at first unrealised, French tendencies.

Also, before you proceed to examine the subsequent specimens of the development of French art, you had better return to the Salon Carré to inspect the portraits by Philippe de Champaigne, as well as the Jouvenet, the Rigaud, and other French works there, which I purposely passed by on our previous visit, as out of harmony with the Italian masterpieces. On your way back, glance at the later Italian pictures in the First Compartment of the Long Gallery (particularly at Bronzino's odiously vulgar Christ and Mary Magdalen, and Rossi's

Doubting Thomas, both skied, on your R) as conspicuous examples of the sort of thing admired at the time when the French School took its first flights and made its earliest experiences. Then observe once more the works of the School of Fontainebleau; and, finally, inspect the pictures in Baedeker's Room IX; after which, you will be in a position to start fair in Room XIII, with the French School in the 17th century.

This Small Room beyond the St. Brunos contains more favourable specimens of *Le Sueur's* faculty (such as 559, 556, and 551), in which a distinctive French tendency still more markedly announces itself. The Ganymede, in 563, in particular, faintly foreshadows at a distance the classic painters of the Empire. We see in this room, in a very vague way, an early stage in the evolution of a David.

Passing through the Landing, at the head of the staircase (with interesting terra-cotta Etruscan sarcophagi) we arrive at the Great Gallery of **French paintings of the 17th century.** These may be examined somewhat in the mass, exhibiting, as they do, rather the courtly tendencies of the age of Louis XIV than any great individual artistic faculty. We must understand them in the spirit which built Versailles and conducted the wars on the north-eastern frontier. They are painted for the most part by the command of His Majesty. Only here and there does a faintly individual work, like *Le Sueur's* Christ and the Magdalen, and Bearing of the Cross, or *Lebrun's* Crucifixion, arrest for a moment one's passing attention. The crudeness of the colour, and the insufficiency of the composition, will be the chief points, in a general survey, to strike the spectator. (On a screen in the centre, out of proper place among its contemporaries, hangs at present *Paul Delaroche's* famous Christian Martyr.)

The student who has courage to attack this mass of uninteresting art in detail, should observe particularly the works of *N. Poussin*, as forming the point of departure for the School in general. His Bacchanal and other mythological works set the fashion of those dreary allegorical scenes which cover so many yards of ceilings in the Louvre. Observe the mixture of religious themes, like *Lebrun's* Martyrdom of Stephen, and

N. Poussin's Holy Family, with classical pictures like the Rescue of Pyrrhus, and the Alexander and Porus, as well as the close similarity of treatment in both cases. Among the best of the lot are *Jouvenet's* Raising of Lazarus, and *Lesueur's* Paul Preaching at Ephesus (partly after Raphael). **Poussin's* " Et in Arcadia ego," a rustic morality, is also famous, and is regarded as the greatest achievement of this artificial School. *Claude's* landscapes, often with a small inserted mythological story by another painter, deserve attention. (Note that landscape has hardly yet vindicated its claim to independent existence.) On the whole, it may be said that this room represents the two prevailing influences in French art of the purely monarchical period of Louis XIV,—either the pictures are quasi-royal and official, or else they are religious, for church or monastery. The mythological scenes, indeed, have often a royal reference—are supposed parallels of contemporary events; and even the religious scenes, wholly destitute of spiritual feeling, are painted in a courtly, grandiose manner. They are saints as conceived by flunkeys. Not till the Revolution swept away the royal patron did the French spirit truly realise itself. This room **reveals the Court,** not the nation.

The next room, in the Pavillon Denon, a connecting passage, contains **Portraits of Painters,** chiefly by themselves, a few of which are worthy of attention. Among them is the famous and touching ** portrait by **Mme. Lebrun** of herself and her daughter, which, in spite of some theatrical sentiment here and there obtruded, is a charming realisation of maternal feeling amply reciprocated.

Beyond it we come to the **French Gallery of the 18th century,** reflecting for the most part the spirit of the Regency and the Louis XV period. Much of it is meretricious; much of it breathes the atmosphere of the boudoir. The flavour of Du Barry pervades it almost all. It scents of musk and powder. The reader will pick out for himself such works as he admires in this curious yet not wholly unpleasing mass of affectation and mediocrity. Indeed, as opposed to the purely official work in the preceding French room, the growth of the **rococo** spirit, to be traced in this gallery, is by no means without interest. The one set of works sets forth the ideal of monarchy as a formal institution; the other displays its actual outcome in royal mistresses and frivolous amusements. Here too the ornate French taste—the Dresden china and Sèvres taste—finds its first faint embodiment. *Greuze's* famous *Cruche Cassée (263), is the chief favourite with visitors to this room. It has about it a certain false simplicity, a pretended virginal innocence, which is perhaps the highest point of art this school could attain. *Drouais's* child portraits (187), are more entirely characteristic, in their red-and-white chubbiness, of the ideas of the epoch. The pastoral scenes by *Watteau* and *Vanloo*, represent nature and country life, as they envisaged themselves to the painted and powdered great ladies of the Trianon. *Coypel's* Esther before Ahasuerus is a not unfavourable specimen of the inflated quasi-sacred style of the period. Some good portraits redeem the general high level of mediocrity in this room, but do not equal those of the daintily aristocratic English School of the end of the 18th century. Two *Greuzes* (267 and, still more, 266), reveal the essentially artificial methods of this superficially taking painter. Most observers begin by admiring him and end by disliking his ceaseless posing. *Boucher's* artificial pink-and-white nudities (as in 24 and 26), have the air of a man who painted, as he did, in a room hung round with rose-coloured satin. He is perhaps the most typical of these rococo artists: he imitates on canvas the coquettish ideals of the contemporary china-painters. *Fragonard*, again, throws into this school the love of display and bravado of a southern temperament. At the far end of the room we find in *Greuze's* later moralising pictures faint indications of the altered and somewhat more earnest feeling which produced the revolutionary epoch, still closely mixed up with the ineradicable affectation and unreality of the painter and his period. Two little stories of a Prodigal Son and his too late return, on either side of the doorway, with their violent theatrical passion and their excessive expression of impossible emotion, illustrate well this nascent tendency. They are attempts to feel where feeling was not really present. *David's* Paris and Helen introduces us, on the other hand, to the beginnings of the cold classicism which prevailed under the Empire.

In order to continue the chronological examination of the

French School the visitor must now return to the Salon Carré and traverse the vulgarly ornate Galérie d'Apollon by its side (which contains objects of more or less artistic interest in the precious metals and precious stones, many of which, especially those in the two last cases, deserve careful inspection. A morning should, if possible, be devoted later to this collection).

A short connecting room beyond (with gold Etruscan jewellery) gives access next to the **Salle des Sept Cheminées**, which contains many stiff but excellent works of the period of the **Empire**. The most noticeable of these are by *David*, whose formal classicism (a result of the revolutionary revolt from Christianity, with its reliance upon Greek, and still more Roman, morality and history) is excellently exemplified in his large picture of the * Sabine Women Intervening between their Husbands and their Fathers. This is considered his masterpiece. Its frigid style, not very distantly resembling that of a bas-relief, and its declamatory feeling do not blind us to the excellence of its general technique and its real advance on the art of the 18th century. *David* imitated the antique, but was always sculpturesque rather than pictorial in treatment. Among other fine examples of this **classic period**—the transitional stage between the 18th century and the distinctively modern spirit—attention may be called to *Gérard's* Cupid and Psyche, and to his fine portrait of the Marquis Visconti. **Mme. Lebrun's* charmingly animated portrait of Mme. Molé-Raymond, the comedian, is full of real vigour. Two good portraits by *David*, of himself and Pius VII, deserve close inspection. *Gros's* Bonaparte at Arcola, is also interesting. *Mme. Lebrun's* earlier portrait of herself and her daughter is less beautiful than the one we have already examined. Several military portraits, such as Gros's Fournier-Sarlovèze, reflect the predominant militarism of the epoch. *David's* huge canvas of the Coronation of Napoleon I in Notre-Dame is typical of another side of the great artist's development. Gradually, the frigidity of the early revolutionary period gave way to the growing **romanticism** of 1830. *Géricault's* Raft of the Medusa (sighting a sail after twelve days out), strikes the first keynote of the modern romantic movement. It created a great sensation in its own day, and gave rise to endless discussion and animadversion. It marks the advent of the **emotional** in modern art. *Gros's* Bonaparte Visiting the Plague-stricken at Jaffa, also indicates in another way a marked modernising tendency. The school of blood and wounds, of the morbid and the ghastly, has here its forerunner. All the works in this room (which modernity forbids me to treat at adequate length) should be carefully studied in detail and comparison by those who wish to understand the various steps which led to the evolution of modern French painting. *Guérin's* Return of Marcus Sextus, and *Girodet's* Burial of Atala, in particular, mark special phases of transition from the coldly classical to the romantic tendency. This room, in one word, begins with the **severe;** it ends with the **melodramatic.**

The room beyond, known as the **Salle Henri II,** is so nearly modern in tone that the reader may be safely trusted to inspect it on his own knowledge. *Giraud's* Slave-dealer and *Chassériau's* Tepidarium are its most popular pictures. It lies outside the scope of the present handbook.

The **Salle La Caze,** however, still beyond, contains a collection kept separately apart by the express desire of the donor, and includes many works both of earlier schools and of the French 17th and 18th century, worthy of the greatest attention. It is especially rich in works of the **rococo** painters, better exemplified here than in the main collection. Beginning on the L, I will merely enumerate a few of the most important works. An excellent *Hondekoeter*, skied. A noble portrait by *Tintoretto* of a Venetian magnate. A most characteristic *Fragonard*, full of the morganatic sentiment of the 18th century. Portraits by *Nattier*, affording more pleasing examples of the early 18th century style than those we have hitherto examined. Above it, a mediocre *Tintoretto* of Susanna at the Bath, not good in colour. Centre of the hall, **Watteau's* Gilles, an excellent embodiment of the innocent fool of traditional French comedy. **Frans Hals's* sly figure of a Gipsy Woman is a fine piece of vulgar character-painting. A good *Greuze*, etc. Examine more particularly the works by *Watteau, Fragonard,* and other boudoir painters, whose pictures on this wall give a more pleasing and fuller idea of the temperament of their school than that which we obtained in other parts of the collection. R wall returning — several good *Watteaus*, *Bouchers*, *Greuzes*, etc. Excellent small Dutch pictures. Fine portrait by *Rembrandt*. Rembrandt's Woman at the Bath is a characteristic example of his strikingly original conception of the nude. *Ribera's* Club-footed Boy is a Spanish pendant to Frans Hals's Gipsy. This room, containing as it does very mixed examples of all the schools, should only be visited after the spectator has obtained some idea of each in other parts of the collection. Its Dutch works, in particular, are admirable. I do not enumerate them, as enumeration is useless, but leave it to the reader to pick out for himself several fine examples.

Now traverse the Galerie d'Apollon, Salon Carré, and Long Gallery till you arrive at the

HALL OF PAINTERS OF THE 19TH CENTURY,

(Room VIII in Baedeker's plan). This hall contains for the most part the works of artists of the period of Louis Philippe and the early Second Empire — almost our own contemporaries. I will therefore only briefly call attention here to the pictures of **the romantic historical school,** then so prevalent in France, of which *Delaroche's* Death of Queen Elizabeth and Princes in the Tower and *Delacroix's* Capture of Constantinople by the Crusaders are conspicuous examples. *Devéria's* popular Birth of Henri IV belongs to the same category. These "picturesque" treatments of history answer in painting to the malign influence of Walter Scott and Victor Hugo in literature. Contrasted with them are such semi-classical works of the school of David, softened and modernised, as *Ingres's* Apotheosis of Homer — the great poet crowned by Fame, with the Iliad and Odyssey at the base of his pedestal, and surrounded by a concourse of ancient and modern singers. It is cold but dignified. *Lethière's* Death of Virginia, and *Couture's* Romans of the Decadence, represent to a certain extent a blending of these two main influences. I will not, however, particularise, as almost every picture in this room deserves some study from the point of view of the evolution of contemporary art. I will merely ask the reader not to overlook *Flandrin's* famous nude figure, the typical landscapes by *Rousseau* and *Millet*, and *David's* exquisite portrait of Mme. Récamier — sufficient in itself to immortalise both artist and sitter. The electric influence of a beautiful and pure-souled woman has here galvanised David for once into full perception and reproduction of truth and nature. Even the severe Empire furniture and background exactly accord with the character of the picture. Ary Scheffer's religious works, in his peculiar twilight style, on a solid blue background, will strike every observer. *Millet's* Gleaners and *Troyon's* group of oxen strike each a new note in art at the period when they were painted. As a whole this Gallery represents all the various strands of feeling which have gone to the production of modern painting. It attains to the threshold of cosmopolitanism in its Arabs, its negroes, and its Algerian women: it is bloodthirsty and sensuous; it is calm and meditative; it dashes with Courbet; it refines with Millet; it oscillates between the world, the flesh, and the devil; it is pious and meretricious; it sums up in itself the endless contradictory and interlacing tendencies of the Nineteenth Century. As regards chronological sequence, one may say pretty fairly that it begins with classicism, passes through romanticism, and ends for the moment in religious reaction.

Come back often to the pictures in the Louvre, especially the Salle des Primitifs, the Salon Carré, and the first two bays of the Long Gallery.

FURTHER HINTS ON THE PAINTINGS IN THE LOUVRE.

The reader must not suppose that these brief notes give anything like an adequate idea of the way in which pictures in such a gallery as the Louvre ought to be studied. My object in these Guides being mainly to open a door, that the tourist himself may enter and look about him carefully, I have given first this connected account of *all* the rooms in chronological order, for the use of those whose time is very limited, and who desire to go through the collection seriatim. But for the benefit of others who can afford to pay **many successive visits,** I will now take one or two particular pictures **in detail,** suggesting what seem to me the best and most fruitful ways in which to study them. Try for yourself afterwards to fill in a similar scheme, as far as you can, for most of the finest works in this Gallery.

I will begin with No. 251, in the Salle des Primitifs—Mantegna's beautiful and glowing **Madonna della Vittoria**. And I take Mantegna first, because (among other reasons) he is a painter who can be fairly well studied by means of the pictures in this Gallery alone, without any large reference to his remaining works in Italy or elsewhere.

Now, first, who and what was **Mantegna,** and what place does he fill in the **history of art** in Italy? Well, he was a **Paduan** painter, born in 1431, died in 1506—about the time when Raphael was painting the Belle Jardinière, in this collection. He was a contemporary and brother-in-law of Giovanni and Gentile Bellini : and if you compare his work with that of the two Bellinis, even as very inadequately represented here, you will see that their art has much in common—that they stood at about the same level of historical evolution, and painted in the same careful, precise, and accurate manner of the second half of the fifteenth century. Contrast them, on the one hand, with their immediate predecessors, such as Filippo Lippi and Benozzo Gozzoli (juniors by roughly about 20 years), in order to mark the advance they made on the art of those who went just before them ; and compare them, on the other hand, with their immediate successors, such as Raphael, and even their more advanced contemporaries, like Lionardo, in order to see what place they fill in the development of painting.

Again, Mantegna was a pupil of **Squarcione of Padua,** who practically founded the Paduan school. Now Squarcione had travelled in Greece and formed a collection of antiques, from which his pupils made drawings and studies. Also **Donatello** (the great Florentine sculptor of the early Renaissance, of whose work you can find some beautiful examples in the Renaissance Sculpture rooms of this museum) had executed several bronzes in the church of Sant' Antonio, the great local saint of Padua ; and these likewise Mantegna studied ; so that much of his work bears traces of the influence of sculpture and especially of bas-relief. He is particularly fond of introducing reliefs, festoons of fruit or flowers, and classical detail into the accessories of his pictures : and these peculiarities are well marked in the Mars and Venus, the Crucifixion, and the Madonna della Vittoria in this collection. Compare all these closely with one another till you think you have formed a fair idea of Mantegna's powerful drawing, strong realism, love of the antique, solemnity and dignity, clear-cut style, and perfect mastery of anatomy and technique. Notice his delicate, careful, conscientious workmanship ; the precision and perfection of his hands and feet ; the joy with which he lingers over classical costume and the painting of armour. Everything is sharp and defined as in the air of Italy, yet never hard, or crude, or angular. Observe, also, the sculpture-like folds of his carefully arranged draperies, and his love for shot colours and melting tints on metal or marble. The St. Michael in this picture, and the Roman soldiers in the Crucifixion, are admirable examples of this tone in his colouring. If you wished to characterise Mantegna in a single phrase, however, you might fairly say he was the most **sculpturesque** of painters.

As to date, the **Crucifixion** (in the Salon Carré) which formed one piece only of the **predella,** or series of small pictures at the base of the great Madonna in the Church of San Zeno at Verona, is the earliest example of Mantegna's work here. It displays the delicate and exquisite finish of his youthful period : but it is much more mediæval in tone—has far less freedom and conscious artistic power—than the Madonna della Vittoria, which belongs to the latest epoch of the great painter's development. Observe the early severity of the figures in the Crucifixion, and the firmness of the drawing : each personage stands out with statuesque distinctness. But note, too, that at this early stage, Mantegna's expression of emotion was still inadequate : in his striving to be powerful, he overdid the passions, sometimes almost to the verge of grotesqueness. On the other hand, do not overlook the dramatic force of the picture, as shewn, for example, in the vivid contrast between the anguish of the Madonna, with her attendant St. John, &c., and the callous carelessness of the soldiers casting lots for the Redeemer's raiment. The Mars and Venus, once more, of his middle period, represents an intermediate stage between the two styles. What is meant by a **predella,** again, you can see by looking at Fra Angelico's Coronation of the Virgin, and other similar pictures in this room—the little figures of St. Dominic and his miracles beneath the main altar-piece being examples of this adjunct. The Crucifixion formed the central picture of three such minor episodes : the Agony in the Garden and the Ascension, to right and left of it, are now in the Museum at Tours. Napoleon I had carried off the entire work from Verona : at the Restoration, the Madonna was returned to San Zeno, but the three pieces of the predella were retained in France and thus distributed. If you go to Tours or Verona, recollect the connection of the various fragments.

Next, what was the **occasion** for painting this Madonna della Vittoria? You will remember that in 1494, Charles VIII of France, invited by Ludovico Sforza, Duke of Milan, invaded North Italy, and conquered a large part of it, including Florence, Pisa, and Rome itself. Marching then on Naples, the boy king achieved a further success, which turned his own head and that of his army. (Read up all this episode in any good French history.) But Venice, trembling for her supremacy, formed a league against him; and soon after, all Italy, alarmed at his success, coalesced to repel the invader. The little Republics united their forces under Giovanni Francesco Gonzaga, Marquis of Mantua, and met Charles, on the 6th of July, 1495, at the pass of Fornova, on **the Taro.** The French king, it is true, forced his way through the hostile army, and made good his retreat : but the allies, though baffled, claimed the victory, and, as a matter of fact, Charles immediately concluded a treaty of peace and returned to Lyons. In commemoration of this event, the Marquis Gonzaga in gratitude erected a church at Mantua as a votive offering to the Madonna, and dedicated it under the name of **Santa Maria della Vittoria.**

At that time and for some years previously Mantegna had been in the service of the **Gonzaga** family at **Mantua,** where he lived for the greater part of his artistic life. In the Castello of that town, he executed several frescoes, illustrating domestic events in the history of the Gonzagas, which are still among the most interesting objects to be visited in Mantua. It was natural, therefore, that he should be invited by Giovanni Francesco Gonzaga to paint the altar-piece for the high altar of the church to commemorate this victory. The picture must have been finished about the year 1498 or 1500. It stood in the building for which it was painted till Napoleon I brought it from Italy to Paris, where it has ever since remained.

These circumstances sufficiently explain the **collection of saints** who figure in the picture. In the centre is the **Madonna of Victory** herself, to whom Gonzaga vowed the church in case he should be successful. She is enthroned, as usual. The garlands of flowers and fruit, and the coral over her head, are favourite accessories with Mantegna: they occur again in the (much earlier) Madonna at San Zeno, Verona, of which the Crucifixion here formed part of the predella. The figures of Adam and Eve, in imitation of relief, on the pedestal, are thoroughly characteristic of Mantegna's style, and recall the Paduan school of Squarcione, and the master's dependence on the work of Donatello. The overloading of the picture with flowers, festoons and architectural decoration is also a Paduan feature of the same school: it comes out equally in the works of Carlo Crivelli—not well seen in this collection. On his knees in the foreground is **Gonzaga** himself, with his villainous Italian Renaissance face, as of a man who would try to bribe Our Lady with presents. And indeed Our Lady stretches out her friendly hand towards him, as if to assure him of favour and victory. Notice that the Marquis wears his armour: he is giving thanks, as it were, on the field of battle.

As often with Mantegna, the minor characters and saints are fuller of life than the two central divine personages: his Madonnas have frequently a tendency to be insipid. On the left of the picture, flanking the Virgin, stands **St. Michael the Archangel,** the "warrior of God," as representing the idea that the Lord of Hosts fought on the side of the Italian confederacy. This beautiful figure, clad in refulgent heavenly armour, is one of the noblest and loveliest that Mantegna ever painted. Compare it with the two St. Michaels by Raphael, the early one in the Long Gallery: the later in the Salon Carré: note the general similarity of type, with the divergence in treatment. A little behind, again, half seen, stands **St. Andrew,** who was both Andrea Mantegna's own name-sake, and also one of the patrons of Mantua. He has an important church dedicated in his honour in that town—a Renaissance church, by Leon Battista Alberti: and in this church of his patron, Mantegna himself is buried. For the altar-piece of this same church, which he had doubtless selected beforehand for his own last resting-place, the great artist also painted a representation of the risen Saviour, with St. Andrew holding the cross of his martyrdom on one side, and St. Longinus (of whom more shortly) with his spear on the other. Thus there was every reason both why St. Andrew should be represented in a picture painted for the Marquis of Mantua, and why he should more particularly appear in a work by Andrea Mantegna. As one of the patron saints of town and painter, he naturally had his share in the thanksgiving for the victory. His features in this picture and in the one at Mantua are closely similar. Mantegna, indeed, imitated an older type, which he made his own, and reproduced like a portrait. Note that St. Andrew bears a cross as his symbol.

On the other side of the Madonna, **St. Elizabeth** kneels in the foreground, representing, I think, the patron saint of the Marchesa, Gonzaga's wife, who was Isabella d'Este, sister of Duke Alfonso of Ferrara. (Isabella and Elisabeth are always regarded as variants of the same name.) Now in the chapel of St. Longinus in the church of St. Andrea at Mantua, aforesaid, where Mantegna is buried, he also painted a Madonna, with this same St. Elizabeth, holding the infant St. John Baptist, while the child Christ blesses him : no doubt a votive offering from Isabella. Here again we have a type of St. Elizabeth repeated in this picture. Behind St. Elizabeth stands the exquisitely wistful **St. George,** the patron saint of the Venetian territory, representing the part borne by Venice and her dependencies in the war of expulsion : the patron receives the thanks of his faithful votaries. (Mrs. Jameson thinks this figure is St. Maurice, another military saint, and patron of Mantua : comparison with various St. Georges and St. Maurices elsewhere makes me disagree with her. Besides, St. George's lance is often broken, as here : you can note it so in the Raphael of the Long Gallery.) In the background stands **St. Longinus,** a Roman soldier, distinguishable by his lance and antique helmet. According to tradition, Longinus was the centurion who pierced the side of Christ : you see him so in the famous Rubens (called the Coup de Lance) at Antwerp, and in almost every mediæval Crucifixion or Calvary. (Look out for him in future.) When he saw the wonders which accompanied the Passion, we are told in scripture that he exclaimed, "Truly this man was the Son of God." Later legend made him be converted, after being afflicted with sudden blindness, and undergo a singular voluntary martyrdom. His relics were brought to Mantua in the 11th century, and he has ever since been the chief patron saint of that city. Mantegna painted him often, and sometimes made a type of him. In the picture already described in the chapel of St. Longinus, he answers, as here, to St. Andrew, and wears a classical costume, on which the painter has lavished his usual care and minute accuracy of drawing. Notice him also in the foreground of Mantegna's Crucifixion in the Salon Carré, bearing his spear—where, however, the type is not followed as usual. Thus not one of the characters grouped around the Madonna in this exquisite picture is without its full relevancy and meaning.

Do not overlook in this military votive offering the preponderance of soldier saints, and their appearance under arms, to commemorate the victory.

Observe also the way in which St. George and St. Michael hold the **Madonna's mantle,** so as to enclose or embrace Gonzaga and his wife's patroness, St. Elizabeth. This is a symbol of the Madonna's protection : in what is called a Madonna della Misericordia Our Lady's robe thus shelters numerous votaries. So, at Cluny, you will find a sculptured St. Ursula (in Room VI) sheltering under her mantle as many of the 11,000 Virgins as the sculptor could manage—as she also does in the Memling at Bruges.

On the **æsthetic side,** note once more the marked distinction which Mantegna draws between the historical portrait of the kneeling Gonzaga—a most ruthless ruffian—and the ideal figures of saints by whom he is surrounded. Remark, again, the angelic sweetness of the round-faced St. Michael, contrasted with the purely human look of longing and strife, and the guarded purity in the countenance of the St. George—who almost foreshadows Burne-Jones and Rossetti. Observe, too, how this romantic saint serves as a foil to the practical Roman Longinus, with his honest and sober face, and his soldierly sense of duty. Study the melting tones of colour throughout, and contrast the simple devotional calm of this religious work with the rapidity and movement of the mundane Mars and Venus beside it. Do not overlook a single detail; every hand and foot, every surface of metal, every fruit and flower is worthy of attention.

As always, I have only tried here to **explain** this picture, not to make you **admire** it. But the longer you look at it the more you will be charmed by its wonderful colour, its poetic grace, and the exquisite beauty of its drawing and composition.

Now, still in the same connection, go on into the Long Gallery, and look, near Andrea del Sarto's Holy Family, at a mannered and theatrical picture of the **Nativity by Giulio Romano.** This is not a Nativity simple, but one with selected saints looking on: it was painted for the altar-piece of the altar of the Chapel of St. Longinus in Sant' Andrea at Mantua—the same in which Mantegna had earlier painted the Longinus pictures noted above. The central portion of this altar-piece consists of a tolerably conventional Nativity, with the adoring shepherds, Raphaelized by Giulio Romano (who was Raphael's favourite pupil) in accordance with the ideas of the early 16th cent. (It is interesting to note, by the way, the nature of these modifications.) In the background is the herald angel appearing to the shepherds: this scene, prior in time to the other, was often so represented in the same picture or carving: look out for it elsewhere, and also for such non-contemporaneous episodes in general. But the attendant saints, to right and left, looking on at the sacred scene, are St. John the Evangelist (known by his chalice and serpent) and **St. Longinus.** The last-named holds in his hands a crystal vase—a pyx or reliquary, containing the sacred blood of Christ, which Longinus caught as it fell, and which was brought with the rest of the relics to **Mantua,** and preserved in the very chapel for which this picture was intended. Compare this dull Longinus with the two by Mantegna in this collection: and when you visit Mantua, remember that these pictures came from these two churches. By thus interweaving your facts, you will get a far clearer conception in the end of **the connection of art** than you can possibly do if you regard the various works in pure isolation.

But what was **Giulio Romano** doing at Mantua? After Raphael's death, his pupils were dispersed; and this his favourite follower settled down in the service of Duke Federigo Gonzaga (the first Duke—the earlier lords were Marquises), for whom he decorated the Palazzo del Tè, with its grotesque Titans. **Primaticcio** and **Niccolo dell' Abbate**, pupils again of Giulio's, were educated at Mantua, and afterwards summoned by François Ier to France, where they became the founders of the **School of Fontainebleau.** They thus passed on the Raphaelesque traditions into the French capital. It is partly for this reason that I have selected for my first examples this particular Mantuan group of paintings, in order that you may realise the close interaction of French and Italian politics, and the continuity of the Italian with the French Renaissance.

It is worth while, too, to enquire **how** the different pictures **came into this collection.** The Madonna della Vittoria, we saw, was brought as a trophy of war from Italy by Napoleon. The Giulio Romano, after hanging for some time in the chapel at Mantua, for which it was painted, was shortly annexed by the Duke of Mantua, who sold it to Charles I of England. That king formed a noble collection of Italian and Flemish works, which, after his execution, was sold by the Commonwealth for a very small price to a dealer named Jabach, who in his turn disposed of most of the pictures to Louis XIV; they formed the nucleus of the Louvre collection. Look out for these works of which Puritan England thus deprived herself, and see how considerable a portion they form of the earlier treasures of this Gallery.

Lastly, return once more to the Mantegnas in the Salle des Primitifs, and notice that the so-called Parnassus—that is to say, the Mars and Venus discovered by Vulcan—as well as the Vices conquered by Wisdom, and the companion pieces by Perugino and Costa, were all painted for **Isabella d'Este-Gonzaga,** to decorate her boudoir at Mantua. Of these works, I think Mantegna's are the oldest, and struck the keynote for figures and treatment. For after Mantegna's death, the Ferrarese painter, Costa, was invited from Isabella's home to become court-painter at Mantua: and the Perugino is one in that master's latest manner, most tinged with the Renaissance. Giulio Romano, again, succeeded Costa. If you will now compare Mantegna's two works in this series with his others in this Gallery, you will be able to form a clearer conception of his admirable fancy, his unvarying grace, and his perfect mastery of execution : while if you contrast them with those by the two contemporary artists—the Umbrian Perugino and the Ferrarese Costa—you will be enabled to observe what was the common note of these early Renaissance masters, and what their distinctive individual characteristics. In particular, you may notice in these works, when looked at side by side with those of earlier painters, the enormous advance Mantegna had made in anatomy and in perspective. He is the **scientific painter** of Upper Italy, as Lionardo is the scientific painter of Florence.

These four pictures again made their way to the Louvre by a different route. They were captured at the sack of Mantua in 1630, and originally came to France to decorate the *château* of Cardinal Richelieu.

Once more, **Duke Alfonso d'Este,** Isabella's brother, is the person whom you see in the portrait by Titian in the Salon Carré, together with his mistress Laura Dianti, painted about 1520. Familiarity with such facts alone can give you any adequate idea of the extraordinary rapidity in the development of art and the modernization of Italy in the 16th century.

For my next example I will take a quite obscure and unnoticed picture, also in the Salle des Primitifs, **Giovanni Massone's altar-piece** in three compartments, number 261.

Savona is an unimportant little town between Nice and Genoa, chiefly noteworthy at the present day as the junction for a branch line to Turin. But in the 15th and 16th centuries it was a flourishing place, which gave employment to many distinguished Piedmontese and Lombard artists, the most famous of whom were Foppa and Brea. It also gave birth to two famous popes, Sixtus IV and Julius II, the latter of whom is familiar to most of us from the magnificent portrait by Raphael, three replicas of which exist, in the Uffizi and the Pitti Palace in Florence, and in the National Gallery in London. Sixtus IV erected for himself a superb sepulchral chapel in his native town of Savona : go and see it, if you pass by there, as well as the modern statue of the pope erected by his fellow-citizens. From that chapel this picture, by an otherwise unknown artist, has been abstracted and brought here. We know its author merely by the signature he has placed on a *cartellino* or strip of paper in the picture itself : Joh[ann]es Mazonus de Alex[andri]a pinxit—shewing that he was born in the Piedmontese town of Alessandria. For the rest, he is a mere name to us.

The picture itself, by no means a masterpiece, has in its centre the Nativity, designed in the usual conventional fashion, and in a somewhat antiquated Lombard style. The Madonna and St. Joseph have very solid haloes : the action takes place in a ruined temple, as often, symbolising the triumph of Christianity over heathendom. In the background are a landscape, and some pleasing accessories. But the lateral subjects give it greater interest. In the compartment to the L stands St. Francis of Assisi, in his usual brown Franciscan robe, as protector of Sixtus IV, who kneels beside him. Notice this way of marking the name of a donor, for the pope was Cardinal Francesco della Rovere. Observe too the stigmata, as far as visible, and compare this much later figure of St. Francis with those in the picture by Giotto and its two imitators. On the R stands a second Franciscan saint, also in the coarse brown garb of his order—the same in whose church Andrea Mantegna studied Donatello, and whom we have seen more than once during our Parisian excursions holding in his arms the infant Christ—St. Antony of Padua. He lays his hand on the shoulder of a second votary—the Cardinal della Rovere, afterwards the stern and formidable pope, Julius II. If you know the National Gallery and the Vatican, see whether you can recognise an earlier stage of the same features which occur in the famous portrait, and also in the figure of the pope, borne on the shoulders of his stalwart attendants into the temple at Jerusalem, in a corner of the famous fresco of the Expulsion of Heliodorus.

Recollect, again, that it was for the tomb of this same Pope Julius II that Michael Angelo produced the two so-called Fettered Slaves, which you have seen or will see in the Renaissance Sculpture Room of this collection. Weave your knowledge together in this way, till it forms a connected whole, which enables you far better to understand and appreciate.

I call your special attention to this picture, among other things, for its historical rather than its artistic value. But I want you also to realise that the man who was painted in this rude and antiquated style in his middle age was painted again in his declining years by Raphael at the summit of his powers, and was a patron of the mighty Michael Angelo at the zenith of his development. This will help to impress upon you better than anything else the necessity for carefully **noting chronology**, and will also supply a needed caution that you must not regard any work as necessarily early on no better ground than because it is comparatively archaic in style and treatment.

Next inspect the two little companion pictures of **St. George and St. Michael** by **Raphael**, on the R wall of the First Compartment in the Long Gallery. These two small works are rare examples of Raphael's very earliest pre-Peruginesque manner. Morelli has shewn that the great painter was first of all a pupil of Timoteo Viti at Urbino, his native town. If you have not visited Bologna and Milan, however, this will tell you little; for nowhere else can you see Timoteo to any great advantage; and I may observe here that the best time to visit the Louvre is *after* you have been in Italy, where you ought to have formed a clear conception of the various masters and their relations to one another. But you can see at least, on the face of them, that these two simple and graceful little works are quite different in style and manner even from the *Belle Jardinière*, and certainly very unlike the much later St. Margaret which hangs close by them. They are still comparatively mediæval in tone : they have a definiteness and clearness of outline which contrasts strongly with the softer melting tones of Raphael's later work : they show as yet no tinge of the affected prettinesses which he learned from Perugino—still less of his later Florentine and Roman manners. They are painted on the back of a chess or draught board, and were produced for Duke Guidobaldo of Urbino about the year 1500.

Look first at the **St. George**. The subject here is the Combat with the Dragon; and Raphael, in representing it, has strictly followed the conventional arrangement of earlier painters. No earlier picture for comparison with his treatment exists in this Gallery, though there are plenty elsewhere : but if you will look downstairs at the majolica relief of the same subject in the Della Robbia Room of the Renaissance Sculpture Gallery, you will see how closely Raphael's work corresponds with earlier representations of the same pretty myth. As you will now have learned, there is always a regular way to envisage every stock subject: whoever produced a Combat of St. George with the Dragon was compelled by custom and the expectations of his patron to include these various elements—a St. George in armour, on horseback, the horse usually white, as here: a wounded dragon, most often to the right: the Princess running away in terror in the distance, or at least crouching abjectly. There is a Tintoretto of this subject, indeed, in the National Gallery, where some critics have blamed the great Venetian painter for making the Princess look away in terror, instead of turning with gratitude to thank her brave preserver. But the conventional representation *demanded* that the Princess should flee or cower: people were accustomed to that treatment of the theme, and expected always to see it repeated. It was their notion of a St. George. We must set down a great deal in early art to this sense of expectation on the part of patrons. Tintoretto, who came much later than Raphael, after the mighty Renaissance painters had accustomed the world to put up with, or even to look for, novelty of composition, often ventured very largely to depart from traditional motives. In his picture, therefore, the Princess occupies the foreground—a most revolutionary proceeding—while the action itself is relegated somewhat to the middle distance. But if you compare the three representations of this scene to be found in the Louvre—this picture and the two reliefs by Della Robbia and Michel Colombe respectively—you will see that the Princess in earlier times is always represented quite small in the distance, and is usually running away, or at best kneeling with clasped hands in abject terror.

In the Raphael, the dragon is already wounded: but he has broken the saint's lance, with part of which he is transfixed, while the remainder lies in fragments on the ground behind him. St. George on his prancing steed is drawing his sword to finish off the monster. In the Michel Colombe, on the other hand (downstairs in the French Renaissance Sculpture), the dragon is biting at the lance, which explains why it is broken here, and also why the St. George in Mantegna's Madonna holds a broken shaft as his emblem or symbol. Observe, however, that while the French sculptor, with questionable taste, makes the dragon occupy the larger part of the field, so as somewhat to dwarf St. George and his steed, the Italian sculptor, and still more the Italian painter, have shewn greater tact in treating the dragon as a comparative accessory, and concentrating attention upon the militant saint, combating with spiritual arms the evil demon. In this picture, as Mrs. Jameson well observes, the conception is on the whole serenely allegorical and religious in spirit. But Raphael himself painted a second St. George, at a later date, for the Duke of Urbino to present to Henry VII of England. In this other picture, which is now in the Hermitage at St. Petersburg, St. George is treated rather as the patron saint of England than as the Champion of Right—to mark which fact he wears the Order of the Garter round his knee, with its familiar motto. As Champion of England, he is rushing on the monster with fiery energy: the picture is in this case more military than spiritual. The moment chosen is the one where he is just transfixing the dragon with his lance: the rescued Princess is here again in the background.

Note once more that these various works are pictures of the **combat** of St. George with the Dragon. In **devotional pictures** of the Madonna, St. George frequently stands by Our Lady's side, in accordance with the wishes of the particular donor, as patron saint of that person himself, or of his town or family. In Venetian pictures, as we have seen, he is very frequent, being one of the patron saints of Venice, and more particularly of the Venetian army and the conquered territory. You will find it interesting, after you have finished the examination of the two Raphaels, to go round the devotional Italian pictures in the Salle des Primitifs, the Long Gallery, and the Salon Carré, in order to note his various appearances. He is usually marked by his lance and his armour: the absence of wings (a point not always noticed by beginners) will enable you at once to discriminate him from St. Michael—as man from angel. The more you learn to look out for such recurrences of saints, and to account for the reasons for their appearance, the more will you understand and enjoy picture galleries, and the more will you throw yourself into the devotional mediæval atmosphere which produced such pictures.

Now turn to the second little Raphael. This represents the closely cognate subject of **St. Michael and the Dragon**—the angelic as opposed to the human counterpart. The two ideas are at bottom identical—the power of good overcoming evil; the true faith combating heathendom. It is a world-wide myth, occurring in many forms—as Horus and Typhon, as Perseus, as Bellerophon. Hence Michael and George, the superhuman and the human soldier of right, often balance one another, as in these two pictures: you have seen them doing so already in the Madonna della Vittoria: look out for them elsewhere in this conjunction. Both are knights; both are in armour; but one is a man and the other an angel. In this second little picture, St. Michael is seen, clad in his usual gorgeous mail, treading on the neck of the dragon and menacing it with his sword. The dark and lurid landscape in the background contains many fearful forms of uncertain monsters: condemned souls are plagued in it by demons, while a flaming town flares murkily towards heaven in the far distance, the details being taken, as in many such works, from Dante's Inferno. Or rather, they and the Inferno represent the same old traditional view of Hades. (The figures weighed down with leaden cowls are the hypocrites, while the thieves are tormented by a plague of serpents.) Close comparison of these two little works will give you a good idea of Raphael's earliest Urbino manner. This fantastic picture, however, though full of imagination, is by no means so pleasing as the dainty St. George beside it.

Go straight from this combat to the **Great St. Michael**, also by Raphael, in the Salon Carré. It bears date 1518. Pope Leo X commissioned Raphael to paint this picture as a present for François Ier: the painter—to whom he left the choice of subject—chose St. Michael, the military patron of France, and of the Order of which the king was Grand Master. (You will find a bronze bust of François, wearing the collar and pendant of St. Michael, in the Renaissance Sculpture.) He chose it also, no doubt, because it enabled him to show his increased mastery over life and action. This great and noble picture, one of the finest as regards dramatic rapidity ever painted by Raphael, is celebrated for the instantaneous effect of its movement. (Compare the demoniac boy in the Transfiguration at the Vatican.) The warrior archangel has just swooped down through the air, and, hovering on poised wings, is caught in the very act of setting one foot lightly on the demon's shoulder. The dragon, writhing, tries in vain to lift his head and turn on his conqueror. The noble serenity of the archangel's face, the perfect grace of his form and attitude, the brilliant panoply of his celestial armour, the sheen of his wings, the light tresses of his hair floating outward behind him (as of one who has traversed space on wings of lightning) cannot fail to be remarked by every spectator. This is Raphael in the fulness of his knowledge and power, yet far less interesting to the lover of sacred art than the boy Raphael of Urbino, the dreamy Raphael of the Sposalizio at Milan, the tender Raphael of the Gran Duca at Florence, or of the Belle Jardinière in this same apartment. Notice that with the progress of Renaissance feeling the demon is now no longer a dragon but a half-human figure, with horns and serpent tail, and swarthy red in colour. He is so foreshortened as not to take up any large space in the composition, which is mainly filled by the victorious figure of the triumphant archangel. The more classical armour bespeaks the High Renaissance. The longer you compare these two extreme phases of Raphael's art, the more will you note points of advance between them—technical advance, counterbalanced by moral and spiritual retrogression.

End by comparing this St. Michael with Mantegna's, and with the playful Lionardesque archangel in the *Vierge aux balances*, the last point in the degeneracy of a celestial conception.

Raphael is one of the painters who can best be studied at the Louvre, with comparatively little need for aid from elsewhere.

Pay a special visit to the Louvre one day in order to make a **detailed study of Madonnas.** Before doing so, however, read and digest the following general statement of principles on the subject

[People who have not thrown themselves, or thought themselves, or read themselves into the mental attitude of early art, often complain that Italian picture galleries, and museums like Cluny, are too full of merely sacred subjects. But when once you have learnt to understand and appreciate them, to know the meaning which lurks in every part, you will no longer make this causeless complaint. As well object to Greek art that it represents little save the personages of Greek mythology. As a matter of fact, though the Louvre contains a fair number of Madonnas, it does not embrace a sufficient number to give a perfectly clear conception of the varieties of type and the development of the subject—not so good a series in many respects as the National Gallery, though it is particularly well adapted for the study of certain special groups, particularly the Lionardesque-Lombard development.

The simplest type of Madonna is that where **Our Lady** appears **alone** with the Divine Infant. This modification of the subject most often occurs as a half length, though sometimes the Blessed Virgin is so represented in full length, enthroned, or under a canopy. Several such simple Madonnas occur in the Gallery. In the earliest examples here, however, such as Cimabue's, and the cognate altar-piece of the School of Giotto, the Madonna is seen surrounded by angelic supporters. This forms a second group—**Our Lady with Angels.** Very early examples of this treatment show the angels in complete isolation, as a sort of framework. (See several parallels in sculpture in Room VI, ground floor, at Cluny.) Grouping as yet is non-existent. No specimen of this very original type is to be found in the Louvre; but in the Cimabue of this Gallery the angels are superimposed, so to speak, while in the Giottesque example close by an elementary attempt is made at grouping them. In later works, the angels are more and more naturally represented, from age to age, singly or in pairs, or else grouped irregularly on either side of Our Lady. You will note for yourself that as the Renaissance developes, the nature of the grouping, both of angels and saints, deviates more and more from the early strict architectural symmetry.

A slight variant on the simple pictures of the Madonna and Child are those, of Florentine origin, in which the **infant St.**

John Baptist, the patron Saint of the City of Florence, is introduced at play with the childish Saviour. This class—the **Madonna and Child, with St. John**—is well represented in the *Belle Jardinière*, and several other pictures in the Louvre.

Most often, however, the Madonna is seen enthroned, in the centre of the altar-piece or composition, and surrounded by one, two, or three pairs of saintly personages. The **Madonna with Saints** thus forms a separate group of subjects. These saints, you will by this time have gathered, are *never* arbitrarily introduced. They were selected and commissioned, as a rule, by the purchaser, and they are there for a good and sufficient reason. Often the donor desired to pay his devotion in this fashion to his own personal patron; often to the patron of his town or village, of the church in which the picture was to be deposited, or of his family or relations. Frequently, again, the picture was a **votive offering,** as against plague or other dreaded calamity: in which case it is apt to contain figures of the great plague saints, Roch and Sebastian. Ignorant people often object that such sets of saints are not contemporary. They forget that this is the Enthroned Madonna, and that the action takes place in the Celestial City, where the saints surround the throne of Our Lady.

As regards **grouping,** in the earlier altar-pieces the selected saints were treated in complete isolation. Most often the Madonna and Child occupy in such cases a central panel, under its own canopy; while the saints are each enclosed in a separate little alcove or gilded tabernacle. Reminiscences of this usage linger long in Italy. Later on, as art progressed, painters began to feel the stiffness of such an arrangement: they placed the attendant saints at first in regularly disposed pairs on either side the throne, and afterwards in something approaching a set **composition.** With the High Renaissance, the various figures, instead of occupying mere posts round the seat of Our Lady, and gazing at her in adoration, began to indulge in conversation with one another, or to take part in some more or less animated and natural action. This method of arrangement, which culminates for the Florentine school in Fra Bartolommeo, degenerates with the Decadence into confused and muddled groups, with scarcely a trace of symbols—groups of well-draped models, in which it is impossible to see any sacred significance. The **Florentine** painters preferred, as a rule, such rather complex grouping: the **Venetians,** influenced in great part by the severer taste of Giorgione and of Titian, usually show a more simple arrangement.

Any one of these various types of Madonna may also be modified by the introduction of a **kneeling donor.** Thus, Van Eyck's glowing picture of the Chancellor Rollin adoring Our Lady is an example of the simple Madonna and Child, enthroned, accompanied by the donor; though in this case, the composition is further slightly enriched by the dainty little floating angel in the background, who places an exquisitely jewelled crown of the finest Flemish workmanship on the head of the Virgin. The Madonna della Vittoria, again, which we have so fully considered, is essentially a Madonna and Saints, with the kneeling donor. In very early pictures, you will observe that the donors are often painted grotesquely small, while Our Lady and the Saints are of relatively superhuman stature, to mark their superiority as heavenly personages. In later works, this absurdity dies out, and the figure and face of the donor become one of the recognised excuses for early portrait painting. Indeed, portraiture took its rise for the modern world from such kneeling figures.

Another point of view from which it is interesting to compare these various Madonnas is that of the **Nationality** or **School of Art** to which they belong. The **early Italian** representations of Our Lady are usually more or less girlish in appearance, refined in features, and comparatively simple in dress and decoration. The Flemish type is peculiarly insipid, one might often say, even with great artists, inane and meaningless; in the hands of minor painters, it becomes positively wooden. The face here is long and rather thin; the features peaky. The Madonna of Flemish art, indeed, like the Christ of all art, is a sacred type which is seldom varied. **Early French** Madonnas, once more, are regal and ladylike, sometimes even courtly. They wear crowns as queens, and are better observed in the Louvre in sculpture than in painting. This Gallery hardly suffices to note in full the peculiarities of the **sub-types** in various **Italian schools**; but they may still be recognised. Of these, the **Florentine** are spiritual, delicate, and strongly ideal; the **Lombard**, intellectual, like well-read ladies; the **Venetian**, stately and matronly oligarchical mothers, degenerating later into the mere aristocratic nobility, soulless and materialised, of Titian and his followers. The **Umbrians** and **Sienese** are distinguished for the most part by their pure and saintly air of fervent piety.

Do not confound with any of these **devotional Madonnas**, with or without select groups of saints, various other classes of picture which somewhat resemble them. Each of these has in early art its own proper convention and treatment: it was a recognised species. A **Holy Family**, for example, consists, as a rule, of a Madonna, the Infant Christ, St. Joseph, St. Elizabeth, and the child Baptist. Like the other subjects, it is sometimes complicated by the addition of selected Saints as spectators or assessors. A **Coronation of the Virgin**, again, is an entirely celestial scene, taking place in the calm of the heavenly regions. The Madonna is usually crowned by her Son, but sometimes by angels or by the Eternal Father. (Several interesting examples of this, for comparison, occur in Room VI, ground floor, at Cluny.) **Nativities**, of course, belong rather to the group of pictorial histories, such as the Life of Christ, or the Seven Joys of Mary. The sculptures in the ambulatory at Notre-Dame give one a good idea of such continuous histories.

One interesting set of Madonnas, largely exemplified here, to take a particular example, is the later Lombard type of the **School of Lionardo**. This type, well distinguished by its regular oval features, its gentle smile of inner happiness, and its peculiar waving hair with wisps over the shoulders, is usually regarded as essentially belonging to Lionardo himself and his immediate followers. It is foreshadowed, however, by Foppa, Borgognone, and other early Lombard painters, specimens of whom are not numerous in the Louvre. Lionardo, when he came to Milan to Ludovico Sforza, adopted this local type, which he transfused with Florentine grace and with his own peculiar subdued smile, as one sees it already in the Mona Lisa. From Lionardo, again, it was taken, with more or less success, by his immediate pupils, Beltraffio, Solario, Cesare di Sesto, and others, as well as by Luini, who was not a pupil of Lionardo himself, but who was deeply influenced by the master's methods and his works in Milan. The number of these Lionardesque Madonnas in the Louvre is exceptionally great, while Lionardo himself can here be better estimated than in Italy. Nowhere else perhaps, save possibly at Milan, can this type as a whole be compared by the student to so great advantage.

While the Madonna herself usually occupies the central panel of votive pictures, it sometimes happens that some **other saint** is, on his own altar-piece, similarly enthroned; and in that case he is flanked by brother saints, often more important in themselves, but then and there subordinated to him. This special honour under special circumstances is well seen in the case of the St. Lawrence at the far end of the Salle des Primitifs. Particular local saints often thus receive what might otherwise appear undue recognition. For the same reason, minor saints in the group surrounding a Madonna often obtain local brevet-rank (if I may be allowed the simile) over others of far greater general dignity, which they could not lay claim to in any other connection. Thus, in the Nativity by Giulio Romano, to which I called attention in connection with Mantegna's Madonna, St. Longinus (with his crystal vase) stood on Our Lady's R, while St. John was relegated to her L—a subordination of the greater to the lesser saint which would only be possible in a chapel actually dedicated to St. Longinus, and where he receives peculiar honour. I now propose to escort you round a few rooms of the Louvre, again calling attention very briefly, from this point of view, to certain special Madonna features only.]

Now, go to the Louvre and test these remarks. Begin at the far end of the Salle des Primitifs. The Cimabue and the Giottesque of the Madonna and Angels we have already considered. Compare them again from our present standpoint. Close to them on the R, beneath the large Giotto of St. Francis, are two pretty little Madonnas, 1620 (I now give the large upper numbers alone) and 1667. The first of these exhibits below two tiny votaries—the small-sized donors—a Franciscan monk and a Dominican nun, with the robes of their orders; the centre consists of St. Paul and St. Catherine, as the attendant saints on the large Enthroned Virgin. The second has the choir of angels, both surrounding and beneath the throne, with St. Peter (keys), St. Paul (sword), St. John Baptist (camel-hair) and St. Stephen or St. Vincent (robed as deacon). St. Peter and St. Paul in 1625 are similar figures, once surrounding a central panel, with the Madonna now missing. Compare with this 1666, with its Enthroned Madonna of the early almond-eyed type, its group of angels round the throne, and its two saints at the base, John Baptist and Peter. Observe that the types of these also can be recognised. Each saint has regular features of his own, which you can learn to know quite as well as the symbols.

Higher up, 1664, another Madonna and Child, Enthroned, with similar angels, but with the addition of the figure of St. Catherine of Alexandria, on whose finger the Christ is placing a ring. This is an early intermediate type of the Marriage of St. Catherine, hardly yet characterized. Most of these Madonnas have the characteristic softness and peculiar cast of countenance of the early School of Siena.

1279, Gentile da Fabriano, is almost a simple Madonna and Child, but for the addition of the smaller donor, Pandolfo Malatesta, Lord of Rimini. This picture shows the bland and round-faced Umbrian type which is closely allied to that of Siena. Both Schools are remarkable for the fervent pietism which blossomed out in full in St. Francis of Assisi and St. Catherine of Siena.

In the beautiful Perugino above, 1564, note the complete transformation in the later Umbrian school of the adoring angels into a graceful pair, and the beginning of an attempt to group in comparatively natural attitudes the accompanying saints, Rose and Catherine.

This feature is still more marked in 1565, also Perugino, (but later) where the Baptist and St. Catherine, well composed, are thrown into the background behind the Madonna. Observe that while earlier piety drapes the Child, in Gentile and still more in Perugino, the growing love for the nude begins to exhibit itself. A study of haloes is also interesting.

On the opposite or R side, 1315 is a good example of the simple Enthroned Madonna of the School of Giotto. Compare it with that next it, 1316, where the angels are grouped with some attempt at composition.

1397, by Neri di Bicci, is also a characteristic half-length simple Madonna, with the Child still draped after the earlier fashion affected by this belated follower of Giottesque models.

1345, beneath it, by Filippo Lippi or his school, shows a characteristic type of features which this painter introduced,— a modification of the older Florentine ideal : the face is said to be that of his model Lucrezia Buti, the nun with whom he eloped and whom he was finally permitted to marry. The angels in the background show well the rapid advance in the treatment of these accessories. Observe, as you pass, their Florentine lilies. Their features are like those of the Medici children, as seen in numerous works at Florence.

In 1295, by Botticelli, we get that individual painter's peculiar mystical and somewhat languid type, while the angels are again like Medici portraits. Study these Botticellis for his artistic personality.

1344, by Filippo Lippi, next to it, exhibits Filippo's very rounded faces, both in Madonna and angels. The type is more human. Here, again, we have the Florentine lily borne by the adoring choir, whose position should be compared as a faint lingering reminiscence of that in the Giottesques and the great Cimabue. Observe, at the same time, the division of the painting as a whole into three false compartments, a suggestion from the earlier type of altar-piece. At the Madonna's feet are two adoring saints, difficult to identify—Florentine and local, probably. Do not fail to gaze close at the characteristic baby cherubs, perhaps Lucrezia's. This picture should be compared in all its details with earlier pictures of angel choirs. It is a lovely work. Its delicate painting is strongly characteristic. The relief of the faces should be specially noted.

The Botticelli next it, 1296, introduces us to the infant St. John of Florence whom we meet again in the *Belle Jardinière* of Raphael's Florentine period. Another young St. John close by is full of suggestions of Donatello in the Sculpture Gallery.

493, above the last but one, is a very characteristic Madonna of the Florentine school, closely resembling the type of Botticelli. This once more is a simple Madonna and Child, without accessories.

In 1662, the sanctity has almost disappeared and we get scarcely more than a purely human mother and baby.

On the opposite side, 4573, is a half-length by Perugino, the affected pose of whose neck and the character of whose face you will now recognise; the Madonna floats in an almond-shaped glory of cherubs, which indicates her ascent to heaven. Several similar subjects exist in sculpture at Cluny.

1540, Lo Spagna, is again a simple half-length Madonna, whose purely Umbrian type recalls both Perugino and the earlier examples. Compare the Peruginos, Raphaels, and Lo Spagnas here, and form from them some conception of the Umbrian ideal.

Of the Bellini beside it I have already spoken sufficiently. Observe, here, the absolute nudity of the Child, and the reduction of the angels to sweet little cherub heads among clouds in the background. The graceful arrangement of the attendant saints strikes a Bellini keynote: it was followed in later developments of this subject by Venetian painters. Such half-lengths are common among the School of Bellini.

The treatment by Cima, 1259, introducing landscape, and the peculiarly high Venetian throne, is one of a sort also very frequent for full-length Madonnas at Venice and in the Venetian territory. The grouping of the saints, also, is here transitional. Compare it with the exquisite Lorenzo di Credi opposite.

On the opposite wall, 1367, by Mainardi, shows us a Florentine face, the St. John of Florence, and the typical sweet-faced Florentine angels, holding lilies; in the background, a view of the city.

Cosimo Rosseli's, 1482, has again the almond-shaped glory of cherubs, the nude Child, the typical Florentine face (which you may now recognise) and also characteristic Florentine angels; but its St. Bernard and the Magdalen are introduced on clouds after a somewhat novel fashion. The St. Bernard is writing down his vision of the Madonna.

I have already called attention to the beautiful grouping in 1263 by Lorenzo di Credi ; but observe now that the exquisite attendant saints, almost statuesque in their clear-cut isolation, still show a reminiscence of the earlier arrangement in tabernacles by the Renaissance archways at their back, combined with the niche in which the Madonna is enthroned. Only by the light of Giottesque examples can we understand the composition of this glorious picture. We do not know the circumstances under which it was produced: but St. Julian was the patron saint of Rimini, as St. Nicolas was of Bari. Both these towns were great Adriatic ports : and I believe it was painted for a merchant of the neighbourhood.

Do not be content in any of these cases with observing merely the points to which I call definite attention ; try to compare each work throughout in all its details with others like it. The evolution of the grouping, in fact, will give you endless hints as to the history and development of the art of composition. This picture of Lorenzo's may be regarded as exemplifying the finest stage in such works : those of later date are less pure and severe—show a tendency to confusion.

This will be quite enough to occupy you for one day. Another morning, proceed into the Long Gallery, where you can similarly compare the High Renaissance types and the Lionardesque Madonnas of the later School of Lombardy.

In the little Madonna of the School of Francia, 1437, observe the position of the attendant saint, the new type of face proper to the art of Bologna, and the way in which, as often, the infant Christ is poised on a parapet.

1553, by Garofalo, shows a later and softer development of a somewhat similar (Ferrarese) type ; but the Child, instead of blessing with his two fingers as in most early cases, here displays the growing Renaissance love of variety and novelty : he is asleep in his cradle. Observe his attitude in this and other instances. With all these changes, however, you cannot fail to be struck by the fairly constant persistence of the red tunic and the blue mantle of the Madonna, as well as by the nature of her head-dress in each great School. Never fail to observe the characteristic head-dresses in the various Schools of Italian art. They will help you, like the faces, to form types for comparison.

1353, by Luini, introduces us at once to the Lombard-Lionardesque class of face and hair. Compare it closely with the Madonnas in the frescoes in the Salle Duchâtel. The introduction of Joseph makes this in essence a Holy Family. Note Luini's development of the halo of Christ, cruciform in early cases, or composed of a cross inscribed in a circle, into a cross-like arrangement of rays of light.

The two works by Marco da Oggiono, close by, betray similar types, far inferior to Luini's, with further loss of primitive reverence.

In 1181, Borgognone's Presentation, an earlier Lombard work, the Madonna faintly foreshadows this Lionardesque type, though the Lionardesque features are far less markedly present than in many other examples by this silvery painter.

1530, by Solario, the famous Madonna of the Green Cushion, may be compared with those by Marco da Oggiono, which it resembles in motive.

In 1599, La Vierge aux Rochers, we get Lionardo's own personal type, which is also seen in the Madonna and St. Anne of the Salon Carré. Compare all these with the Mona Lisa, for touch and spirit. Then continue your examination through the rest of this room with the Lionardesque types: after which, turn to the School of Venice, beyond them, and note the evolution of the Titianesque types from the primitive Venetians.

On the opposite side of the same room, observe, once more, how Fra Bartolommeo and his School arranged their extremely complex groups of saints into a composition resembling a state ceremonial. From this point on in the evolution of the Santa Conversazione you will see that the arrangement of the saints entirely loses all sense of sacred meaning. Artificial ecstasies replace natural piety. An attempt to be artistic, and a desire to introduce a mode of treatment fitter for the theatre than for the church, at last entirely obscure the original meaning of these groups, which are so full of ardour in Fra Angelico, so full of stateliness in Lorenzo di Credi.

Another day may well be devoted to the quaintly girlish

Madonnas of the **Flemish School.** Begin by observing carefully the Van Eyck of the Salon Carré, which is a Madonna with donor, and the Memling of the Salle Duchâtel, which is a Madonna with donors, not one with saints; the patrons here being merely brought in to introduce the votaries to Our Lady's notice. From these, proceed to the Early Flemish section of the Long Gallery, and note in detail the evolution of the type in later pictures. I need hardly call attention to the Flemish love for crowns, jewellery, and costly adjuncts. These reflect the wealthy burgher life of Bruges, Ghent, and Antwerp. The translucent colour of the Flemish painters, too, lends itself well to these decorative elements.

The best example of an **Early French Madonna** is the beautiful one which hangs by the R hand side of the door in the Salon Carré, leading into the Salle Duchâtel. This exquisite figure, a true masterpiece of its School, should be compared with later French developments in painting, as well as with the admirable collection of plastic works of this School in the Renaissance Sculpture Gallery down stairs. With these may also be mentioned, as a typical French example, the famous miracle-working Notre-Dame-de-Paris, a statue of the thirteenth or fourteenth century, which stands under a canopy against the pillar by the entrance to the choir in the south transept of Notre-Dame, and is popularly regarded as the statue of Our Lady to which the church is dedicated. The close connection between royalty and religion in France, well exemplified in the number of saints of the royal house at St. Germain l'Auxerrois, St. Germain-des-Prés, St. Denis, and elsewhere, is markedly exhibited in the extremely regal and high-bred character always given to French Madonnas. The Florentine, which form in this respect the greatest contrast, are often envisaged as idealised peasant girls, full of soul and fervour, but by no means exalted.

Finally, note as far as is possible with the few materials in this collection, the round-faced, placid type of the **German Madonna**—placid when at rest, though contorted (as the Mater Dolorosa) with exaggerated anguish. The fine wooden statue in the room of the Limoges enamels at Cluny will help to strike the key-note for this somewhat domestic national ideal. The early

German Madonna is as often as not just a glorified housewife.

Many other subjects for similar comparative treatment may be found in the Louvre. Pick out for yourself a special theme, such as, for example, the Adoration of the Magi, the Nativity, the Presentation in the Temple, or the Agony in the Garden, and try to follow it out through various examples. Choose also a saint or two, and pursue them steadily through their evolution. Do not think that to examine paintings in this way is to be absorbed by the subject rather than by the art of the painter. Only superficial observers fall into this error. You will find on the contrary that the characteristics of each School and of each artist can best be discovered and observed by watching how each modifies or alters pre-existing and conventional conceptions. In order to thoroughly understand any early picture, you must look at it first as a representation of such-and-such a **given subject,** for which a relatively fixed and conventional set of figures or accessories was prescribed by tradition. The number and minuteness of the prescribed accessories will grow upon you as you watch them. You have then to observe how **each School as a whole** treats such works; what feeling it introduces, towards what sort of modification in style or tone it usually tends. Next, you must consider it relatively to **its age,** as exemplifying a particular stage in the progress of the science and art of painting. Last of all you must carefully estimate what peculiarities are due to the taste, the temperament, the hand, and the technique of the **individual artist.** For example, Gerard David's Marriage at Cana is thoroughly Flemish in all its details; while Paolo Veronese's is thoroughly Venetian. You may notice the Flemish and Venetian hand, not merely in the figures and the composition as a whole, but even in the extraordinarily divergent treatment of such details as the jars in the foreground, which for David are painted with Flemish daintiness of detail, though coarse and rough in themselves; while Veronese approaches them with Venetian wealth of Renaissance fancy, both in decoration and handling. But the David, again, is not merely Flemish: it has the distinctive marks of that particular Fleming, and should be compared with his lovely portrait of a kneeling donor with his three patron saints in the National Gallery : while the Veronese is noticeable for the voluptuousness, the over-richness, the dash and spirit, of that large free master of the full Renaissance, the Rubens by comparison among the Venetians of his time. So too, if you study attentively the Botticellis in the Salle des Primitifs, you can notice a close similarity of type in many of his faces with the types in certain pictures by Filippo Lippi and still more in those by other Florentines of the same period ; while you are yet even more distinctly struck by the intense individuality and refined spiritual feeling of this very original and soulful master.

In order to study the Louvre aright, in short, you must be **continually comparing.** In a word, regard each work, first, as a representation of such-and-such a subject, falling into its proper place in the evolution of its series : second, as belonging to such-and-such a school or nationality : third, as representing such-and-such an age in the historical evolution of the art of painting : fourth, as exhibiting the individuality, the style, the characteristics, the technique, and the peculiar touch of such-and-such an individual painter. Only thus can you study art aright in this or any other gallery.

Try this method on Van Eyck's Madonna, on Titian's Entombment, on Sebastiano del Piombo's Visitation, and on Memling's little John Baptist, which is one attendant saint from a triptych whose Madonna is missing.

Some other time, consider in detail the two delicately luminous **frescoes by Luini,** in the Salle Duchâtel. Before doing so, however, read on the spot the following remarks.

I have spoken here for the most part from the point of view of those visitors who have not travelled much in Italy or the Low Countries. And, as a matter of fact, the Louvre is the first great picture gallery on the Continent visited by nine out of ten English or Americans. In reality, however, since this collection contains several isolated masterpieces of all the great schools, together with several unconnected pictures of minor artists, it requires, almost more than any other great gallery, to be seen by the light of information acquired elsewhere. It ought, therefore, to be examined *after* as well as, and even more than, *before* visits to other countries. This collection, for example, includes works by Van Eyck, by Memling, by Giotto, by Fra Angelico. But Van Eyck can only be fully understood by those who have visited Ghent ; Memling can only be fully understood by those who have visited Bruges : it is impossible really to comprehend Giotto unless you have seen his great series of frescoes in the Madonna dell' Arena at Padua : it is impossible really to comprehend Fra Angelico unless you have examined the saintly and ecstatic works at San Marco in Florence. Thus you have to bear in mind that the works in the Louvre are only **stray examples** of masters and schools with whom an adequate acquaintance must be obtained elsewhere. It was for this reason that I began these notes with special examples of Mantegna, because he is one of the very few artists, other than French, of whom you can form some tolerably fair conception in Paris alone, to be pieced out afterwards by observation in Italy.

Furthermore, it must be recollected that many artists can only be seen to advantage under the **conditions amid which** their works were produced. This is especially the case with the Italian painters of the 14th and 15th centuries. They were **a school of fresco-painters**. Their altar-pieces and other separate panels give but a very inadequate idea of their powers, and especially of their composition. Giotto and Fra Angelico, in particular, cannot possibly be estimated aright by any of their works to be seen north of the Alps. The altar-pieces, being more especially sacred in character, were relatively very fixed in type : they allowed of less variation, less incident, less action, than the histories of saints which frequently form the subjects of frescoes. You can judge of this to a slight extent in the Louvre itself, by comparing the Madonnas at the far end of the Salle des Primitifs with Giotto's St. Francis which hangs by : for the Madonna was the most sacred and therefore the most bound by custom of any type. You will at once observe how much freer and more naturalistic is the treatment in the episode of the Stigmata than in the comparatively wooden figures of Our Lady by which it is surrounded. Still more is this the case when we come to compare any of these altar-pieces with frescoes such as those of the Arena at Padua, or Santa Croce at Florence. Similarly with Fra Angelico: the little crowded works which he produced as altar-pieces give a totally different conception of his character and powers than that which we derive from the large and relatively spacious frescoes at San Marco, or in Pope Nicolas's Chapel at the Vatican. In such works, we see him expand into a totally different manner. Now frescoes, by their very nature, cannot easily be removed from the walls of churches without great danger. Therefore, the school of fresco-painters—that is to say, the Early Italian school—is ill represented outside Italy.

Now Luini, though he belongs to the 16th century, and though he produced some of his most beautiful works as cabinet or panel pictures, was yet almost as essentially a painter in fresco as Fra Angelico or Ghirlandajo. He can best be appreciated in Milan and its neighbourhood. And I will add a few notes here for the benefit of those who know Italy, and who can recall the works they have seen in that country. At the Brera in Milan, an immense number of his frescoes, cut out from churches, can be seen and compared to great advantage. Everybody who has visited that noble gallery must recall at least the exquisite figure of St. Catherine placed in her sarcophagus by angels, as well as the lovely Madonna with St. Antony and St. Barbara, where the face and beard of the aged anchorite somewhat recall the treatment of the old bearded king in the Adoration of the Magi in this gallery. Still better can Luini's work be understood by those who know the Sanctuary at Saronno, where a splendid series of his frescoes still exists on the wall of the great church in which they were painted. The two frescoes here in the Salle Duchâtel are not quite so fine either as those at Saronno or as the very best examples among the collection at the Brera. Nevertheless, they are beautiful and delicately-toned specimens of Luini's work, and, if studied in conjunction with other pictures by the same artist in the adjoining rooms, they will serve to give a tolerably just conception of his style and genius.

Luini is essentially a **Lionardesque** painter. He was not actually a pupil of Lionardo; but like all other Lombard artists of his time, he was deeply influenced by the temperament and example of the Florentine master. If you wish to see the kind of work produced by the Lombard school *before* it had undergone this quickening influence of Lionardo,—been Tuscanised and Lionardised—look at the Borgognones in the Long Gallery. These, again, are not at all satisfactory specimens of that tender, delicate, and silvery colourist. To appreciate Borgognone as he ought to be appreciated, however, you must have seen him at home in the Certosa di Pavia: though even those who know only his exquisitely spiritual altar-piece of the Madonna with the two St. Catherines (of Alexandria and Siena) in the National Gallery will recognise how inadequately his work is represented by the specimens in the Louvre. Nevertheless, these examples, inferior though they be in style and feeling, will serve fairly well to indicate the point to which art had attained in Lombardy *before* the advent of Lionardo. I need not point out their comparatively archaic character, and their close following of earlier methods and motives. Again, if you compare with Borgognone the subsequent group of Lionardesque painters,—Solario and his contemporaries,—whose works hang close by on the left-hand wall of the Long Gallery, you will see how immense was the change which Lionardo introduced into Lombard art. From his time forward, the Lionardesque face, the peculiar smile, the crimped wisps of hair, the subtle tones of colour, and as far as possible the touch and technique of the master, are reproduced over and over again by the next generation of Milanese painters. Among them all, Luini stands preeminently forward as the only one endowed with profound original genius, capable of transfusing the Lionardesque types with new vitality and beauty of his own conceiving. The others are imitators: Luini is a disciple.

These attributes are well seen in the two beautiful frescoes of the Salle Duchâtel. They came to Paris from the Palazzo Litta, that handsome rococo palace in Milan which stands nearly opposite the church of San Maurizio, itself a museum of Luini's loveliest frescoes, including the incomparable Execution of St. Catherine. The Adoration of the Magi is the most satisfactory of the two. In it the kings,—Caspar, Melchior, Balthasar,—representing, as ever, the three ages of man and the three old continents,—are treated with a grace and soul and delicacy which Luini has hardly surpassed even at Saronno. The eldest king, as most often, kneels next to the Madonna, who occupies the conventional R hand of the picture. He has removed his crown, also an habitual feature, and is presenting his gift, while the others are caught just before the act of offering theirs. The exquisite face of this eldest king is highly typical ; so is the gently-smiling Lionardesque Madonna. The youngest king is represented as a Moor, as always in German, Flemish, and North Italian art, though this trait is rarer, if it occurs at all, in the Florentine and Central Italian painters. I take it that the notion of the Moor was derived from Venice ; for the Three Kings were great objects of devotion in Lombardy and the Rhine country. Their relics, which now repose at Cologne, made a long stay on their way from the East at Milan ; and it is to this fact, I fancy, that we must attribute the exceptional frequency of this subject in the art of Northern Italy, as of the Rhenish region. In the background, the usual caravans are seen descending the mountain. Such long trains of servants and attendants are commonly seen in Adorations of the Magi. Camels and even elephants frequently form part of them. Recollect the charming procession in the exquisite Benozzo Gozzoli in the Riccardi Palace. A study of this subject, from the simple beginnings in Giotto's fresco in the Arena at Padua (where a single servant and a very grotesque camel, entirely evolved out of the painter's imagination, form the sole elements of the cortége beyond the Three Kings), down to the highly complex Ghirlandajo in the Uffizi at Florence, (a good copy of which may be seen at the Ecole des Beaux Arts,) and thence to Luini, Bonifazio and the later Italians, forms a most interesting subject for the comprehension of the historical evolution of art in Italy. Go straight from this picture to the Rubens in the Salon Carré in order to observe the way in which the theme has been treated, with considerable attention to traditional detail, yet with highly transformed feeling, by the great and princely Flemish painter.

The Nativity, in Luini's second fresco, is also full of traditional features,—a beautiful work in the peculiar spirit of this gentle artist. Note every one of the accessories and details, observing how they have come from earlier pictures, and also how completely Luini has subordinated them to his own art and his delicate handling. Comparison of these two with the other Luinis in other rooms will give you some idea of his varying manners in fresco and oil-painting. Note that the frescoes represent him best, and are fullest of Luini.

Another picture, which in a wholly different direction exemplifies the need for knowledge of works of art elsewhere, and especially under the conditions in which they were originally painted, is to be found in Carpaccio's **Preaching of St. Stephen,** on the R hand wall, shortly after you enter the Salle des Primitifs. This is one of a series of the Life of St. Stephen,—a form of composition of which the only good example in the Louvre is Lesueur's insipid and colourless set, recounting the biography and miracles of St. Bruno. In Italy, such histories of saints are everywhere common, as frescoes or otherwise. Those who know Venice, for example, will well remember Carpaccio's own charming series of the Life of St. Ursula, now well arranged round the walls of a single room in the Venice Academy. Still better will they understand the nature of these works if they have seen Carpaccio's other delicious series of the Life of St. George, in San Giorgio dei Schiavoni, where the pictures still remain, at their original height from the ground, and in their original position, on the walls of the church for which they were painted. Only in such situations can works of this kind be properly estimated. That they can less easily be understood in isolation, you can gather if you look at the four cabinet pictures from the boudoir of Isabella d'Este, by Mantegna, Perugino, and Costa, which hang not far from this very St. Stephen in the same room of the Louvre. The size of the figures, in particular, is largely dictated by the shape of the room, the distance from the eye, and the character of the space which the painter has to cover.

This St. Stephen series, again, once existed entire as five pictures, all by Carpaccio, in the Scuola (or Guild) of St.

Stephen at Venice. Similar sets of other saints still exist in the Scuola di San Rocco and other Guilds in the city. The first of the group, which represents the saint being consecrated as deacon by St. Peter, is now in the Berlin Gallery. The second, the Preaching of St. Stephen, is the one before which you are now standing. The third, St. Stephen disputing with the Doctors, is at the Brera in Milan. The fourth, the Martyrdom of St. Stephen, is at Stuttgardt. The fifth and last, St. Stephen Enthroned, between St. Nicolas and St. Thomas Aquinas, has disappeared from sight, or at least its present whereabouts is unknown to me. It is interesting to look out for such companion works in widely separated galleries.

Rightly to understand this picture, once more, one should know Carpaccio. And fully to know him one must have spent some time in Venice. But even without that knowledge, it is pleasant here to remark the familiar acquaintance with oriental life, which is equally visible in the neighbouring picture of the School of Bellini representing the reception of a Venetian Ambassador at Cairo. The mixed character of the architecture and the quaint accessories are all redolent of Carpaccio's semi-mediæval and picturesque sentiment. The pellucid atmosphere, the apparent realism, the underlying idealism, the naïveté of the innocent saint in his deacon's robes, counting his *firstly*, *secondly*, and *thirdly* on his fingers, irrespective of persecution, and the glow and brilliancy of the Venetian colouring, here approaching its zenith, all combine to make this daintily simple picture one of the most attractive in this part of the Louvre. Recollect it when you go to Milan and Venice, and let it fall into its proper place, in time, in your mature conception of the painter and the epoch in which he lived.

Nor is this all. It must be borne in mind that while the Louvre is one of the noblest collections of pictures in Europe, it differs from most other fine collections in the fact that its most important and valuable works are **not of native origin,** nor of one race, school, or period. The pictures at Florence are almost all Florentine: the pictures at Venice are almost all Venetian. At Bruges and Antwerp we have few but Flemish works: at the Hague and Amsterdam, few but Dutch. In the Louvre, on the contrary (as at Dresden and Munich), we get several masterpieces of *all* the great schools, with relatively few minor works of the groups to which they belong, by whose light to understand them. In short, this is a gallery of purple patches. The gems of the collection are the Raphaels, the Titians, the Lionardos, an exquisite Van Eyck, a splendid Memling, a few fine Murillos, a number of great Rubenses. To understand all these, we must know something of Florentine art, Umbrian art, Venetian art, Flemish art, Spanish art, and so forth. The finest pictures of any in the collection are not French at all, and cannot wholly be comprehended by the light of works in this gallery alone. Therefore it is best, if possible, **to return to the Louvre** after visiting every other great school of art in Europe. On the other hand, a few great artists are here very amply represented; among them I may particularise Raphael, Titian, Mantegna, Lionardo and the Lionardesque school, Gerard Dou, and Rembrandt.

As a further example of the light cast by pictures elsewhere on those in this Gallery, however, I prefer to take a single little subject from the predella of **Fra Angelico's** glorious **Coronation of the Virgin:** I mean the compartment which represents St. Dominic and his brethren being fed by angels in the monastery of St. Sabina at Rome. Anybody who looks at Fra Angelico's painting, even in these smaller works, can recognise at once his tender, saintly, and devout manner. He is permeated by a spirit of adoring reverence, which comes out in every one of his angels and martyrs. Fewer people, however, note that the angelic friar was also a loyal and devoted **Dominican.** Whatever he paints is to the glory of God; but it is also to the glory of St. Dominic and of the order that he founded. This beautiful altar-piece, for instance, was produced by the Dominican painter of Fiesole for the Dominican church of St. Dominic at Fiesole. The saint himself, with his little red star, is everywhere apparent: and those who have visited Fra Angelico's own Dominican monastery of San Marco at Florence will recollect that the founder and his red star similarly occur in almost every fresco in that beautiful building. They will also recollect that this very subject of the brethren fed by angels forms the theme for a beautiful but much later fresco by Sogliani in the Great Refectory of the same monastery. Such an episode is admirably adapted for one of those large pictures representing a repast of some sacred character which it was usual to place on the end wall of conventual dining halls. Compare it also with a Spanish treatment of a similar miracle by Murillo, in the Cuisine des Anges. Note the simplicity and sobriety of the Early Italian work, as contrasted with the strained feeling and insistence upon mere effects of luminosity and glory in the showy Spanish painting. The moral of all such half-allegorical miracles is clearly this:—Our order is sustained by God's divine providence.

I have said already that a **German Last Supper** in this collection (German Room) betrays the influence of Lionardo's great fresco on the wall of the monastery of Santa Maria delle Grazie at Milan, of which an early copy by a pupil of Lionardo's exists in the Louvre (L wall of the Long Gallery). But in order thoroughly to understand Lionardo's Last Supper, again, we must similarly compare it with many previous representations of the same sacred scene. The type, in fact, was begun among nameless Byzantine and early Christian artists, whose work can best be studied in Italy. It found its first notable artistic expression in Giotto's fresco at Santa Croce at Florence, where the traditional type is considerably transformed: and this Giottesque Last Supper was repeated over and over again by many copyists, who each introduced various modifications. Ghirlandajo once more transformed the type at San Marco and the Ognissanti; and from Ghirlandajo, Lionardo borrowed part of his arrangement, while transfusing it with an entirely new element of life and action, at a dramatic moment, which marks this great painter's style, and is a distinct move forward in the art of composition. Each work of art down to the end of the 16th century can thus only be fully understood by considering it in its proper place, as one of a continuous evolutionary series. Every painter took much from those who went before: his individuality can best be gauged by observing how he transformed and modified what he borrowed.

Now take **Ghirlandajo's Visitation** in the Salle des Primitifs as an example of a work which in quite a different way, requires to be understood by light from elsewhere. Note how admirably the figures here are balanced against the sky and the archway in the background. In itself, this is a beautiful and striking picture; but it is also a good illustration of those subjects which cannot adequately be understood by consideration of works in this Gallery alone. The attitudes and costumes of the two principal personages are strictly conventional: nay, if you compare the St. Elizabeth in this Visitation with the same saint in the Mantegna almost opposite, you will see that her dress and features remain fairly typical, even in two such very distinct schools as the Paduan and the Florentine. The relative positions of the Madonna and her elder cousin have come down to Ghirlandajo from a very remote antiquity: they were adopted, with modification, by Giotto, in his fresco of this subject in the Madonna dell' Arena at Padua. But Giotto also introduced an arch in the background, which persists in almost all later representations. His arch, however, is blind—you do not see the sky through it. So is Taddeo Gaddi's, in his closely similar Visitation at Santa Croce in Florence: but the figures here still more nearly approach the positions of the Ghirlandajo, and they stand more directly framed, as it were, by the arch behind them. Skipping many intermediate examples, each of which leads up to this picture, we come to this beautiful embodiment of Ghirlandajo's, which, while retaining the simplicity of composition in the earlier examples, shows a fine artistic instinct in the way in which the chief characters are silhouetted in the gap of the archway. Ghirlandajo accepted the older tradition, while transforming it with the skill and taste of the early Renaissance after his own fashion. Those who have visited Florence will remember how Pacchiarotto, in his admirable presentation of the same subject, now in the Belle Arti in that town—which, like this one, is a Visitation with selected saints as spectators—has closely followed Ghirlandajo's treatment with still further modifications: while the noble embodiment of the same scene by Mariotto Albertinelli, in the Uffizi, consists of the two central figures in the Ghirlandajo or the Pacchiarotto, cut out, as it were, and presented separately with noble effect against a background of sky seen through the archway. In such a case we see distinctly how the individual work can only fairly be judged as a development of motives borrowed from others which have preceded it, and how in turn it gives rise later to still further modifications of its own conception. If you have not yet visited Florence, bear in mind this work when you see the Pacchiorotto and the Albertinelli. It is a good plan for the purposes of such comparison to carry about photographs of other pictures in the same series. You may go straight from the Ghirlandajo here to the Sebastiano del Piombo in the Salon Carré; and thence again to a copy of Pontormo's Visitation in the Long Gallery (R side, near the Fra Bartolommeo), which is interesting as showing a survival of the arch, treated with far less effect, and thrown away as an element in the composition. Here the attendant saints have become a confused crowd, and the degradation of Fra Bartolommeo's balanced grouping is very conspicuous. Make one picture thus cast light upon another.

II. SCULPTURE

[The **Sculpture** at the Louvre falls into three main divisions, each of which is housed in a separate part of the building. The **Classical Sculpture** is approached by the same door as the Paintings, and occupies the basement floor of Jean Goujon's part of the Old Louvre, with the wing beneath the Galerie d'Apollon. The **Renaissance Sculpture** is approached by a separate door in the eastern half of the same side, and occupies the corresponding suite opposite the Classical series. The **Modern Sculpture** is also approached by a special door in the north wing of the W side in the old Cour du Louvre, and occupies the suite beyond the Pavillon de l'Horloge.

The importance of these three divisions is very different. Without doubt, the most valuable collection, intrinsically and artistically speaking, is that of the **Classical or Antique Sculpture**: and this should be visited in close detail by all those who do not contemplate a trip to Rome, Naples, and Florence. Nobody can afford to miss the " Venus of Milo, the "Diana of Gabii," or the Samothracian Nikè. On the other hand, these exquisite Greek and Roman works, models of plastic art for all time, including two or three of the greatest masterpieces which have come down to us from antiquity, have yet no *organic connection* with French history, or even, save quite indirectly, with the development of French art. At the same time, thoroughly to understand them is a work for the specialist: those who have little or no classical knowledge, and who desire to comprehend them, must be content to buy the new official catalogue (not yet issued), to follow closely the excellent labels, and also to study the subject in detail in the various excellent handbooks of antique sculpture, such as Lübke's or Gardner's.

The discrimination of the different schools, and the evidence (usually very inferential) as to the affiliation of the various works on the great masters or their followers, are so much matters of expert opinion that I do not propose to enter into them here. I shall merely give, for the general reader, a brief account of the succession and evolution of antique plastic art, as exemplified in the various halls of this gallery, referring him for further and fuller details to specialist works on the subject.

The **Renaissance Sculpture,** on the other hand, is largely French; and, whether French or Italian, it bears directly on the evolution of Parisian art, and has the closest relations with the life of the people. Every visitor to Paris should therefore pay great attention to this important collection, which forms the best transitional link in Western Europe between Gothic Mediævalism and the modern spirit.

The collection of **Modern Sculpture,** again, is both artistically and historically far less important. It may be visited in an hour or two, and it is chiefly interesting as bridging the lamentable gap between the fine Renaissance work of the age of the later Valois, and the productions of contemporary French sculptors.]

1. ANTIQUE SCULPTURE

[Few or none of the most famous masterpieces of the great classical artists have come down to us with absolute certainty. The plastic works which we actually possess are for the most part those which have been casually preserved by accidental circumstances. Almost all the greatest productions of the greatest sculptors have either been destroyed or else defaced beyond recognition. We therefore depend for our knowledge of ancient sculpture either upon those works which were situated on comparatively inaccessible portions of huge buildings like the Parthenon and other temples, and which have consequently survived more or less completely the ravages of time, the mischief of the barbarian, and the blind fury of early Christian and Mahommedan fanatics ; or else upon those which have been preserved for us in the earth, under the débris of burnt and ruined villas and gardens, or in the ashes of buried cities like Pompeii. Under these circumstances, the wonder is that so much of beautiful and noble should still remain to us. This is mainly owing to the fact that in antiquity **a fine model,** once produced, was repeated and varied *ad infinitum,*—much as we have seen at Cluny and in the paintings upstairs each principal scene from the Gospels or the legends of the saints, once crystallized by custom, was reproduced over and over again with slight alterations by many subsequent artists. The consequence is that most of the statues in this department fall into well-marked groups with other examples here or elsewhere. We have not the originals, in most cases, but we have **many copies**; and few of these copies are servile reproductions : more often, they show some touch of the individual sculptor. The best antiques are therefore generally those which happen most nearly to approach in spirit and execution a great and famous original. (See later, for example, the Apollo Sauroctonos.) You must compare these works one with another, in this collection and elsewhere, in this spirit, recollecting that often even an inferior variant represents in certain parts the feeling of the original far better than another and generally finer example may happen to do. Nay, such splendid works as the so-called Venus of Milo itself must thus be regarded rather as fortunate copies or modifications of an accepted type by some gifted originator than as necessarily originals by the best masters. With the exception of the few fragments from the Parthenon by Pheidias and his pupils, hardly anything in this gallery can be set down with certainty to any first-class name of the very best periods. But many statues can be assigned to groups which took their origin from certain particular famous sculptors: we know the *school*, though not the *artist*. And several are judged by the descriptions of ancient writers to be copies or variants of works assigned to sculptors of the first eminence.

Many of the statues found in the Renaissance period, and up to the close of the eighteenth century, have been freely and often injudiciously restored: others have really antique heads, which do not however in every case belong to them. Not a few have been considerably altered and hacked about in the course of restoration, or of arbitrarily supplying them with independent faces. This reprehensible practice has *not* been followed in more recent additions such as the "Venus of Milo" and the Samothracian Nikè.]

Enter by the same door as for the paintings. Proceed along the corridor (Galerie Denon) and dive, right or left, under the great staircase. (Good new room to the R, containing excellent Roman mosaics from French North Africa.) Pass some good sarcophagi and other objects, and enter the **Rotonde**, which contains for the most part works of a relatively late period. In the centre, the *Borghese Mars (or, in Greek, Ares), a celebrated statue, less virile than is usual in figures of this god. Round the room are grouped many fairly good statues, not a few of them almost duplicates. Among them should be noticed (beginning from the door) on the R a fine Melpomene; then, the Lycian Apollo, with harmless serpent gliding from a tree-trunk; and especially the famous *Silenus nursing the Infant Bacchus, of the School of the great sculptor Praxiteles— perhaps the most pleasing of the many representations of Faun and Satyr life which antiquity has bequeathed to us. This work should be studied as showing that later stage of easy Greek culture when sculpture was not wholly religious and monumental, but when the desire to please by direct arts and graces was distinctly present. Close by are two or three good draped female figures; and another Lycian Apollo, which should be closely compared with the one opposite it, as indicating the nature of the numerous copies or replicas commonly made of famous works of antiquity. Beside this, a couple of Hermæ, or heads on rough bases, in later imitation of the archaic Greek style, with its curious stiff simper : the type was doubtless too sacred to be varied from : a portrait statue of a lady with the attributes of Ceres ; a charming Nymph, carrying an amphora ; excellent figures of athletes, etc. Many of the statues in this and succeeding rooms are much restored, and in some cases with heads that do not belong to them. They are interesting as showing the general high level of plastic art among nameless artists of the classical period.

The next room, **the Salle Grecque, or Salle de Phidias, is interesting as containing a few works of the great artist after whom it is called, as well as many specimens of **archaic** Greek art, before it had yet attained to the freedom and grace of the age of Pheidias. In the **centre** are fragments of the early half-prehistoric figures (6th century B.C.) commonly known as Apollos, but more probably serving in many cases merely as funereal monuments—a man in the abstract, to represent the deceased, like a headstone. They exhibit well the constrained attitudes and want of freedom in the position of the arms and legs, which are characteristic of the earliest epoch. These very old features are still more markedly seen in the mutilated draped Herè in the centre ; it well illustrates the **starting-point** of Hellenic art. The admirable *bas-reliefs from Thasos on the entrance wall, on the other hand—removed from a votive monument to Apollo, the Nymphs and the Graces, and still retaining the dedicatory inscription graven over their portal,— exemplify the gradual increase in freedom and power of modelling during the early part of the 5th century B.C. This improvement is very noticeable in the Hermes with one of the Graces on the first of these reliefs. Still somewhat angular in movement, they herald the approach of the Pheidian period. From this time forward the advance becomes incredibly rapid.

Next, examine the work of the **perfect period.** Above is a mutilated fragment of Athenian girls ascending the Acropolis to present the holy robe to Athenè, from the **frieze of the Parthenon,** of the great age of Pheidias (not a century later than these archaic attempts) : with portions of a Metope of the same temple. The first may be possibly by Pheidias himself : the second by his pupil Alcamenes. Close by, **Metope of the**

temple of Zeus at Olympia (about 450 B.C.), whose subjects are sufficiently indicated on the labels: almost equal in power to the Athenian examples. The fine bas-relief of Orpheus and Eurydice, of the best period (falsely named above, later) should also be observed. (But the works of the archaic and transitional periods are far better exemplified at Munich and in London; while the fragments of Pheidias cannot of course compare with the magnificent series in the British Museum. See the copies of both in the École des Beaux Arts.) By the next window, lion and bull, somewhat recalling remote Assyrian influence; with numerous small reliefs of the best age, which should be carefully studied. These, for the most part of the finest early workmanship, admirably illustrate the extraordinary outburst of artistic spirit during the age which succeeded the wars with Persia. The reliefs on the **end wall**, chiefly from Athens and the Piræus, as well as those by the last window, belong in most instances to this splendid age of awakening and culminating art-faculty. I do not enumerate, as the labels suffice; but every one of the works in this room should be closely followed. Do not miss the charming, half-archaic, funereal relief of Philis, daughter of Cleomedes, from Thasos.

Continue on through the Long Gallery, flanked by inferior works—but what splendid inferiority!—to the room of the **Medea sarcophagus**, a fine stone tomb, containing scenes from the legend of Medea and the children of Jason. Round the room are grouped several small statues, much restored, indeed, and not of the best period, but extremely charming. The most noticeable is the dainty little group of the Three Graces, characteristic and pleasing, though with modern heads. The next compartment—that of the **Hermaphrodite**—includes one of the best and purest of the many versions of this favourite subject, from Velletri, couched, by the window. (Another in the Salle des Caryatides, for comparison.) The Farnese Eros is a pretty work of a late period. The room also possesses several works of the Satyr class, two of which, close by, are useful as instances of repetition. The four statues of Venus (Aphroditè), at the four corners (in two closely similar pairs) are also very interesting in the same manner, being variants based upon one original model, closely resembling one another in their general features, but much altered in the accessories and details. The same may be said of the good figures of Athenè by the far wall.

The Hall of the **Sarcophagus of Adonis** contains several excellent sarcophagi, the reliefs on which well illustrate the character of the class; among them, one to the L has interesting reclining figures of its occupant and his wife, an early motive, late repeated. The relief from which the room takes its name, on the wall to the right, represents, in three scenes, the departure of Adonis for the chase; his wounding by a wild boar; and Aphroditè mourning over the body of her lover. Such reliefs afforded important hints in mediæval times to the sculptors who first started the Renaissance movement. As we pass into the next compartment, notice another variant of the Aphroditè.

The **Salle de Psyché** contains, opposite the window, the famous figure from which it takes its name (too much restored to be freely judged): together with two characteristic dancing Satyrs, after models of the school of Praxiteles. The fine sculptured chairs of office by the window should also be noticed.

We now come to the Hall of the so-called **Venus of Milo**—an absurd mistranslation of the French name: the idiomatic English would be either "the Melos Venus," "the Melian Venus," or, better still, "the Melian Aphroditè." This is undoubtedly the finest plastic work in the whole of the Louvre. Its beauty is self-evident. It was found in 1820 in the island of Melos in the Greek Archipelago. The statue is usually held to represent the Greek goddess of love, and is a very noble work, yet *not* one by a recognised master, nor even mentioned by ancient writers among the well-known statues of antiquity. Nothing could better show the incredible wealth of Greek plastic art, indeed, than the fact that this exquisite Aphroditè was produced by a nameless sculptor, and seems to have been far surpassed by many other works of its own period. In type, it belongs to a school which forms a transition between the perfect early grace and purity of Pheidias, with his pupils, and the later, more self-conscious and deliberate style of Praxiteles and his contemporaries. Not quite so pure as the former, it is free from the obvious striving after effect in the latter, and from the slightly affected prettinesses well illustrated here in the group of Silenus with the infant Bacchus. The famous series of Niobe and her Children, in the Uffizi at Florence (duplicates of some elsewhere), exhibits much the same set of characteristics. Those works have been attributed on reasonable grounds to Scopas, a contemporary of Demosthenes : and this statue has therefore been ascribed with little hesitation to one of his pupils. It is, however, purer in form than the Niobe series, and exhibits the perfect ideal, artistic and anatomical, of the beautiful, healthy nude female form for the white race. Its proportions are famous. As regards the missing portions, which have happily *not* been conjecturally restored, it was originally believed that the left hand held an apple (the symbol of Melos), while the right supported the drapery. It is more probable, however, that the figure was really a Nikè (or Victory) and that she grasped a shield and possibly also a winged figure on an orb. Comparison with the other similar half-draped nude statues described as Venuses in the adjoining rooms is very instructive : their resemblances and differences show the nature of the modifications from previous types, while the immense superiority of this to all the rest is immediately apparent. Notice in particular the exquisite texture of the skin ; the perfect moderation of the form, which is well developed and amply covered, without the faintest tinge of voluptuous excess, such as one gets in late work ; and the intellectual and moral nobility of the features. No object in the Louvre deserves longer study. It is one of the finest classical works that survive in Europe.

Pass to the R into the next suite of rooms, the first of which contains the colossal figure of **Melpomene,** the tragic muse—a splendid example of this imposing type of antique sculpture, so well represented in the Vatican. Round the room are ranged several minor works, including a charming Flute-Player, doubtfully restored, and some excellent busts.

The long series of rooms which follows this one contains in many cases Græco-Roman works, imitated from the great Greek models, and often showing more or less decadent spirit. Among them, however, are some of the finest specimens of ancient sculpture, Greek included : and indeed it must be admitted that the grounds upon which such Greek works are distinguished by experts from later copies are often sufficiently delicate and inferential. Centre, a beautiful Genius of Sleep. Behind it, good figures of Eros (Love) drawing his bow, again indicating the nature of the replicas and variations of established models which were so familiar to antique sculptors. The little mutilated fragment by their side, well placed here for comparison, excellently illustrates the nature of the evidence on which such works are frequently restored. Further on—a Venus, which is a variant (probably Roman) of the type of the Venus of Arles, just beyond it. Behind this, a little in front in the room, the noble *Pallas from Velletri—the finest and most typical representation of the goddess: a good Roman copy of a Greek work of the best period. Then the famous *Venus of Arles itself, a Greek original, which may be instructively compared with the replica or variant close to it. (The labels well indicate to the student who cares to proceed further in this study the extent of the restorations in every case.) This figure, after the Melian Aphroditè, is probably the most beautiful female form in the entire collection. Behind it, the graceful and exquisitely-draped Polyhymnia (replica of a well-known type), a model of perfect repose and culture, but largely modern. Then, good bust of Homer. Next, the *Apollo Sauroctonus or Lizard-Slayer, a copy in marble of a famous work in bronze by Praxiteles. This is once more one of the many reproductions (not necessarily always actual copies) of types which are mentioned by classical authors. By the archway, Euterpe, and a Votary. Among the sarcophagi, one of Actæon torn by his dogs: another representing the Nine Muses. Most of the figures in this room are marked by a calm and classical repose; while those in the next compartment,

The **Salle du Héros Combatant,** indicate in many cases a later tendency to rapidity of motion and violent action, which is alien to the highest plastic ideal. Among the most successful works of this group is the light and airy Atalanta, under the archway,—a beautiful figure of a young girl, running, caught at the most exquisite statuesque moment. Near it, a fine Venus Genetrix. By the window, admirable figure of a wounded Amazon. Next window, the celebrated Borghese Centaur and Bacchus, a charming realization of this mythological concep-

L

tion. Note the playfulness of developed Greek fancy. The centre of the room is occupied by a powerful and anatomically admirable figure of a Fighting Hero (formerly called a Gladiator), by Agasias of Ephesus,—one of the few statues here on which the sculptor has inscribed his name. It is a triumph of its own "active" type of art (where movement and life are aimed at), but wholly lacking in beauty or ideality. It belongs to the age of Augustus or a little earlier. Behind it, Marsyas flayed alive, a repetition of a frequent but unpleasant subject. Centre again, the Faun of Vienne, a young satyr, retaining traces of colour, vigorous and clever. Then, **exquisite ideal statue of a young girl fastening her cloak, commonly but incorrectly known as the Diana of Gabii; for simple domestic grace this dainty work is unrivalled. It is probably of the age of Alexander the Great : and is well worth study. It almost suggests the Italian Renaissance. By the archways, a Hermes known as the Richelieu Mercury, with a closely similar replica. Under the archway leading to the next room, fine portrait statue of the age of Hadrian, representing Antinous, the Emperor's favourite, in the guise of Aristæus, the mythical hero of agriculture: the features are much less beautiful than in most other instances of this well-known face, several examples of which occur later. Such representations of historical characters in the form of gods or mythical heroes were common at Rome : probably in most cases the sitter's head and figure were accommodated or adapted to a well-known model.

The **Salle du Tibre**, which we next enter, contains in its centre the celebrated figure of *Artemis (Diana) known as "Diane à la Biche" or the "Diane de Versailles," one of the antique statues acquired by François Ier, the influence of which on later art will be very distinctly felt when we come to examine the French sculpture of the Renaissance. It is a charming, graceful, and delicate figure of the age of declining art, exactly adapted to take the French fancy of that awakening period. It was probably executed at Rome by a Greek sculptor about the time of Julius Cæsar. At the end of the room, colossal recumbent figure of the Tiber, represented as the benignant Father Tiber of Rome, bearing the oar which symbolizes the navigable river, and the cornucopia denoting the agricultural

III.]   RENAISSANCE PARIS (THE LOUVRE)   163

and commercial wealth of the Tiber valley : by its side nestles the wolf, with Romulus and Remus ; a pretty allegorical conception of Rome and the stream which made it : itself doubtless a pendant to the similar recumbent figure of the Nile in the Vatican. Close by, two Satyrs, imitated from Praxiteles. Behind, four Satyrs as Caryatides, from the theatre of Dionysus, Athens, 3rd cent. B.C. Round the wall, good draped figures of goddesses. Walk through these rooms often, in order to gain an idea of the astonishing wealth and purity of Hellenic sculpture.

Now, return through the Salle Grecque and the Rotonde, and turn to the L into the **Roman Galleries,** which contain for the most part statues and busts of the imperial epoch.

In the first room are reliefs of sacrifices, and fronts of sarcophagi, together with a fine portrait-statue of Sulla. By the second window, the famous and noble head of Mæcenas, the great Etruscan statesman and minister of Augustus, who practically organised the Roman Empire. The astute features, very Tuscan in type, which in some degree recall those both of Bismarck and Möltke, are full of practical vigour and the wisdom of statecraft. A more characteristic or finer head has not been bequeathed to us by antiquity. Contrast this magnificent and thoughtful bust of the best Roman age, instinct with meaning, with the coarse and coarsely-executed colossal head of Caracalla, the cruel and sensuous Emperor of the decadence, in the next window,—as crude as a coarse lithograph. In the corner, a Mithra stabbing a bull, of a class to be noted again in greater detail later. By the passage into the next room, masks of Medusa with the snaky hair.

Walk straight through the following rooms, without stopping, till you arrive at the **Salle d'Auguste** on the right, at the end, so as to take the works in historical sequence. This hall is the first in chronological order of the **Roman period.** It contains portrait-statues and busts of the Julian Emperors and their families, and of the Flavian dynasty. Begin down the centre. *Bust of Julius Cæsar, indicating well the intellectual character and relentless will of the man : a speaking likeness. Next to it, the famous **Antinous (eyes removed ; once jewels), a much idealised colossal portrait-bust of the beautiful young favourite of the Emperor Hadrian, who drowned himself in the Nile in order to become a protecting genius for his patron; he is here represented in a grave and rigid style somewhat faintly reminiscent of Egyptian art, and with the attributes of Bacchus or (more correctly) Osiris; Hadrian deified him and erected a temple in his honour in a town in Egypt which he named after him. Observe the lotus entwined in the hair. Fine portrait-statue of a Roman orator, probably Julius Cæsar, one of the best works of its class of the best period of revived Greek art under the early Roman Empire: signed by Cleomenes. The figure is that conventionally attributed to Hermes or Mercury. Near it, Agrippa, the son-in-law of Augustus and builder of the Pantheon; full of the statesmanlike characteristics of the early empire. Ideal bust of Rome, cold but beautiful: Romulus and Remus on the helmet. Under the tribune, famous *portrait-statue of Augustus, a very noble representation. It is flanked by two good portrait-statues of the Emperor himself, and of his successor, Tiberius. In front of it are Roman boys of the imperial family, the one to the L admirable in execution. They wear the golden bulla round their necks, which marked lads of noble family; the faces and figures are thoroughly patrician. Windowless wall, members of the imperial (Julian and Claudian) family,—Agrippina, Tiberius, Drusus and Germanicus, etc.; Caligula, showing incipient traces of Cæsarian madness; Octavia, Antonia, and others. Study these carefully. Then, a most malignant Nero, with less unpleasant ones further: a Messalina, whose gentleness of face belies her reputation; a grandiose Claudius; and a selfish Galba, in whom we begin to see traces of the traits produced by ruthless struggle for empire. Near him, a vain-glorious Otho, still fine and classical. Notice the dainty profiles of the women. All the statues and busts in this room, indeed, are conceived in the fine classical spirit, with no trace of the coming decadence. Most of them have the old close-shaven, clear-cut Roman features, contrasting strongly with the weaker, bearded types we shall see later. By the window wall, statues, not so good, of the coarse bull-necked Vitellius; hard, practical, businesslike Vespasian; capable Titus, and one or two less satisfactory busts or statues of Julius Cæsar. Observe even already how both types and art begin to show less perfect finish. The men are more vulgar: the artists less able.

The **Salle des Antonins**, next, contains a fine series of busts and statues of this second prosperous epoch of the empire. Facing the river, a very noble seated portrait-statue of Trajan, contrasting well with the other more decadent emperors at the further end. We have here still the old Roman severity, and the close-shaven type, admirably opposed to the more sensuous degenerate faces further on, which herald the decadence. These are the builders-up, the others the destroyers, of a great empire. In the corner close by, two erect Trajans. Notice how clear an idea of the personalities of the emperors comparison of these statues and busts affords one. Close to the archway, a beautiful Faustina Junior, one of the loveliest portrait-busts of the second Roman period. Further on, bearded and weaker emperors of the Antonine age; among them, a capital Lucius Verus, holding the orb of empire. Near it, a fine statue of the philosophic emperor, Marcus Aurelius, seen here rather as the soldier than as the sage. In the centre—the same emperor nude—or rather, a nude figure, on which his head has been placed by a modern restorer. By the middle window, colossal busts of Lucius Verus and Marcus Aurelius, and a very big head of Lucilla, wife of the former. These all deserve study, by comparison with the simpler and nobler types of the Julian period.

The **Salle de Sevère**—age of the early decadence—contains in the centre a fine statue of the Emperor's mother, Julia Mammæa, figured after the common fashion as Ceres—a half deification. Near it, another (less pleasing) bust of Antinous. Excellent statue of Pertinax. Round the walls, portrait-busts of the Antonine family and their successors, in sufficient numbers to enable one to form clear conceptions of their personality. This is especially the case with Caracalla and Plautilla by the last window; Septimius Severus himself—a weak face, gaining somewhat with age; and Lucius Verus, selfishly vicious, with a distinct tinge of conscious cruelty. Near the last, a fine portrait-statue of Faustina Senior. Beside it, pleasing bust of the boy Commodus; his subsequent development may be traced round the rest of the window. All these busts, again, should be viewed by the light of their dates; they are identified by means of coins, where the same faces occur with their names—most interesting for comparison.

The **Salle de la Paix** contains mixed works, some of them of the extreme decadence. Among them, a good figure of Minerva in red porphyry, the flesh portions of which have been restored in gilt bronze as Rome. By the window, the Emperor Titus as Mars. A half-length of Gordianus Pius near the archway is an unusually fine and classical example for its age. Fine figure of Tranquillina, his wife, and nude of Pupianus, less successful. In many of these works the decadence triumphs.

The **Salle des Saisons** contains busts, mostly of the extreme **decadence,** and works with a **semi-barbaric** tinge. The bust of Honorius, by the far door, shows the last traces of classical work rapidly passing into **Byzantine** stiffness and lifelessness. Note the feebleness of the eyes and general ineffectiveness of plastic treatment. Eugenius, opposite him, equally displays decadence in a somewhat different direction, provincial and Gaulish, foreshadowing barbaric Romanesque workmanship. A fine Muse, however, stands next to Honorius. There are also several very decent reliefs from sarcophagi. The figure of Tiridates, wearing the barbaric trousers, is a fine example of Greco-Roman art applied to a member of an alien civilisation. Close to it, the famous **Mithra** of the Capitol, stabbing a bull, with other representations of the same subject beneath and beside it. These reliefs are extremely illustrative of a most interesting phase of the later Empire. Rome was then a cosmopolitan city, crowded with Syrians, Jews, Egyptians, Asiatic Greeks, and other Orientals. Many of these people introduced into Italy and the Provinces the worship of their own local deities: the cult of Isis, of Serapis, and of other Eastern gods competed with Christianity for the mastery of the Empire. Among these intrusive religions, one of the most successful was the worship of Mithra, which came to Rome indirectly from Persia, and directly from the southern shores of the Black Sea. The mystic deity himself is always represented in an underground cave, stabbing a bull; he was regarded as a personification or avatar of the Sun God. His worship spread rapidly to every part of the Roman world, and was immensely popular: similar reliefs have been found in all Romanized regions from Britain to North Africa. The best of those in this room comes from the cave of Mithra in the Capitol at Rome itself, where the eastern god was permitted even to invade the precincts of the Capitoline Jupiter. Notice the barbaric Oriental dress and the voluptuous, soft Oriental treatment; also, the action in the cave, and the personages on the upper earth above it. Compare all these reliefs with one another, and notice their origin as given on the labels. Observe also the close similarity and religious fixity of the representations. They should be studied with care, as illustrative of the conflict of new religions with old in the Roman Empire, out of which Christianity at last emerged triumphant. Their number and costliness shows the strength of this strange faith; their inferior art betokens both eastern influence and the approach of the decadence. Compare the Oriental tinge in the Mithra reliefs with that of some Early Christian works in the small Christian room of the Renaissance Sculpture.

In the centre, Roman husband and wife, in the characters of Mars and Venus, an excellent and characteristic group of the age of Hadrian; contrast the somewhat debased proportions with those we have seen in the best Greek period. Round the wall and by the windows, many inferior portrait-busts of emperors of the decadence; observe their dates, and note the gradual decrease in art and truth, and the slow return to something resembling archaic stiffness. We have thus followed out the rise and culmination of antique art, and watched its return to primitive barbarity. Conspicuous among the works of the better age here are the charming features of Julia Mammæa, wife of Alexander Severus, especially as shown in the bust nearest to the first window. The fine Germanicus, holding the orb of empire, is also an excellent example of the portrait nude of the best period.

Leave this portion of the Museum by the **Salle des Caryatides** beyond, so called from the famous Caryatides by Jean Goujon (French Renaissance; see later), which support the balcony at its further end—very noble examples of the revived antique of the age of François Ier—majestic in their serenity. Above them is a cast from Cellini's Nymph of Fontainebleau, to be noticed later. The room contains good Greek and Roman work of the culminating periods. In the **vestibule** to the L, by the window, the *Borghese Hermaphrodite, a variant on the Velletri type, voluptuous and rounded, belonging to the latest Greek period; the mattress was added (with disastrous effect) by Bernini. In the **body of the hall** colossal Jupiter of Versailles, an impressive Hermes-figure. To the L, noble and characteristic *Demosthenes. In the centre, Hermes and Apollo of the School of Praxiteles: boy fastening his sandals. Dionysus, known as the Richelieu Bacchus. By the right wall, Aphroditè at the bath, in a crouching attitude; a nymph is supposed to be pouring water over her. All the works in this room deserve examination; they are sufficiently described, however, by the labels.

2. RENAISSANCE SCULPTURE.

[This collection, one of the most important and interesting among the treasures of the Louvre, occupies a somewhat unobtrusive suite of rooms on the Ground Floor, and is therefore too little visited by most passing tourists. It contains three separate sets of plastic work: first, sculpture of the **Italian Renaissance,** on which the French was mainly based; second, sculpture of the **Middle Ages** in France, leading gradually up to the age of François Ier, and improving as it goes, though uninfluenced as yet by external models; third, and most important of all, in Paris at least, the exquisite sculpture of the **French Renaissance,** a revolt from mediævalism, inspired from above by kings and nobles, based partly on direct study of the antique (many specimens of which were brought to France by François Ier), but still more largely on Italian models, made familiar to French students through the work of artists invited to the Court under the later Valois, as well as through the Italian wars of Charles VIII, Louis XII and François Ier (of which last more must be said when we visit St. Denis). At least **one whole day** should be devoted by every one to this fascinating collection: those who can afford the time should come here often, and study *au fond* the exquisite works of Donatello, Michael Angelo, and (most of all) Jean Goujon, Germain Pilon, and their great French contemporaries. The Italians can be seen to greater advantage at Florence and elsewhere; only here can one form a just idea of the beauty and importance of the French Renaissance.]

Enter by Door D, in Baedeker's plan—centre of the South-Eastern wing in the (old) Cour du Louvre. Pass straight through the vestibule, and Salle de Jean Goujon; then turn to your R, traversing the Salle de Michel Ange, and enter that of the **Italian Renaissance** (numbered VI officially).

The Renaissance in France being entirely based upon that in Italy, we have first to observe (especially in the case of those who have not already visited Venice and Florence) what was the character of the **Italian works** upon which the French sculptors and architects based themselves. Here you get, as it were, the original: in French sculpture, the copy. This small hall—the hall of **Donatello**—contains works of sculpture of the 13th to the 15th centuries in Italy. Contrast it mentally with the purely mediæval objects which you saw at Cluny, unrelieved for the most part by classical example, in order to measure the distance which separates the Italians of this epoch from their contemporaries north of the Alps. Recollect, too, that the Italian Renaissance grew of itself from within, while the French was an artificially cultivated exotic.

R and L of the door, early squat figures of Strength and Prudence, Italian sculpture of the 13th century, still exhibiting many Gothic characteristics, but with a nascent striving after higher truth which began with the school of the Pisani at Pisa. Opposite them, Justice and Temperance, completing the set of the four cardinal virtues. These may be looked upon as the point of departure. They show the first germ of Renaissance feeling. L of doorway, good Madonna from Ravenna; flanked by two innocent-faced angels, in deacon's dress, drawing aside a curtain from a tomb—beautiful work of the Pisan school of the 14th century: contrasted with the best French reliefs at Cluny (such as the legend of St. Eustace), these works exhibit the early advance of art in Italy. Between them (contrasting well with the early French style, as much more idealised), terra-cotta painted Madonna and Child. Beneath, good Madonna in wood, and painted gesso Madonnas, later. Near the window, **beautiful bust of a child, by Donatello, exhibiting the exquisite unconscious naïveté of the early Renaissance. Most of these works are so fully described on their pedestals that I shall only call attention to a few characteristics. The emaciated figure of the Magdalen, in a Glory of Cherubs, below, is the conventional representation of that Saint, when a penitent in Provence, being daily raised aloft to the beatific vision: many examples occur at Florence. The beautiful little terra-cotta Madonna under a canopy close by is admirable in feeling. Opposite it, characteristic decorative work of the Renaissance. Then, **Donatello's naif Young St. John, the Patron Saint of Florence, is another exquisite example of this beautiful sculptor. The open mouth is typical. A Lucretia, near it, indicates the general tendency to imitate the antique, still more marked in the relief of a funeral ceremony, where the boy to the R is especially pleasing. Do not overlook a single one of the Madonnas in this delightful room: the one above the funeral relief, though skied, is particularly pleasing. Even the large painted wooden Sienese Madonna in the centre, though the merest church furniture, has the redeeming touch of Italian idealism. The busts of Roman emperors, imitated after the antique, betray on the other hand the true spring of Renaissance impulse.

The room beyond—to the R—No. VII—is filled for the most part with fine coloured terra-cottas or **majolicas** of the **School of Della Robbia.** Centre of L wall, at the end (as you enter), Madonna and Child, with St. Roch showing his plague spot, and St. Francis pointing to the stigma in his side—a votive offering. Fine nude figure, L of it, of Friendship, by Olivieri. Exquisite little cherubs and angels. Bronze busts, instinct with Renaissance feeling. Window wall—centre—a Della Robbia of the Agony in the Garden: the arrangement is conventional, and occurs in many other works in this Gallery. It is flanked by two good Apostles of the Pisan school (the first to imitate the antique) from the Cathedral of Florence. Far L, a voluptuous figure of Nature by Tribolo, from Fontainebleau, characteristic of the works collected by François I$^{er.}$ R wall, several Madonnas, all of which should be closely studied. In the centre, terra-cotta of the School of Donatello. R and L of it, fine busts of the Italian Renaissance, with most typical faces. Near the door, portrait-statue of Louis XII, by Lorenzo da Mugiano: this king was the precursor of the French Renaissance: note the fine decorative work on his greaves and knee-caps. In the centre, a fine St. Christopher, his face distorted by the weight of the (non-existent) Christ Child. I note these in particular, but *all* the works in these two rooms should be closely followed, both as exhibiting the development from traditional forms, and as illustrating the style of art on which the French Renaissance was grafted. Notice for instance (as survival, modified) the quaint little St. Catherine, in the corner by the window, bearing her wheel, and laying her hand with a caressing gesture on the donor—a special votary, evidently. Observe, again, the three little scenes from the life of St. Anne, in gilt wood, under the large Della Robbia of the Ascension, on the wall opposite the windows. They represent respectively the Rejection of Joachim's Offering (he is expelled from the Temple by the High Priest, because he is childless: notice his servant carrying the lamb for sacrifice); the Birth of the Virgin (with the usual details of St. Anne in bed washing her hands, the bath for the infant, and the attendant bringing in a roast chicken to the mother); and the Meeting of Joachim and Anne at the Golden Gate—a scene which you may often recognise elsewhere (it comes immediately after the first, the Birth being interposed as principal subject: the servant here bears the rejected lamb less ceremonially). Beneath them, once more, a characteristically dainty St. George and the Dragon—with the beautiful Princess most heartlessly fleeing (as always) in the distance—should be carefully noted for comparison later with Michel Colombe and Raphael (St. George's lance is accidentally broken: you can still see the stump of it). To the L, again, is a beautiful Tabernacle of the Della Robbia school—angels guarding relics. To the R, a terra-cotta angel, most graceful and beautiful. Further L, charming Madonna: I need hardly call attention to the frames of fruit, which were a Della Robbia speciality. Further R,

Baptism of Clovis, gilt, and very spirited, though over-crowded. Do not overlook the skied St. Sebastian.

(The little room beyond again contains a small but interesting collection of **Early Christian works** which must be visited and studied on some other occasion. These very ancient Christian sculptures, antique in conception, antedate the rise of the conventional representations.)

Now return through Room VI to the **Salle de Michel Ange** (Room V), containing for the most part still more developed works of the Italian Renaissance, which therefore stand more directly in connection with French sculpture of that and the succeeding period. The *doorway by which we enter is a splendid specimen of a decorated Italian Renaissance portal, removed from the Palazzo Stanga at Cremona; it was executed by the brothers Rodari at the end of the 15th century, and is decorated with medallions of Roman Emperors, a figure of Hercules (the mythical founder of Cremona), and of Perseus, together with reliefs from the myths of those heroes and others. Identify these. Above the name of Perseus, for example (to the R), is a relief representing the three Gorgons and the head of Pegasus. Above that of Hercules (L) are the heads of the Hydra which he slew (as also represented in a bronze on the end wall not far from it). This gateway you should mentally compare, when you visit the École des Beaux-Arts, with that of Diane de Poitiers' Château d'Anet now erected in the courtyard and with the *façade* of the Château de Gaillon at the same place. The beautiful Italian Renaissance fountain in the centre of the room comes itself from the same Château de Gaillon: it was given to Cardinal d'Amboise (who built the Château) by the Republic of Venice.

The most beautiful works in this room, however, are the two so-called ***Fettered Slaves,** by Michael Angelo—in reality figures of the Virtues, designed for the monument of Julius II. It was Michael Angelo's fate seldom to finish anything he began. This splendid monument, interrupted by the too early death of the Pope who commissioned it, was to have embraced (among other features) figures of the Virtues, doomed to extinction by the death of the pontiff. These are two of them: the one to the right, unfinished, is of less interest: **that to the left, completed, is of the exquisite beauty which this sculptor often gave to nude youthful male figures. They represent the culminating point of the Italian Renaissance, and should be compared with the equally lovely sculptures of the Medici tombs in San Lorenzo at Florence. Observe them well as typical examples of Michael Angelo's gigantic power and mastery over marble.

You will note in the windows close by several exquisite **bronze reliefs**; eight of them, by Riccio, are from the monument of the famous anatomist, Della Torre, representing his life and death in very classical detail. (L window) Della Torre lecturing at Verona; dangerously ill; sacrifice to the gods for his recovery; his death and mourning: (R window) his obsequies; passage of the soul (as a naked child with a book) in Charon's boat (pursued by Furies); apotheosis (crowned by Fame); and celebrity of the deceased on earth; all designed in a thoroughly antique manner. (Souls of the recently dead are frequently represented leaving the body like new-born children.) This work shows the Renaissance not only as secular and humanist but even as pagan: early ages would have considered such treatment impious. All the other reliefs in this very important room should be carefully noted. By this (R) window, the Annunciation (from Cremona); Judgment of Solomon (now wholly conceived in the classical spirit); Adoration of the Magi, in bronze; figures of Galba and Faustina, entirely antique in tone; Paul shaking off the snake, etc. A portrait medallion of Ludovico il Moro of Milan (also by this window) may be instructively compared with those in contemporary Italian paintings upstairs. The next (L) window (with a rosso antico and marble imitation of the Wolf of the Capitol) contains the beginning of the reliefs from the tomb of Della Torre, in the same classical style, together with two exquisite Madonnas by **Mino da Fiesole**, and other charming works of the same period The infantile simplicity of Mino has an unspeakable attraction Between the windows, a Pietà from Vicenza, with St. Jerome, beating his breast as always with a stone, and St. Augustine (I think) writing. On the far wall, note a fine wooden Annunciation in two figures, from Pisa, of the Florentine 14th cent. The angel Gabriel and the Madonna are frequently thus separated. Between them, admirable equestrian figure of Robert Malatesta, of Rimini, where the action of the horse is particularly spirited. Fine bust of Philippo Strozzi by Benedetto da Majano on a pedestal close by. (You will find many works by this artist for this patron at Florence.) The various Virgins on the R wall should also be carefully studied, as well as the fine wooden Circumcision—a good rendering of the traditional scene, where the artist triumphs over his intractable material—and the exquisitely dainty bust of the Florentine **Baptist, instinct with the tender simplicity of Mino da Fiesole, whose decorative fragments above must not be overlooked. Do not leave this room without having carefully examined everything it contains, as every object is deserving of study. [For instance, I have omitted to mention works so fine as the self-explanatory High Renaissance Jason, the relief of Julius Cæsar, the splendid bust of Beatrice d'Este (see for this family the Perugino, etc., upstairs), and the spirited bronze of Michael Angelo, lined with the lines of a thinker who has struggled and suffered.] Finally, sit long on the bench between the windows, and look well at the **Nymph of Fontainebleau**, with stag and wild boar, by Benvenuto Cellini, the great Florentine metal-worker whom François Ier commissioned to produce this work for Fontainebleau. (But Henri II gave it instead to Diane de Poitiers, for her Château d'Anet.) Cellini's work gave an immense impetus to French sculpture, and it is largely on his style that Jean Goujon and the great French sculptors we have shortly to examine formed their conceptions. Voluptuous and overlithe, this fine relief is a splendid example of its able, unscrupulous, deft-handed artist—seldom powerful or deep, yet always exquisite in tone and perfect in handicraft.

Now, in order to form a just conception of the rise of the **French school of sculpture**, traverse the Salle de Jean Goujon and the other rooms which succeed it, till you come to the last room of the suite—officially No. I—the **Salle d'André Beauneveu.** This vault-like hall contains works of the **Early French School** of the 13th, 14th, and 15th cent., still for the most part purely Gothic, and uninfluenced in any way by Italian models. Among them we notice, at the far end of the room, near the door which leads into the Egyptian Museum, several statuettes of Our Lady and Child, of a character with which Cluny has already made us acquainted. Invariably crowned and noble, they represent the Madonna as the Queen of Heaven, not the peasant of Bethlehem. This regal conception and, still more, the faint simper, are intensely French, and mark them off at once from most Italian Madonnas. Further on, by the end window, the figures of angels, of St. John Baptist, and of a nameless king, are also thoroughly French in character; while the dainty little Burgundian choir of angels, holding, as they sing, a scroll with a Gloria, is in type half German. Note also the numerous **recumbent effigies from tombs,** among the best of which are those of Catherine d'Alençon and of Anne of Burgundy, Duchess of Bedford. The tombs at this end have still the stiff formality of the early Gothic period. The strange recumbent figure in the centre, supported by most funereal mourners (placed too low to be seen properly), is the tomb of Philippe Pot, Grand Seneschal of Burgundy under John the Good, from the Abbey of Citeaux. Such mourners are characteristic of the monumental art of Burgundy. One more occurs under a canopy near the middle window: you will recollect to have seen others (from the tomb of Philippe le Hardi) at Cluny. Further on in the room we get more Madonnas whose marked French type you will now be able to recognise. Good recumbent figures of a bishop, and of Philip VI, sufficiently described by the labels, and other excellent statues, one of the best of which is the child in the centre. The king and queen by the doorway are also fine examples of the art of the 15th cent. Notice the dates of all these figures, as given by the labels, and convince yourself from them (as you can do still more fully in the next room) that French art itself made **a domestic advance** from the 11th cent., onward, wholly independent of Italian influence. This advance was due in the main to national development, and to the slow recovery of trade and handicraft from the barbarian irruption. What was peculiar to Italy was the large survival of antique works, which the School of Pisa, and others after them, strove to imitate. In France, till François Ier, no such classical influence intervenes: the development is all home-made and organic. But if you contrast the busts by the W doorway, or the tombstone of Pierre de Fayet, near them, with the ruder work by the first window in the next room, the reality of this advance will become at once apparent to you. The artists, though still hampered by tradition, are striving to attain higher perfection and greater truth to nature. Do not miss in this connection the excellent wooden Flagellation by the middle window : nor the Madonna opposite it ; nor the donor and donatrix close by ; nor the fine mutilated Annunciation (with lily between the figures) by the W window ; nor the well-carved Nativity (clearly Flemish, however) near the seat by the doorway. In this last, observe the quaint head-dress of the donatrix in the background (an unusual position) as well as the conventional ox and ass, and the Three Kings approaching in the upper right-hand corner, balanced by the shepherds listening to the angels. St. Joseph's candle is, however, a novelty. I merely note these points to show how much there may often be in seemingly unimportant objects. This is officially called an Adoration of the Shepherds, but if you look into it, you will see, erroneously. The person entering from behind is a mere modern spectator. Study well the works in this room and the next, regarded as a **starting-point.**

In the **passage** leading into the next room are a truncated statue of St. Denis, from his Basilica (to be visited later), and, beyond it, a group of Hell from the same church. Notice the usual realistic jaws of death, vomiting flame and swallowing the wicked. Observe also that souls are always represented as nude. Opposite this, a mutilated fragment of St. Denis bearing his head, and accompanied by his two deacons, St. Rusticus and St. Eleutherius. I have not hitherto called attention to these two attendant deacons, but you will find them present in almost all representations of St. Denis. (Look for them among the paintings.) Try to build up your knowledge in this way, by adding point to point as you proceed, and afterwards returning to works earlier visited, which will gain fresh light by comparison with those seen during your more recent investigations.

Enter Room II : **Salle du Moyen Age.** Notice, first, the fragments by the window ; those numbered 19 to 22 are good typical examples of the rude work of the Romanesque period (10th to 12th cents.). 23, beside them, shows the improvement which came in with the Gothic epoch, as well as the distinctive

Gothic tone in execution,—softer, and rounder, with just a touch of foolish infantile simplicity or inanity. Observe all the other heads here, and compare their dates, as shown on the labels. Two beautiful angels, from the tomb of the brother of St. Louis, will indicate this gradual advance in execution, wholly anterior to any Renaissance influence. On the R side of the window, notice particularly an admirable head of the Virgin, 76, and another near it, from the cathedral of Sées. On the pillar, St. Denis bearing his head. Every one of these capitals and heads should be closely noted, with reference to the dates shown on the label. In the little Madonna on the L hand window, observe a nascent attempt to introduce an element of playfulness which is characteristically French. This increases later. It develops into the grace—the somewhat meretricious grace— of more recent French sculpture.

Now turn to the body of the room. R wall, 53, an excellent angel. Beyond it, the Preaching of St. Denis; observe that he is here attended by his two faithful deacons; the gateway indicates that he preaches at Paris. Such little side-indications are common in early art: look out for them. Above it, Christ in Hades, redeeming Adam and Eve, as the firstfruits of the souls, from Limbo; the devil bound in chains on the ground beneath them; you saw several similar works at Cluny. Further on, another Madonna and Child, with the same attempt at playfulness; notice here Our Lady's slight simper, a very French feature; the Child carries a goldfinch, which you will frequently find, if you look for it, in other representations, both French and Italian. The coloured relief of Pilate recalls those in the ambulatory at Notre-Dame. (Read in every case the date and place whence brought here.) Beneath it are the Flagellation, Bearing of the Cross, Crucifixion, and Entombment, which may be profitably compared with other examples.

(If, after observing the French type of Madonna in these rooms, and the few Burgundian works they contain, you have time to revisit the Mediæval Sculpture at Cluny—Room VI, ground floor—as I strongly advise you to do, you will find that **Burgundian art** in the Middle Ages was quite distinct from French, and had types of its own, approximating to the Flemish, and still more to the German. This is well seen in the Burgundian Madonna and St. Catherine at Cluny. For study of the style, it is a good plan to stop at **Dijon** on your way to or from Switzerland.)

The end of the room is occupied by a Gothic doorway from a house in Valencia (Spain), which may be contrasted with the scarcely later Renaissance example from the Palazzo Stanga. On its top is an Annunciation, representations of which are frequent in similar situations; we saw one on the façade of St. Étienne du Mont; in such cases, the Madonna is almost always separated by some form of wall, door, or ornament from the angel Gabriel; here, the finial represents the usual pot of lilies. Below it, a very characteristic French Madonna, again slightly smirking, and with the Child bearing the goldfinch. Note once more the royal air, the affected lady-like manner, given to the Madonna in early French sculpture and painting. To its L, a similar regal painted Madonna. To the R, gorgeous coloured statue of King Childebert, of the 13th cent.: this once stood at the entrance to the beautiful refectory of the Abbey of St. Germain-des-Prés (see later) which Childebert founded, and where the king was buried. L wall, fragment of a coloured stone relief, Judas receiving payment: of the same type as those in Notre-Dame. Further on, a similar Kiss of Judas. (Compare this with several specimens at Cluny.) The mutilated state of many of these fragments is in several instances due to the Revolution. All the other statues and fragments in this compartment should be carefully examined, including the strange scene from a Hell, and the stiff wooden Madonna, on pedestals in the centre. By the doorway, painted Virgin and Child,—the Madonna under a little canopy, and very typical of French conceptions.

Room III, **Salle de Michel Colombe,** represents the **advance** made **in French plastic art** during the last half of the 15th cent., and the beginning of the 16th cent., in some cases independently of the Italian Renaissance. The bust of François Ier, in bronze, on a pedestal near the door, may be compared, both for spirit and likeness, with the (very wooden) contemporary portraits of the same king in the French School upstairs. It has all the stiffness and archaic fidelity of early portraiture, with the usual lack of artistic finish.

Note such little points as that the king wears the collar of his order, with the St. Michael of France as a pendant. Near the window, fragments of work displaying Renaissance influence. One, a relief of the Return of the Master, from the Château de Gaillon (built by Cardinal d'Amboise, minister of Louis XII, and one of the great patrons of the Renaissance in France), exhibits the beginning of a taste for secular, domestic, and rustic subjects, which later became general. (Early work is all sacred—then comes mythical—lastly, human and contemporary.) Note on the opposite side, the fine bronze of Henri Blondel de Rocquencourt, under Henri II. The Apollo and Marsyas is strongly Renaissance—a mythic subject (see the Perugino upstairs). The Massacre of the Innocents exhibits Renaissance treatment of a scriptural scene. The **centre of the room** is occupied by fine **bronzes** of the school of Giovanni da Bologna, a Frenchman who worked in Italy and forms a link between the art of the two countries. Observe the decorative French slenderness and coquetry of form, combined with the influence of the Italian Renaissance. The Mercury—light and airy—is a replica of Giovanni da Bologna's own famous statue in the Bargello at Florence. The Mercury and Psyche beside it is a splendid example of Giovanni da Bologna's school, by Adrian de Vries. Notice the French tinge in the voluptuous treatment of the nude, and the slenderness and grace of the limbs. The bronze statue of Fame, from the tomb of the Duc d'Epernon, exhibits in a less degree the same characteristics. It is obviously suggested by Giovanni's Mercury.

Along the wall to the L, the most noticeable work is the splendid ** marble relief of St. George, by the great French sculptor Michel Colombe, produced for the chapel of the Château de Gaillon; recollect all these Gaillon objects, and their connection with one another: the château was erected under Louis XII, at the dawn of the French Renaissance, and much of its work, like this fine relief, shows a considerable surviving Gothic feeling. You will see the façade of the château later at the École des Beaux-Arts. It is interesting to compare this splendid piece of sculpture with the little Della Robbia in the Italian rooms, and the painting by Raphael upstairs : the dragon here is a fearsome and very mediæval monster; but the St. George and his horse are full of life and spirit; and the fleeing Princess in the background is delicately French in attitude and conception. The dragon is biting the saint's lance, which accounts for its broken condition in the Raphael and the Mantegna. ' Comparison of the various St. Georges in this collection, indeed, will give you an admirable idea of the way in which a single conventional theme, embracing always the very same elements, is modified by national character and by the individuality of the artist. To understand this is to have grasped art-history. (Note that the legend of St. George itself is in one aspect a Christianisation of the myth of Perseus and Andromeda.)

Beneath the St. George stands a fine Dead Christ, also exhibiting characteristic French treatment. The somewhat insipid but otherwise excellent Madonna and Child, on a pedestal close by, is admirable as exemplifying the transformation of the smirking Madonnas of the Middle Ages into the type of the Renaissance. The Death of the Virgin, near it, from St. Jacques-de-la-Boucherie (of which only the tower now remains), suggests to one's mind the riches which must once have belonged to the demolished churches of Paris,—mostly, alas! destroyed at the great Revolution. Observe in this work the figures of the attendant apostles, the Renaissance architecture of the background, and the soul of the Madonna ascending above, escorted by angels, to heaven. More naïve, and somewhat in the earlier style, is the Nativity above it, flanked by the two St. Johns, the Baptist and the Evangelist. The tomb of Philippe de Commynes also illustrates the older feeling, as yet little influenced by the Italian irruption. Note that the works which betray the greatest Italian influence are chiefly connected with the **royal** châteaux and palaces of François Ier and his Italianate successors, or their wives and mistresses; the **nation** as yet is little touched by the new models.

The bronze tomb of Alberto Pio of Savoy, by Ponzio, on the other hand, exhibits strongly the Italian tendency, and should be compared with the earlier recumbent tombs, behind in Room I, as showing the survival of the mediæval type, transmuted and completely revivified. The same may be said of the tomb of Philippe de Chabot, which, however, is more distinctively French and much less markedly Italian. See how the early prostrate effigies become here recumbent : the figure, as it were, is trying to raise itself. In comparing the various works in this room, endeavour to note these interlacing points of resemblance and difference. The beautiful Genii above are parts of the same tomb, and are exquisite examples of the minor work of the French Renaissance. Passing the Italian Tacca's admirable bust of Giovanni da Bologna, we come to an excellent Entombment, of the French School, from St. Eustache, which should be compared with earlier specimens in the adjacent rooms. Beneath it, a fine fragment by Jean Cousin. Still lower, a Passage of the Red Sea, beginning to display that confused composition and lack of unity or simplicity which spoiled the art of the later 16th and 17th centuries. The fine Madonna and Child close by should be compared with the very similar example opposite, as well as with its predecessors in other centuries. (Comparison of varying versions of the *same* theme is always more instructive than that of different subjects.) The tomb of Abbot Jean de Cromois, with its Renaissance framework, shows a survival of earlier tendencies ; as does also that of Roberte Legendre, though the figures of Faith and Hope (Charity is missing) are distinctly more recent in type than the recumbent effigy. Those who have time to notice and hunt up the **coats of arms** on the various tombs will often find they shed interesting light on their subjects. Observe also the **churches** from which these various monuments have been removed, a point which will fit in with your previous or subsequent knowledge of the buildings in many cases.

The **last window** contains a few works of the **German School,** which it is interesting to compare with their French contemporaries. Thus, the shrewd, pragmatical, diplomatic head of Frederick the Pacific, a coarse, cunning self-seeker, is excellently contrasted with the French portrait-busts. The little scene of the Holy Family, after Dürer, which should be closely studied, is essentially German in the domestic character of its carpenter's shop, in the broad peasant faces of its Madonna and attendant angels, in the playful touches of the irreverent cherubs, and in the figure of the Almighty appearing in clouds at the summit of the composition. The Kiss of Judas, opposite it, is also characteristically German; notice the brutal soldiers, whose like we have seen in woodwork at Cluny: the bluff St. Peter with the sword is equally noteworthy; in the background are separate episodes, such as the Agony in the Garden; though officially ascribed to the French School, this is surely the work of a deft but unideal German artist. Do not neglect the many beautiful **decorative fragments** collected in this room, nor the fine busts, mostly of a somewhat later period.

Now enter Room VIII, the **Salle de Jean Goujon.** The magnificent collection of works contained in this room embraces the **finest specimens of French Renaissance work** of the school of the great artist whose name it bears, and of his equally gifted contemporary, Germain Pilon. They represent the plastic side of the School of Fontainebleau. In the centre is Jean Goujon's **Huntress Diana, with her dogs and stag; it was probably executed for Diane de Poitiers, and comes from her Château d'Anet, presented to her by her royal lover. (Note all the works from the Château d'Anet, which is a destroyed museum of the art of the Renaissance.) Observe on the base the monogram of H. and D., which recurs on contemporary portions of the Louvre. The decorative lobsters and cray-fish on the pedestal should also be noted. Diana herself strikes the keynote of all succeeding French sculpture. Beautiful, coquettish, lithe of limb, and with the distinctive French elegance of pose, this figure nevertheless contains in it the germs of rapid decadence. It suggests the genesis of the 18th century, and of the common ormolu clock of commerce. Step into the next room and compare it with the Nymph of Fontainebleau, by Benvenuto Cellini. You will there see how far the Florentine artist approached the French, and how much the Frenchman borrowed from the Florentine. Walk round and observe on either side this the most triumphant work of the French Renaissance. Observe also its relations to the Diana of Versailles, in the Classical Gallery—brought to France by François Ier,—and its general debt to the antique, as well as to contemporary Italy.

Perhaps still more beautiful is the exquisite **group of the Three Graces, supporting an urn, by Germain Pilon, intended to contain the heart of Henry II, and commissioned by Catherine de Médicis. It once stood in the Church of the Celestines. Here again one sees the delicacy and refinement of the French Renaissance, with fewer marks of its inherent defects than in Jean Goujon's statue. Sit long and study this exquisite trio— which the Celestines piously described as the Theological Virtues. Walk round it and observe the admirably natural way in which the figures are united by their hands in so seemingly artificial a position. The charming triangular pedestal is by the Florentine sculptor, Domenico del Barbiere.

The third object in the centre of the room is the exquisite group of the **Four Theological Virtues, in wood, also by Germain Pilon, which, till the Revolution, supported the reliquary containing the remains of Ste. Geneviève, in St. Étienne-du-Mont, and earlier still in the old church now replaced by the Panthéon. These are probably the finest figures ever executed in this difficult material. The faces and attitudes deserve from every side the closest study. If you have entered into the spirit of these three great groups in the centre of this room, you have succeeded in understanding the French Renaissance.

Now, begin at the further wall, in the body of the Salle, and observe, first, the exquisite reliefs of *Tritons and Nereids, with **Nymphs of the Seine, by Jean Goujon. Read the labels. We shall visit hereafter the Fountain of which these graceful and delicate reliefs once formed a portion. The Nymph to the L is one of the loveliest works ever produced by its sculptor, and is absolutely redolent of Renaissance spirit. It indicates the change which had come over French handicraft, under the influence of its Italian models, at the same time allowing the national spirit to shine through in a way which it never succeeded in doing in contemporary painting. Beneath it are two noble figures in bronze, from the tomb of Christopher de Thou, attributed to an almost equally great artist, Barthélemy Prieur. Frémin Roussel's Genius of History still more markedly anticipates more recent French tendencies. It is intensely modern. Germain Pilon's monumental bronze of René Birague prepares us for the faults of the French works of this style in the Louis XIV period. Mere grandiosity and ostentation are here foreshadowed. The centre of the next wall is occupied by Germain Pilon's fine chimney-piece, with Jean Goujon's bust of Henri II as its central object. The decorative Renaissance work on this mantel should be closely studied, as well as that—so vastly inferior—on the adjacent later columns of the age of Louis XIV. Barthélemy Prieur's exquisite bronzes from the tomb of the Constable Anne de Montmorency also breathe a profoundly French spirit. The figures represent Justice, Courage, and Abundance. Germain Pilon's too tearful Mater Dolorosa (painted terra-cotta) close by, from the Sainte Chapelle, indicates the beginnings of modern French taste in church furniture. His recumbent tomb of Valentine Balbiani, on the other hand, is admirable as portraiture; but the genius of the artist is only fully displayed in the repulsive figure of the same body seen emaciated in death and decomposition beneath it. Barthélemy Prieur's recumbent figure of Anne de Montmorency shows survival of the older type, doubtless due to the prejudices of patrons.

Above it is an admirable piece of Renaissance sculpture, by Jean Goujon, for the decoration of the rood-loft (now removed) in St. Germain l'Auxerrois. The rare beauty of the existing one at St. Étienne-du-Mont (by a far inferior artist) enables us to estimate the loss we have sustained by its disappearance. The Deposition, in the centre, marked by the highly classical style and secular or almost sensuous beauty of its Maries, and the anatomical knowledge displayed in its Dead Christ, should be contrasted with earlier specimens in adjacent rooms. In the accompanying figures of the four Evangelists, notice how earlier conceptions of the writers and their attendant symbols have been altogether modified by a Raphaelesque spirit. You would scarcely notice the eagle, angel, bull, and lion (compare Sacchi upstairs), unless you were told to look for them. Germain Pilon's Agony in the Garden displays an exactly similar transformation of a traditional subject.

Some interesting works are placed **near the windows.** In the **first** is a fragment from the pulpit of the Church of the Grands Augustins in Paris, by Germain Pilon, representing

Paul Preaching at Athens. The bald head and long beard of the Apostle of the Gentiles are traditional; the figure is modelled on Italian precedents; here again the female auditors are introduced entirely in the classical spirit, and treated with Renaissance love for exuberant femininity. Nominally sacred, such works as this are really nothing more than sensuous and decorative in their tendencies. The Church accepted them because they were supposed to be artistic. Other fragments opposite exemplify the same baneful tendency, pregnant with decadence. Christ and the Woman of Samaria (with her classical urn) is a subject we have already met with elsewhere: here, it is much permeated by Renaissance feeling. The Preaching of St. John Baptist gives the artist an opportunity for introducing two attractive female listeners. In the **second window**, the contrast between the comparatively archaic St. Eloi from Dijon, and the Nymphs of the school of Jean Goujon, is sufficiently abrupt to point its own moral. Germain Pilon's Entombment may be instructively compared with Jean Goujon's and others; the Magdalen here is an admirable figure. Glance across from one to the other and note the resemblance. Even at this late date, how close is the similarity in the attitudes of the chief actors! They almost correspond figure for figure:— Joseph of Arimathæa, and then Nicodemus, supporting the dead Christ; next, the fainting Madonna, in the arms of one of the Maries; then, the Magdalen at the foot, with her box of ointment, and the mourning women; all stand in the same relations in the two reliefs. If you will compare both paintings and sculptures in this manner, you will learn how much the artist borrowed in each case from predecessors, and exactly how much is his own invention. Opposite the Entombment are other Nymphs of the school of Jean Goujon, and a characteristic transitional figure of a Donor and his Family, showing a distinct attempt to treat an old motive by the new methods; L the Donor, kneeling, introduced by his patron, St. John Baptist; R, two ladies of his family, introduced by a sainted bishop and an abbot; near them, their children, kneeling, but with some genial allowance for the sense of tedium in infancy; in the background, Renaissance architecture, with quaint bas-reliefs of Samson carrying off the gates of Gaza; the Resurrection and Appearance to the Apostles; the Supper at Emmaus; and Jonah emerging from the mouth of the whale. Works like these, often artistically of less importance, nevertheless not infrequently throw useful light on the nature of the conditions under which the sculptor worked—the trammels of tradition, the struggle to wriggle out of the commands of a patron, who desires to see reproduced the types of his childhood. The **third window** contains some charming but mutilated fragments from the tomb of the Duc de Guise : more figures by Germain Pilon; and a thoroughly Renaissance Awakening of the Nymphs, attributed (with little doubt) to Frémin Roussel. Germain Pilon's good bust of Charles IX strikes the keynote of the king's vain and heartless character. The baby Christ, by Richier, though evidently suffering from water on the brain, is otherwise a charming early French conception of soft innocence and infantile grace. Notice, above this, a somewhat transitional Pietà, placed as a votive offering (like so many other things) in the (old) church of Ste. Geneviève, with the kneeling donor represented as looking on, after the earlier fashion. The Judgment of Daniel, attributed to Richier, though splendid in execution, forms an example of the more crowded and almost confused composition which was beginning to destroy the unity and simplicity of plastic art. As a whole, the works in this room should be attentively and closely studied, illustrating as they do the one exquisite moment of perfect fruition, when the French Renaissance burst suddenly into full flower, to be succeeded almost at once by painful degeneracy and long slow decadence. I would specially recommend you to compare closely the more classical works of this room with those in the adjoining Salle de Michel Ange in order to recognise the distinctively French tone as compared with the Italian. The importance of these various rooms, of both nationalities, to a comprehension of Paris and French art in general, cannot be over-estimated. By their light alone can you fully understand the fabric of the Louvre itself, the Luxembourg, the Renaissance churches, the tombs at St. Denis, and above all, Fontainebleau, St. Germain, Versailles itself, and the entire development of architecture and sculpture from François Ier to the Revolutionary epoch. Especially should you always bear in mind the importance of works from the Château de Gaillon (early) and Château d'Anet (full French Renaissance).

In the **vestibule**, as you pass out, notice a copy in bronze, probably by Barthélemy Prieur, of the antique Huntress Diana, the original of which we have already noticed in the Classical Gallery. It helps to accentuate the direct dependence of French Renaissance sculpture upon the classical model as well as upon that of the contemporary Italians. Observe that while each of these arts is based upon the antique, it necessarily follows the antique models *then and there* known to it—not the "Venus of Milo" discovered in 1820, or the figures from Olympia of quite recent discovery.

3. MODERN SCULPTURE.

This collection is entered by a separate door in the Cour du Louvre, marked E on Baedeker's plan. It takes up the development of French plastic art at the point where the last collection leaves off. It is, however, of vastly inferior interest, and should only be visited by those who have time to spare from more important subjects. The decline which affected French painting after the age of the early Renaissance had even more disastrous effects in the domain of sculpture. I will not, therefore, enumerate individual works in these rooms, but will touch briefly on the characteristics of the various epochs represented in the various galleries.

The **Salle de Puget** contains sculptures of the age of Louis XIII and XIV, for the most part theatrical, fly-away, and mannered. They are grandiose with the grandiosity of the school of Bernini; unreal and over-draperied. Like contemporary painting, too, they represent official or governmental art, with a courtier-like tendency to flattery of monarchy, general and particular. A feeble pomposity, degenerating into bombast, strikes their keynote. Few works in this room need detain the visitor.

The **Salle de Coyzevox** continues the series, with numerous portrait-busts of the celebrities of the age of Louis XIV, mostly insipid and banal. The decline goes on with accelerated rapidity.

The **Salle des Coustou**, mostly Louis XV, marks the lowest depth of the degradation of plastic art, here reduced to the level of Palais Royal trinkets. It represents the worst type of 18th century handicraft, and hardly contains a single passable statue. Its best works are counterparts in marble of Boucher and Greuze, but without even the touch of meretricious art which colour and cleverness add to the craft of those boudoir artists. Few of them rise to the level of good Dresden china. The more ambitious lack even that mild distinction.

The **Salle de Houdon,** of the Revolutionary epoch, shows a slight advance upon the preceding (parallel to the later work of Greuze), and is interesting from its portrait-busts of American statesmen and French republican leaders. Some of the ideal works, even, have touches of grace, and a slightly severer taste begins to make itself apparent. The classical period is foreshadowed.

The **Salle de Chaudet,** of the First Empire, answers in sculpture to the School of David in painting. It is cold, dignified, reserved, and pedantic. It imitates (not always at all successfully) the antique ideals. The best works in this room are Canova's; but the intention is almost always better than the execution. A sense of chilly correctness distinguishes these blameless academic works from the natural grace and life of antique Greek sculptors. They lie under the curse which pursues revivals.

The **Salle de Rude** contains plastic work of the Restoration, the July Monarchy, and the Second Empire. It answers roughly to the romantic School of Delaroche in painting. Several of these almost contemporary works have high merit, though few of them aim at that reposeful expression which is proper to sculpture. Some, indeed, trench upon the domain of painting in their eager effort to express passing emotion and action. Picturesqueness and sensuousness are their prevailing features. Nevertheless, the room, as a whole, exhibits the character of a real renaissance, such as it is, from the mediocrity of the last century, and the bleak propriety of the classical revival. Too many of the works, however, are aimed at the taste of the Boulevards. They foreshadow that feeling which makes too much modern sculpture attempt to catch the public by flinging away everything that is proper to the art. The desire for novelty is allowed to override the sense of beauty and of just proportion : repose is lost ; dignity and serenity give place to cleverness of imitation and apt catching at the momentary expression.

III. THE SMALLER COLLECTIONS.

The **other collections** at the Louvre appeal for the most part rather to the **specialist** than to the general public. They are for workers, not for sight-seers. The **Egyptian Museum**, for example, to the L as you enter the Cour du Louvre by the main entrance, contains, perhaps, the finest collection of its sort in all Europe. You must, of course, at least walk through it—especially if you have not seen the British Museum. The objects, however, are sufficiently indicated for casual visitors by means of the labels ; they need not be enumerated. The opposite wing, to the R as you enter, contains the **Assyrian Collection**, inferior on the whole, especially in its bas-reliefs, to that in the British Museum. Beyond it, again, to the left, lie a group of rooms devoted to the **intermediate region** between the sphere of **Assyrian and Greek art**. These rooms ought certainly to be examined by any who wish to form some idea of the origin and development of Hellenic culture. The first two rooms of the suite contain **Phœnician** works,—important because the Phœnicians were the precursors of the Greeks in navigation and commerce in the Mediterranean, and because early Greek art was largely based on Phœnician imitations of Assyrian and Egyptian work, or on actual Egyptian and Assyrian objects imported into Hellas by Phœnician merchants. These Semitic seafarers had no indigenous art of their own ; but they acted as brokers between East and West, and they skilfully copied and imitated the principal art-products of the two great civilisations on whose confines they lay, though often without really understanding their true import. The Phœnicians were thus the pioneers of civilisation in the Eastern Mediterranean.

Room IV, beyond these two, contains more Phœnician antiquities, and others from **Cyprus**, an island inhabited by Greeks or half Greeks, but one in which this imported Oriental culture earliest took root and produced native imitations. Examine these objects as leading up to, and finally correcting, the *archaic* Greek work ill represented by a few objects in the Salle de Phidias. The **Salle de Milet,** beyond, contains Greek antiquities from **Asia Minor,** some of which indicate transition from the Assyrian to the Hellenic type. Examine these from the point of view of development. The reliefs from the temple of Assos in Mysia show an early stage in the evolution of Asiatic Greek art. Compare them with the archaic objects in the Salle de Phidias. It must be borne in mind that civilised art entered Greece from Assyria, by way of Phœnicia, the Hittites, Lydia, Phrygia, the Ionian cities in Asia Minor, and the Islands of the Archipelago. These intermediate rooms should therefore be studied in detail from this point of view, dates and places being carefully noted, as illustrating the westward march of art from Nineveh to Athens. The last hall of the suite, the **Salle de Magnésie,** on the other hand, contains works from **Ephesus** of a late Greek period, representing rather a slight barbaric deterioration than a transitional stage. These collections, most important to the student of Hellenic culture, may be neglected by hurried or casual visitors.

The **Salle Judaique,** to the right, under the stairs, contains the scanty remains of the essentially inartistic Jewish people, interesting chiefly from the point of view of Biblical history. The famous and much-debated **Moabite Stone,** recording the battles of King Mesa of Moab with the Jews in B.C. 896, is here preserved. It is believed to be the earliest existing specimen of alphabetic as opposed to hieroglyphic or ideographic writing.

There is, however, one group of objects in the Louvre, too seldom visited, which no one should omit to inspect if time permits him. This is the admirable **Dieulafoy Collection of **Persian Antiquities.** To arrive at it, go to the front of the Old Louvre, facing St. Germain l'Auxerrois, as for the previously noted series. Enter by the principal portal, and turn to the R, through the Assyrian collection, whose winged bulls and reliefs of kings you may now inspect in passing, if you have not done so previously. Mount the staircase at the end, and, at the landing on the top, turn to your L, when you will find yourself at once face to face with the collection.

The **First Room** contains merely Græco-Babylonian objects (of a different collection) which need only be inspected by those whose leisure is ample. They illustrate chiefly the effect of Hellenic influence on Asiatic models. On the entrance wall of the **Second Room** is the magnificent *****Frieze of Archers** of the Immortal Guard, in encaustic tiles, with cuneiform inscriptions, from the Throne Room of Darius I. This splendid work, mere fragment though it is of the original, gives in its colour and decorative detail some idea of the splendour of the Palace of the Persian monarchs. The colours are those still so prevalent in Persian art, showing a strong predominance of blues and greens, with faint tones of yellow, over red and purple, which latter, indeed, are hardly present. Round the rest of the walls are ranged decorative fragments from the Palace of Artaxerxes Mnemon. Opposite the archers is another magnificent frieze of **angry lions**, from the summit of the portals in the last-named palace. The next compartment of the same room contains the *****Base of a Column** and a ******Capital** of the same, also from the Palace of Artaxerxes Mnemon:—two figures of bulls supporting between them the enormous wooden rafters of the ceiling. These gigantic and magnificent figures form perhaps the most effective and adequate supports for a great weight to be found in any school of architecture.

The next room contains the admirable **reconstruction** of the Palace, when entire, showing the position on the walls of either pylon, and the manner in which the columns supported the colossal roof. If, from inspection of this model, we return to the base and capitals themselves, we shall be able to judge what must have been the magnificent and gigantic scale of this Titanic building, the effect of which must have thrown even the Temple of Karnac into the shade. At the side are a **lion** and **winged bull**, which help to complete the mental picture. This collection, unique in Europe, serves to give one an idea of the early **Persian civilisation** which can nowhere else be obtained, and which helps to correct the somewhat one-sided idea derived from the accounts of Greek historians. On no account should you miss it.

The **minor art-objects** of the Louvre, though of immense value and interest in themselves, may be largely examined by those who have the time in the light of their previous work at Cluny. The collection of **drawings,** one of the finest in Europe, is mostly interesting to artists. That of **smaller Mediæval and Renaissance Objects** contains works closely similar to those at Cluny, including admirable **ivory-carvings,** fine **pottery** (the best of which is that by **Palissy,** and the **Henri II ware**), together with Oriental faïence, bronzes, etc. The **Greek Vases,** again, of which this Museum contains a magnificent collection, are mainly interesting to Hellenic specialists. For the casual visitor, it will suffice to examine one or two of them. The **Etruscan Antiquities** give a good idea of the civilisation of this ancient race, from which, both in earlier and later times, almost all the art, poetry, and science of Italy has proceeded. Though entirely based upon Greek models, the Etruscan productions betray high artistic faculty and great receptive powers of intellect. Among the **minor Greek works,** none are more interesting than the beautiful little terra-cotta **figures** from **Tanagra** in Bœotia, which cast an unexpected light on one side of Greek art and culture. Examine them as supplementing the collection of antique sculpture. These **figurines,** as they are called, were produced in immense quantities, chiefly in Bœotia, both for household decoration and to be buried with the dead. They were first moulded or cast in clay, but they were afterwards finished by hand, with the addition of just such accessories or modifications as we have seen to obtain in the case of the statues in the antique gallery. Finally they were gracefully and tastefully coloured. Nothing better indicates the universality of high art-feeling among the ancient Greeks than the extraordinary variety, fancy, and beauty of these cheap objects of every-day decoration; while the unexpected novelty given by the slightest additions or alterations in what (being moulded) is essentially the same figure throws a flood of light upon the methods of plastic art in higher departments. Look out for these exquisite little figures as you pass through the (inner) rooms on the South Side of the old Cour du Louvre, on the First Floor. Most of them will be found in Room L of Baedeker's plan. Almost every visitor is equally surprised and charmed by their extremely modern tone of feeling. They are alive and human. In particular, the **playfulness** of Greek art is here admirably exemplified. Many of them have touches of the most graceful humour.

Here, again, do not suppose that because I do not specify, these minor works of art are of little importance. If you have time, examine them all : but you must do so by individual care and study.

The neighbouring **Salle des Bijoux** contains beautiful antique jewellery ; do not miss the very graceful gold **tiara** presented to the Scythian King Saitaphernes by the Greek city of Olbia in the Crimea—a lovely work of the 3rd century B.C. Its authenticity has been disputed, but not its beauty.

The **Galerie d'Apollon** contains, among many objects of considerable interest, the Reliquary which encloses the Arm of Charlemagne—who, having been canonized, was duly entitled to such an honour. The Reliquary of St. Henry, and the Chasse of St. Louis are also well worthy of inspection. Notice, too, the Hand of Justice, used at the coronation of the French Kings. But all these objects can only be properly studied, by those who wish to investigate them, with the aid of the official catalogue. I shall recur at greater length to a few of them after our return from St. Denis.

When you have learnt Paris well, go often to and fro between these rooms of the Louvre, the Mediæval and Renaissance Sculpture, the halls at Cluny (particularly Room VI, with its French architectural work), and the older churches, such as St. Germain-des-Prés, Notre-Dame, St. Denis, etc. Thus only can you build up and consolidate your conceptions.

A special small collection, to which part of a day may well be devoted, is the **Early Christian Sculpture**, to which I have already briefly alluded, in the first room to the R as you enter the Renaissance Galleries in the Cour du Louvre.

The centre of the hall is occupied by a good Early Christian **sarcophagus**, with a cover not its own, sufficiently described as to origin on the label. The front towards the window represents the True Vine, surrounding the "X P," which form the first two letters of the name of Christ in Greek, inscribed in a solar circle, and with the Alpha and Omega on either side of it. This figure, repeated on various works in this room in slightly different shapes, is known as a **Labarum.** It forms, after Constantine (who adopted it as his emblem and that of the Christianized Empire), the most frequent symbol on early Christian monuments. Note modern reproductions on the frieze of this apartment. Its variations are numerous. At the ends, are other True Vines and a better Labarum, with a Star of Bethlehem. The back has the same devices repeated.

Wall nearest the entrance, several **inscriptions,** among which notice the frequency of the Labarum, with the two birds pecking at it,—a common Early Christian Symbol. Below them, good early **sarcophagus.** On its end, remote from window, Daniel in the Lions' Den, a traditional representation, of which an extremely rude barbaric degradation may be noticed, high up, near the door which leads into the Della Robbia room, adjacent. In Early Christian art certain subjects from the Old and New Testaments became conventionalised, and were repeated on numerous works; of which this scene of Daniel is an example. Observe here that Old Testament subjects are frequent; while Madonnas are rare, and saints almost unknown. Further on, on the ground, sarcophagus representing **Christ with the Twelve Apostles.** The treatment here, in spite of slight Oriental tendencies (compare the Mithra reliefs) is on the whole purely classical. Now, the great interest in this room is to watch the way in which classical styles and figures passed slowly from pagan types into Christian, and again from the debased classical types of the later Empire into those of Romanesque or Gothic barbarity. As an example of this surviving pagan element, see, on the wall to the R of this sarcophagus, **Elijah taken up to Heaven** in a chariot of fire, and leaving his mantle to Elisha. Here, the Jordan is represented, in truly pagan style, by a river-god reclining on an urn and holding water-weeds. Such river-gods were the conventional classical way of representing a river (see the Tiber here, and the Nile of the Vatican, reproduced in the Vestibule): and Christian artists at first so represented the

III.] *RENAISSANCE PARIS (THE LOUVRE)* 195

Jordan, as in the Baptism of Christ (in mosaic) in the Baptistery of the Orthodox at Ravenna.

Above the sarcophagus of Christ and the Twelve Apostles is an extremely beautiful **altar-front** from the abbey of St. Denis (read label) with a cross and palm trees, the True Vine interlacing it, and the characteristic wave-pattern, which you may note on many other works in this room. This is the most beautiful piece of early Romanesque or intermediate Christian carving in this collection.

In the centre of the Elijah wall, below, a sarcophagus with a very Oriental figure of the **Good Shepherd**—a frequent early Christian device. Compare this figure with the plaster cast of a similar statue from Rome, near the Della Robbia doorway. Compare the marked Orientalism of face, form, and foot-gear with the Mithra reliefs. Above it, Scenes from the Life of Christ:—Blessing the Children, Christ and Peter, the Woman of Samaria, etc.; treatment quite classical. Still higher, sarcophagus-front of Christ and the Twelve Apostles; workmanship becoming decadent; architecture, classical in the centre, passing at the sides into early Romanesque or Constantinian and Diocletianesque, as in some of the other examples in this room. L of it, Abraham's Sacrifice of Isaac, with rather late architecture.

All the other objects in this room should be carefully examined, and their place of origin noted. The symbols and the frequent Oriental tinge should also be observed. Likewise, the absence of several ideas and symbols which come in later. Note that there are no crucifixions, sufferings, or martyrdoms; the tone is joyous. Many of the minor objects have their own value. Thus, the fish, by the entrance door, is a common Early Christian symbol, because the Greek word ΙΧΘΥΣ formed the initials of the sentence, "Jesus Christ, Son of God, the Saviour"; and its sacred significance is here still further emphasised by the superimposed cross—a symbol, however, which does *not* belong to the very earliest ages of Christendom. So, on the opposite wall of the window, notice the little Daniel in the Den of Lions, and the youthful beardless Christ with a halo. The longer you study these interesting remains, the more will you see in them.

Those who have had their interest aroused in Early Christian art from the examination of this room will find the subject best pursued at Rome (Catacombs and Lateran) and Ravenna, where we can trace the long decline from classical freedom to Byzantine stiffness and Gothic barbarism, as well as the slow upward movement from the depths of the early Romanesque style to the precursors of the Renaissance. For the chronological pursuit of this enticing subject the best order of visiting is Rome, Ravenna, Bologna, Pisa, Siena, Florence. For a list of the extensive literature of the subject, see Dean Farrar's *Christ in Art*.

IV

THE NORTH BANK (RIVE DROITE)

PARIS, **north of the river,**—which is for most purposes the practical Paris of business and pleasure (and of the ordinary tourist) at the present day—has grown by slow degrees from small beginnings. The various rings of its growth are roughly marked on the Map of Historical Paris. The wall of **Philippe Auguste** started from near the easternmost end of the existing Louvre, and, after bending inland so as just to enclose the Halles Centrales, reached the river again near the upper end of the Île St. Louis. It thus encircled the district immediately opposite the primitive islands: and this innermost region, the Core of the Right Bank, still contains most of the older buildings and places of interest N. of the river. **Étienne Marcel's** walls took a slightly wider sweep, as shown on the Map; and by the time of **Louis XIII**, the town had reached the limit of the **Great Boulevards**, which, with their southern prolongation, still enclose almost everything of historical or artistic interest in modern Paris. The fact that the kings had all their palaces in this northern district was partly a cause, partly perhaps an effect, of its rapid predominance. The town was now spreading mainly northward.

The increase of the royal power brought about by Richelieu, and the consequent stability and internal peace of the kingdom, combined with the complete change in methods of defence which culminated in Vauban, enabled Louis XIV to **pull down the walls** of Paris altogether, and to lay out the space covered by his predecessor's fortifications in that series of broad curved avenues which still bears from this circumstance the name of Boulevards ("bulwarks" or ramparts). The original line so named, from the Bastille to the Madeleine, is ordinarily spoken of to this day simply as "the Boulevard." All the others called by the same have borrowed the title, mostly at a very recent date, from this older girdle. Gradually, the **Faubourgs** which gathered beyond the line of the inner city, as well as beyond the artificial southern prolongation of the Boulevards by which Louis continued his circle, with true French thoroughness of system, on the southern bank, have entirely coalesced with the central town, and at last enormously outgrown it. Nevertheless, to the end, the Paris of Louis XIV continues to enclose almost all that is vital in the existing city. Especially is **Paris within the Great Boulevards** to this day the Paris of **business and finance**: it includes the Bourse, the Banque de France, the Bourse de Commerce, the chief markets, the Post Office, the Ministries of Finance, Marine, and Justice, the Hôtel de Ville, numerous Government Offices, the principal wholesale warehouses, financial firms, and agencies, and almost all the best shops, hotels, banks, and business houses.

Even the inner circle itself, again, *within* the Boulevards, has been largely transformed by modern alterations, especially in that extensive reorganisation of the city inaugurated under Napoleon III by Baron Haussmann. In the brief itinerary which follows, and in which I have endeavoured to give the reader in two short walks or drives some general idea of the development of the Right Bank, with its chief points of interest, I shall indicate roughly the various ages of the great thoroughfares, and note with needful conciseness the causes which at various times led to their construction.]

A. THE CORE OF THE RIGHT BANK

Start from the **Place de la Concorde**, and walk eastward along the Rue de Rivoli, in the direction of the Louvre. (If you like, the top of an omnibus will suffice as far as the Hôtel de Ville.) The Place de la Concorde itself, though old in essence, is, in its present form, quite a modern creation, having been laid out in 1854 under the Second Empire, when it was decorated with the 8 seated stone figures, wearing mural crowns, and representing the chief cities of France (including Strasbourg). The Luxor obelisk (age of Rameses II) was erected in the Place, in its simpler form, by Louis Philippe, in 1836. The two handsome large buildings on the N. side are still earlier in date, age of Louis XV : one of them is occupied by the Ministère de la Marine—that nearest the Tuileries.

Proceed along the **Rue de Rivoli,** driven through this part of Paris by Napoleon I. He was a Corsican, and admired his native Italian arcaded streets, which he transplanted to Paris in this thoroughfare, and in the Rues Castiglione, and des Pyramides, all of which commemorate his victories. The form, however, is ill-adapted to the North, being draughty and sunless : and Frenchmen have never cared for the Rue de Rivoli, which is the street of strangers and especially of Englishmen. The native Parisian has always preferred to sun himself on the Boulevards. To your R are the **Gardens of the Tuileries,** still much as they were laid out under Louis XIV by Le Nôtre, in the formal style which well accorded with that artificial epoch. They contrast markedly with the newer portion, further E., on the site of the Palace, laid out by the present Republic in something like the English manner.

L, as you proceed, lies the Rue Castiglione, another of Napoleon's arcaded streets, leading up to the Place and Colonne Vendôme. R, a little further on, you come abreast of the Louvre, the first Pavillon being part of the connecting wing of the Tuileries. L, the Rue des Pyramides, again Napoleonic : and further L, opens up the **Place du Palais-Royal,** with the façade of the Palace showing behind it. This part, marked **Conseil d'Etat,** is the original building (much restored and rebuilt) : it was erected by Richelieu for his own occupation, and bore at first the name of Palais-Cardinal. Occupied after his death by the widow of Louis XIII, it took its present name : and was later the residence of the notorious Regent, Philippe d'Orléans, and of his scheming grandson, Philippe Égalité. The garden behind, with an arcade of shops, now half deserted and uninteresting, which also bears the name of Palais-Royal (almost to the exclusion of the original building) was laid out and let in this curious way by the Regent, as a commercial speculation. As a relic of the past, it is worth ten minutes' visit, some time in passing.

Continue along the Rue de Rivoli, eastward, till you reach

the Rue du Louvre. So far, you have been passing through the Paris of Louis XIII, Louis XIV, and the Empire; but now you are abreast with the wall of Philippe Auguste, and enter **the Core of the Right Bank.** Old as this part is, however, by origin, few of its buildings are mediæval; almost everything has been re-made in the Renaissance period. To your R lies the site of the old *château* of the Louvre, and opposite it, the mediæval Church of St. Germain l'Auxerrois, one of the few remaining, which thus announces your arrival in early Paris from the town of Napoleon and François Ier. (The Rue du Louvre itself is of very recent origin, and leads to the L to the new Post Office.) Still going east, you have on your R the tower of St. Jacques, once another fine mediæval church, now demolished. (Near it, on the L., opens out the modern Boulevard de Sébastopol, forming part of the great trunk line from N. to S., which was a principal feature in the Haussmannizing plan. It is known, further N., as the Boulevard de Strasbourg, and S. as the Boulevard du Palais, and the Boulevard St. Michel.) Keep on till you come to the **Hôtel de Ville**, the centre of the town on the North Bank.

The old Hôtel de Ville, which this building replaces, was erected in 1533, under François Ier, by an Italian architect, in emulation of the similar buildings in Italy and the Low Countries. It was afterwards largely added to at various times, and played an important part in the history of Paris. This first Hôtel de Ville, however (a handsome Renaissance building), was unfortunately burned down during the internal struggles of 1871. The present edifice was erected shortly after, in much the same style, but on a larger scale; a walk round the **exterior** will help to piece out the visitor's conception of Renaissance Paris. Note here once more the *pavillons* at the angles, and other features which recall the Louvre. A visit to the interior is quite unnecessary for any save those hardened sightseers who desire to inspect the decorations and arrangements of purely contemporary buildings. The sole reason for coming to the Hôtel de Ville at all, indeed, is the desirability of recognising its historic site, and understanding that here, by the hall of the old Prévôt des Marchands and the seat of the revolutionary Commune of Robespierre's period, you stand at the heart of La Ville—the Paris of the merchants. The building is occupied by the Préfet de la Seine—the Department which practically coincides with Paris. The Place in front of it, now called after the Hotel itself, is the old Place de Grève, the famous place of execution under the old Monarchy,—almost equally conspicuous in the history of the great Revolution.

Earlier still than the building of François Ier, a " Hostel de Ville " had stood upon the same site, purchased for the purpose by Étienne Marcel, Prévôt des Marchands, the real founder of the Paris municipality—to whom, therefore, a bronze equestrian statue has been erected in the little square facing the river.

The Hotel de Ville forms a convenient centre from which to begin the exploration of the core of the northern city. Walk round to the back (with a second fine *façade*) and, between the two handsome barracks, you see towering before you the front of the church of

St. Gervais.

This is an old church, remodelled: and, unlike most of the churches in the older part of Paris, it does *not* commemorate a local saint. Gervasius and Protasius, to whom it is dedicated, were two very doubtful martyrs of the persecution under Nero, whose names, bodies, and resting-place were miraculously and conveniently revealed to St. Ambrose at Milan (A.D. 387) at the exact moment when he needed relics for the church he had built, and which is now dedicated to him—the most interesting building in that beautiful city. St. Germain, bishop of Paris, brought back some relics of these saints in 560: and thenceforth St. Gervais and St. Protais became great objects of cult, like St. Stephen, in the Frankish city. (They are frequent subjects of French pictures in the 17th century.) This church, dedicated to them, probably occupies the site of one built by St. Germain in their honour. It was begun in 1212, added to and completely altered in 1420, and finally remodelled in front in the later Renaissance or classic manner. Most of the building as it stands is late Gothic; but you must go to the side to see it: the incongruous classic *façade*, illustrating the Doric, Ionic, and Corinthian orders, was added by Debrosse in 1616. Notice the coldness and bareness of this pseudo-classical front, as compared with the rich detail of the earlier mediæval exteriors. Almost the only breaks are the figures, on either side, of the two martyrs to contain whose relics the church was built. The sides, enclosed in houses which go close up to the wall, show the earlier architecture. Most churches in Paris were so walled up during the 17th century. The tower, and the aspect of the streets at the side, are very characteristic of a set of old effects now seldom visible.

The **interior** is chiefly noticeable for its great height, and for its interesting Late Gothic architecture. The patron saints, with their palms of martyrdom, stand on either side of the High Altar. The chapels at the S. side should be examined separately: in one is a good stained glass window by Pinaigrier (restored) of the Judgment of Solomon. Notice to what saint each is dedicated. The beautiful flamboyant Lady Chapel, behind the choir, contains good modern frescoes, illustrating the mystic titles of the Blessed Virgin, whose history is shown in the stained glass of the windows, also by Pinaigrier, but very much restored. These scenes the reader will now, I trust, be able to follow for himself—the birth, education, marriage, etc., of the Virgin, with the events of her life as recorded in the Gospels, and her death and assumption. Good Pietà (Christ mourned by angels) as you return on the N. side, with some excellent paintings—Martyrdom of St. Juliet, etc. I do not enlarge, as I hope the reader is now able to follow the lead I have given him in previous churches.

From St. Gervais, walk a little way along the N. side of the church, enclosed in its curious envelope of houses, till you come to the Mairie of the IVth Arrondissement. Then, turn up into the Rue de la Verrerie, along which continue till you reach the side of the church of **St. Merri**, almost hidden from view by a wall of houses. The *façade* is round the corner, in the Rue St. Martin. This is one of the few remaining mediæval churches in this district. St. Merri (Abbot Mederic of Autun) was a (historical) saint of the 7th century, local and early. He had a hermitage on this spot (then in the woods), and was finally buried here. The shrine over his tomb became the centre of a Parisian cult, and several churches rose successively above his body. The present one was not built till 1520; it is nevertheless a good late Gothic building. But notice the decline from the purity of Notre-Dame and the exquisite lightness of St. Louis's chapel. Handsome flamboyant doorway, one mass of sculpture : statues of 12 Apostles, with symbols of their martyrdoms, all restored, after being destroyed in the Revolution. The **interior** is interesting, but spoilt in 17th century : good stained glass, badly injured. I bring you here mainly for the sake of the reminiscences.

Continue straight on through characteristic old streets, to the modern Boulevard de Sébastopol, which cuts right through the core of Paris. Cross it and take the first turn to the left (as you walk northward) observing the marked contrast of the modern thoroughfare to the narrow streets we have just been traversing. Go along the Rue de la Reynie, and continue for one block, till you see, a little obliquely to your right, the

Square des Innocents.

In the centre rises the **Fontaine des Innocents,** designed by Pierre Lescot, with beautiful and appropriate sculptured figures of nymphs, bearing urns of water, by Jean Goujon. The fountain originally stood with its back to the Church of the Innocents, demolished in 1783. It has been re-erected here, with a fourth side added (to the S.), and has been much altered by the addition of a base and cupola. Nevertheless, it still remains a beautiful and typical example of French Renaissance architecture and sculpture. The coquettish reliefs, indeed, are not perhaps more lovely than those which adorn Jean Goujon's portion of the Louvre ; but they are nearer to the eye, and the scale enables one to judge of the entire effect more truthfully. The other exquisite nymphs which we saw in the Renaissance Sculpture at the Louvre, were originally part of the same fountain. The pretty little square in which the fountain stands is characteristic of the many democratic public gardens of Paris.

Proceed diagonally across the square, and continue along the North side of the Halles Centrales, till the east end of

St. Eustache

with its characteristic French *chevet*, comes in view before you. At the Pointe St. Eustache, as you cross the roadway, look up the vistas of un-Haussmannized Paris, again contrasting vividly with the broad Rue de Turbigo, which runs hence to the Place de la République. Do not enter at the first door at which you arrive—the one in the *chevet*—a rather good one—but continue along the South side of the church, observing as you pass the beautiful transept, with fine rose window, noble Renaissance portal, and a stag's head with the crucifix (emblem of St. Eustace) surmounting the gable. Go on round the corner to the gaunt, bare, lumbering, and unimposing late Renaissance or classical *façade*. In this you see the worst aspect of the decadent Renaissance architecture of Louis XIV—no saints, no archways. The door to the R gives access to the **interior**. In any other town but Paris, so splendid a building, rivalling many cathedrals, would attract numerous visitors. Here, it is hardly noticed. This is the church of the "Dames de la Halle" or market-women, who may often be observed in it.

We have already seen in brief at Cluny the main elements of the story of **St. Eustace**, the saint who was converted by the apparition of the Christ between the horns of the stag he was pursuing. Though not a local martyr, St. Eustace early obtained great consideration in Paris. But the first church here was one to St. Agnes : look out for memorials of her throughout the building. St. Eustace had practically supplanted her as early as 1223 : his church, after many enlargements, was finally pulled down under François Ier, and the present splendid Renaissance edifice erected in its place in 1532 ; completed in 1640. It is a strangely picturesque and unique building. St. Eustache, indeed, displays Renaissance architecture in a **transitional state**, endeavouring vainly to free itself from the traditions of the Gothic. In general plan, and in the combination of all its parts, it is in essence a Gothic cathedral ; but its arches are round, and its detail and decorative work are all conceived in the classical spirit of the Renaissance. If you wish to see the difference between such a church and one in which developed Renaissance methods have finally triumphed, you must visit St. Sulpice.

Note three things about St. Eustache : (1) it replaces a church to St. Agnes, who is still one of its two patronesses ; (2) it is the great **musical** church of Paris ; (3) it is the church of the markets.

Immediately on entering, stand in the centre of the nave,

and look up the church towards the choir and *chevet*. The enormous size of the building will at once strike you. Notice, too, the tall, round arches of the nave and aisles, the triforium above them (best seen from the aisles), and, higher still, the clerestory rising above the aisle-vaulting. The proportions are admirable. Observe also the roof, essentially Gothic in plan, though with an incongruous substitution of round for pointed arches. But note that all these quasi-Gothic constructive features are combined with **classical columns** and pilasters of the three great orders—Doric, Ionic, Corinthian —superimposed, and with such Renaissance detail as masks, cherubs, and other later decorative features.

Now walk up the **R aisle.** Everything in this church is, of course, comparatively modern, but still rich in symbolism. Most of the chapels have their names inscribed upon them —an excellent feature. The first, containing Franciscan Saints, has a good modern stained-glass window, representing the Saints and Patrons of the Order—St. Francis, St. Louis, etc. Observe the frescoes in the various chapels, and note their applicability to the saints to whom they are dedicated. I need not now enlarge upon this point. For example, the chapel of the Souls in Purgatory has a relief of Christ bound to the pillar—*His* purgatory—(a portion of it is preserved here) and a fresco representing mourning souls below, with triumphant ones in heaven. Observe from this point the beautiful Renaissance detail of the aisles and of the vaulting in the ambulatory, or passage behind the choir. Do not overlook the chapels of St. Agnes (co-patroness) and St. Cecilia, the inventress of the organ and patroness of music. The **transepts** are very short, but are decorated with good rose-windows and other excellent semi-Gothic detail. Walk round the **ambulatory**, noticing as you go the various chapels with their polychromatic decoration and their appropriate frescoes. Thus, that of St. Anne contains a representation of the Saint educating her daughter the Virgin. Note also on your L as you go the delicate work of the choir-screen, and the excellent vaulting and decoration of the lofty **choir.** The Lady Chapel behind the choir is not wholly pleasing. It contains a good 18th century statue of the Virgin and Child by Pigalle.

Observe particularly in the North part of the ambulatory the chapel of Ste. Geneviève, with scenes from her legend. The chapel of St. Louis, next it, contains excellent modern frescoes from his life, by Barrias, and a fine stained-glass window of his education, with his mother, Blanche of Castille, looking on, beneath a canopy marked with fleurs-de-lis and the three castles of Castille. One fresco represents him taking the Crown of Thorns to the Sainte Chapelle. Observe these little historical reminiscences: they add interest. Pleasing reliefs in the **North transept** of St. Cecilia and King David, representing music, for which this church has always been celebrated, especially on St. Cecilia's Day and Good Friday. They stand for Psalms and Hymns—the Jewish and the Christian psalmody. Notice, again, the figure of St. Agnes with her lamb, between the doorways, a tribute to the earlier dedication of the building. Above it, good stained-glass window of the Annunciation, with traditional details. (Do not be content to notice merely the points to which I call attention, but observe for yourself as you go the other figures, with their meaning and connection. To spell it all out is half the pleasure.) Above the Holy Water vessel in this Transept is a figure of Pope Alexander I, who first sanctioned the use of Holy Water, accompanied by angels. Beneath it, the baffled and disappointed demons, fleeing from the consecrated water. The next chapel contains the **relics of St. Eustace** and his children, martyrs. It is, perhaps, a little characteristic of modern feeling that the half-mythical namesake saint of the church should thus be relegated to a subordinate chapel in the edifice originally erected to his honour. The pictures are imitated from those in the Catacombs at Rome. Notice, in particular, the fresco of St. Eustace kneeling before the stag, which displays between its horns the miraculous image; also, the subsequent scenes of his legend (for which, see Mrs. Jameson). Beautiful view from this point of the choir and ambulatory.

Do not leave this interesting building without having examined all its details. It contains enough to occupy you for several hours, and is rich in illustrations of modern Catholic sentiment. Even the most tawdry bits of its modern church furniture become of interest when examined as parts of a consistent whole, falling into their due place in a great system of belief and the government of conduct. You have not really understood a church till you have grasped this connection between its various members. Ask yourself always, "Why is this here?" and though you may not always be able to see, the longer you proceed to investigate in this spirit, the more will the meaning of the whole come home to you. For example, return to the S. Transept and observe the figure of St. Gregory: he is the musical Father from whom the Gregorian chants take their name, and as such deserves commemoration in the musical church.

Quitting St. Eustache, you can continue westward a few steps, and then turn down a short street on the left, which leads you obliquely to a curious circular building, the Bourse de Commerce. Skirt round this till you come to its ugly *façade*, and then continue your way into the Rue du Louvre.

This short walk will have enabled you to take your bearings in the heart of the old district north of the river. You can prolong it a little, if you choose, through the town of Louis XIV, by walking northward along the Rue du Louvre as far as the new Post Office, and then turning to the left into the little circular **Place des Victoires** with its clumsy rearing equestrian statue of the Grand Monarch. The Place dates from his reign, and was designed by Mansart. Originally known as the Place Louis XIV, it was decorated by an earlier statue of the king, destroyed in the Revolution. The Restoration replaced it by the present ugly monument. A few steps to the N.-W. stands the Church of Notre-Dame des Victoires, begun in 1656, to commemorate the taking of La Rochelle, the Huguenot stronghold. It is instructive to compare this building of the worst period with the Mediæval and Renaissance churches you have just been examining. The Rue Notre-Dame des Victoires will lead you hence up to the Bourse (adequately viewed from outside), whence the brand-new Rue du 4 Septembre takes you straight back to the Opéra and the centre of modern Paris.

I have only walked you here through a small part of this older town; but if you care to explore the interesting district, rich in Renaissance and even Mediæval buildings, which lies to the east of the Hôtel de Ville, you cannot do better than take Mr. Augustus Hare's *Paris* as your guide—a valuable book, especially rich in historical reminiscences of the Renaissance period, the epoch of Louis XIV, and the Great Revolution. Mr. Hare will lead you to many forgotten nooks of old Paris, which the modest dimensions of the present handbook are insufficient to deal with. But I advise you only to explore these less-known byways after you have examined all the objects of first-rate importance here enumerated.

The **Musée Carnavalet,** also in this district, you had better defer visiting till after you have seen the École des Beaux-Arts, in the St. Germain Quarter, south of the river. It will be noticed later.

B. THE OUTER RING OF LOUIS XIV

A second, and doubtless to the reader by this time more familiar walk, round the **Great Boulevards,** will suffice to give a hasty conception of the Paris of Louis XIV and his immediate successors. Even if you are already well acquainted with the route, go over it once more, if only on the top of an omnibus, at this stage of your investigation, in order to take your bearings more fully. It must be borne in mind for the purposes of this walk or ride that in the earlier mediæval period the district between the Boulevards and the central core consisted, for the most part, of gardens and fields, among which were interspersed a few rural monasteries and suburban churches. These last have long since, of course, become wholly imbedded in modern Paris, but I will note as we pass a few earlier objects which it may be interesting for those who have time to diverge and visit.

Start from the Luxor Obelisk in the Place de la Concorde (noting here and elsewhere the Roman reminiscence of the bronze ships of Paris on the gas-lamps—as you see them at the Thermes), and walk up the **Rue Royale,**—the first portion of the great ring of streets which girdles the city of Louis XIV. The Rue St. Honoré, to your R, was, before the construction of the Rue de Rivoli and the Champs Elysées, the chief road which led westward out of ancient Paris. The

Porte St. Honoré stood on this site, where it crossed the barrier by the modern Rue Royale. Beyond it, the street takes the characteristic name of the Rue du Faubourg St. Honoré; and all the other streets which cross the girdle similarly change their name to that of the corresponding Faubourg as they pass beyond it. These long straggling roads, lined with houses on the outskirts (Faubourg St. Honoré, Montmartre, St. Denis, du Temple, etc.), have finally become the chief residential quarters of the city at the present day.

The handsome classical building in front of us is the **Madeleine**—(Church of St. Mary Magdalen)—the last stage in the classical mania which substituted Græco-Roman temples for Christian churches and other edifices. (See previous stages in St. Paul and St. Louis, the Sorbonne, the Invalides, the Panthéon, etc.) Begun under Louis XV, it was not completed till the Restoration. In style it follows the late Roman variation on the Corinthian-Greek model. Notice, however, as you approach, that even this Grecian building bears on its purely classical pediment the stereotyped Parisian subject of the Last Judgment, with the Angel of the Last Trump, and the good and wicked to R and L of the Redeemer. Only, in this case, St. Mary Magdalen, under whose invocation, as the inscription states, the church is dedicated, kneels by the L side of Christ, imploring mercy for the wicked. Compare this last term in the treatment of this old conventional portal-relief with its naïf beginnings at Notre-Dame and St. Denis. It is also worth while to enter and inspect the chapels, the paintings and sculpture in which will reveal their dedications. (See also Baedeker.)

The Rue Royale forms the first part of the girdle of Louis XIV. From the Madeleine onward, we enter that wider part of this girdle which still distinctively bears the name of the **Boulevard**. To our L, Baron Haussmann's quite modern Bd. Malesherbes opens up a vista of the recent and unsatisfactory Church of St. Augustin—a great ornate pseudo-Romanesque building, unhappily accommodated to the space at the architect's disposal. Proceeding along the Bd. de la Madeleine, and then the Bd. des Capucines, we arrive in a few minutes at the Place de l'Opéra, undoubtedly the central nodal point of modern Paris. To our L stands the great **Opera House,** erected at vast expense in the gaudy meretricious style of the Second Empire, and decorated with good, but too voluptuous modern sculpture. Two new streets branch R and L of it. Walk round them, and so take the measure of the building. To our R the **Avenue de l' Opéra** has been run diagonally across the older streets of Louis XIV's town, towards the Palais Royal and the Théâtre Français. This is now one of the finest thoroughfares of the existing town. Nevertheless, the old Boulevard, above all in this part of its circuit, remains the centre of Parisian life, thought, and movement. Especially is it the region of cafés and theatres. Here also the older **Rue de la Paix,** one of the earliest fine open thoroughfares in Paris, leads to the irregular octagonal **Place Vendôme,** laid out under Louis XIV, and said to owe its canted corners to the king's own personal initiative. [This Place is a good example of the best domestic architecture of the Eighteenth Century. Its centre is occupied by the great **bronze column** (Colonne Vendôme) originally erected by Napoleon to commemorate his victories. It was pulled down by the Commune, but (the fragments having been preserved) was re-erected after the triumph of the National party. Round it in a long spiral run a series of reliefs, suggested by those on Trajan's Column at Rome: but while the Roman pillar was surrounded by a Forum of several stories, with open porticoes from which the sculpture could be inspected, the sculpture on Napoleon's is quite invisible, except just at the base, owing to the lack of any similar elevated platform from which to view it.] The other great street diverging from the Place de l'Opéra to the R, the Rue du 4 Septembre, leads to the **Bourse** (uninteresting), and is part of the modern arterial system.

Continuing along the line of Louis XIV's Boulevards, we reach next the Bd. des Italiens, and then turn obtusely round into the Bd. Montmartre. To our L lies the Faubourg of that name, long since swallowed up by the engulfing city. At the Rue St. Denis (the great north road of Paris), we arrive at one of the debased classical **triumphal arches** (Porte St. Denis) which Louis XIV erected in place of the ancient castellated gates.

It is (more or less) decorated with contemporary reliefs representing his victories; these, and the inscriptions, are worth examining. Beyond the gate, the road to St. Denis, much traversed in earlier times by pilgrims, takes the significant name of Rue du Faubourg St. Denis. A little further on, the modern trunk line of the (Haussmannesque) Bd. de Sébastopol, hewn straight through the heart of the earlier town, intersects the old fortifications, leading R to the Cité, and L to the Gare de l'Est, in which direction it is known as the Bd. de Strasbourg. The next corner, the Rue St. Martin, which similarly changes its name to that of its Faubourg as it crosses the limit of the earlier town, is marked by a second of Louis XIV's arches, the **Porte St. Martin** (not *quite* so ugly), whose sculpture is again worthy of notice on historical grounds, if not on artistic. [A little way down the Rue St. Martin to the R lies the **Conservatoire des Arts et Métiers** (uninteresting internally) which occupies the site of the former **Cluniac Priory** of St. Martin-des-Champs, after which the street is still called. This was one of the principal old monasteries in the belt outside the girdling walls of Philippe Auguste, though included within those of Étienne Marcel. It was founded as early as the 11th century. The Conservatoire itself, as an industrial exhibition, is hardly worth a visit (except for technical purposes), but it ought to be inspected for the sake of the old **church** of the monastery which it contains (enter it to view interior; open on Sundays, Tuesdays, and Thursdays only) as well as for the fine **Refectory** of the 13th century, a beautiful Gothic hall, probably erected by Pierre de Montereau, the architect of the Sainte Chapelle, who also built the other Refectory, now destroyed, at St. Germain-des-Prés in the southern Faubourg. A little further on in the same street is the interesting Gothic church of **St. Nicolas-des-Champs,** with rather picturesque Renaissance additions. It stood, when first built, far out in the country. The fine west porch is of the 15th century. These buildings are chiefly worth notice as enabling the visitor mentally to restore the outer ring of monasteries and churches during the early mediæval period, afterwards englobed in the town of Louis XIV, and now in many cases adapted to alien modern uses.]

Return to the main line of the Boulevards, which here become distinctly shabbier and pass through a poorer district. This part of Paris is destitute of immediate interest, but should be traversed in order to give the visitor a just idea of the extent and relations of the eighteenth century city. We arrive before long at the Place de la République, formerly **Place du Château-d'Eau,** now adorned with a new bronze statue of the Republic. From this Place several more new Boulevards in various directions pierce through the poorer and densely-populated regions of eastern and north-eastern Paris. Along the main line, the Bds. du Temple, des Filles du Calvaire, and Beaumarchais lead hence through increasingly poorer-looking districts to the **Place de la Bastille,** where stood the famous strong castle of that name (Bastille St. Antoine), destroyed in the Revolution. Its site is now occupied by the **Colonne de Juillet,** erected to commemorate the Revolution of 1830. Hence the Rue St. Antoine leads R in one line into the Rue de Rivoli near the Hôtel de Ville. Beyond the line of the Boulevards, L, it takes the name of Rue du Faubourg St. Antoine. This was the region of the poorer and fiery revolutionists of 1789–93.

The district **within** the Boulevards in this direction was in the Valois period the most fashionable part of Paris. It contained the old royal palace of the Hôtel St. Paul, together with numerous other *hôtels* of the French nobility. From the Place de la Bastille, also, new Boulevards diverge in several directions. You had better return to the centre of the town by the Rue St. Antoine, where the third turning to the R will lead you direct into the **Place des Vosges,** a curious belated relic of the Paris of Henri IV. Its interesting architecture and quiet stranded air will well repay you for the slight détour, and will suggest to you the possibility of many similar agreeable walks in the same district. Mr. Hare will prove a most efficient guide to this quaint district, for those who have time to explore it thoroughly. Remember always that the *least* important part of Paris, historically speaking, is the western region which alone is known to most passing strangers.

V

THE FAUBOURG ST. GERMAIN

(LUXEMBOURG, ETC.)

THE town on the North Side, we saw, was early surrounded by a **suburban belt** of gardens and monasteries. A similar zone encircled the old University on the South Bank. The wall of Philippe Auguste, you will remember, bent abruptly southward in order to enclose the abbey of Ste. Geneviève; but an almost more important monastic establishment was left outside it a little to the west. This was the gigantic abbey of **St. Germain-des-Prés,** whose very name betokens its original situation. This rich and powerful community, whose building covered an enormous area of ground on the Left Bank, and grew at last into a town by itself, was originally founded by Childebert I as a thank-offering for his victory over the Visigoths in Spain in 543. Childebert, it may be remarked, was one of the most religious-minded among the Frankish monarchs,—which is why we have more than once met with his effigy in Gothic sculpture. He was also one of those few Merovingian kings who especially made his residence in Paris. On the portal of the other St. Germain (l'Auxerrois), which has numerous points in common with this one, we saw him represented with his wife Ultrogothe and the earlier St. Germain, a naïve way of expressing the fact that the King and Queen first gave that church to the sainted bishop. At the Louvre, too, we saw his statue from this very monastery. Among the sacred objects which Childebert brought back from Spain was the tunic of **St. Vincent,** the patron saint of prisoners. When he was besieging Saragossa, he saw the inhabitants carry this tunic in unarmed procession round the walls; which so convinced him of its value that he raised the siege, on condition that he might take the holy object home with him. He also brought a large rich gold cross, ornamented with precious stones, from Toledo,—a piece of jeweller's work which might probably be compared with the crowns of the Gothic kings preserved at Cluny. **St. Germain,** Bishop of Paris (who must not be confounded with his earlier namesake of Auxerre), recommended to the king the foundation of a new church and abbey, in order fitly to receive these holy relics. A church was therefore built in the garden belt outside the wall, and was originally dedicated (as was natural) to the Holy Cross and St. Vincent. The latter thus became one of the local saints of Paris, through its possession of his tunic; and his effigy may often be seen, with or without that of his brother deacon St. Stephen, on many of the older buildings of the city. We noticed him in particular on the portal of St. Germain l'Auxerrois, and on the frescoes within, though it was premature then to explain his presence. Note here that possession of the body of a Saint (St. Denis, Ste. Geneviève) or of some important relic (St. Vincent's tunic, St. Martin's cloak at St. Severin) almost invariably gives rise to local churches, and decides the cult of local patrons.

Later on, **St. Germain of Paris** having died, was buried in turn in Childebert's church of St. Vincent. His body being preserved here (as it still is), and working many miraculous cures, it came about in time that St. Vincent and the Holy Cross were almost forgotten, and the local bishop whose bones were revered on the spot grew to be the acknowledged patron of the mighty abbey which surrounded his shrine. Such of the early Merovingian kings as were buried in Paris had their tombs in this first church: their stone coffins may still be seen at the Hôtel Carnavalet. The abbey, which belonged to monks of the Benedictine order, grew to be one of the most famous in Europe: its name is still bestowed upon the whole of the **Faubourg** (long since imbedded in the modern town) of which it forms the centre. It was to the South Bank what St. Denis was to Northern Paris.

The existing **church,** of course (save for a few small fragments), is of far later date than the age of Childebert. Most of the Paris churches and monasteries suffered severely at the hands of the Normans: even those which were not then burnt down or sacked, were demolished and rebuilt in a more sumptuous style by the somewhat irreverent piety of later ages. This, the present church of St. Germain-des-Prés, belongs for the most part to the 11th century. It is therefore older than Notre-Dame or the Sainte Chapelle, and even as a whole than the greater part of St. Denis. It exhibits throughout that earlier **Romanesque** style which formed the transitional term between classical architecture and the pointed arches of the Gothic period. (What we call "Norman" in England is a local modification of Romanesque.) Portions of the building, however, show Gothic tendency; and the upper part is pure Pointed. Most of the Abbey has long since been swept away; a small part of the building still remains in the rear of the existing church. St. Germain should be visited if only on account of the fact that it is the earliest large ecclesiastical building now standing in or near Paris. Flandrin's noble modern frescoes have given it of comparatively recent years another form of attractiveness.

During the Renaissance period, while many of the nobility fixed their seats in the eastern and north-eastern part of Paris-within-the-Boulevards on the Right Bank, not a few erected houses for themselves in the open spaces of the **Faubourg St. Germain.** The most magnificent of these later buildings is the **Palais du Luxembourg,** erected for Marie de Médicis, after the death of Henri IV, by Jacques Debrosse, one of the best French architects of the generation which succeeded that of Jean Goujon and Philibert Delorme. It was built somewhat after the style of the Pitti Palace at Florence, where Marie was born, and it exhibits the second stage of French Renaissance architecture, when it was beginning to degenerate from the purity, beauty, and originality of its first outburst, towards the insipid classicism of Louis XIII and Louis XIV. It was for this building that Rubens executed his great series of pictures from the life of Marie, now in the Louvre; while Lesueur painted his St. Bruno legends for a Carthusian monastery within the grounds. The gardens which surround it are interesting in their way as being the only specimen now remaining in Paris of Renaissance methods of laying out;

most of the other palaces have gardens designed by Le Nôtre in the formal style of Louis XIV. The Palace is now occupied by the Senate: it is practically difficult of access, and the interior contains so little of interest that it may well be omitted save by those who can spend much time in being ushered round almost empty rooms by perfunctory officials. But the exterior, the gardens, and the Medici fountain should be visited by all those who wish to form a consistent idea of Renaissance Paris.

In the same excursion may be easily combined a visit to **St. Sulpice**, a church which occupies the site of an old foundation, but which was entirely rebuilt from the ground in the age of Louis XIV, and which is mainly interesting as the best example of the cold, lifeless, and grandiose taste of that pompous period.

The **Faubourg St. Germain** and the quarter about it, as a whole, are still the region of the old noble families. The western end of this Faubourg, especially about the Quai d'Orsay, is given over to embassies and political machinery, particularly that connected with foreign affairs. The South Bank is also the district of the **Legislature**, in both its branches. The Quartier Latin, however, has largely overflowed of recent years into the Luxembourg district and that immediately behind it, which are now to a great extent occupied by the students, artists, and other Bohemian classes.]

Cross the river, if possible, by the Pont de la Concorde. The classical building which fronts you proclaims itself legibly on its very face as the **Chambre des Députés**. But it has borne in its time many other names. This *façade* towards the river is of the age of the First Empire; the main edifice, however, is much older, being the **Palais Bourbon**, built in 1722 for the Duchesse de Bourbon. In 1790, it was confiscated, and has ever since been the seat of one or other legislative body, according to the Government of the moment.

You can go round to the back, as you pass, to inspect the original *façade*, in the style of Louis XIV, facing the little Place du Palais Bourbon. The interior is uninteresting, but has a few good pictures, which should only be visited by those whose time is unlimited.

The river front is on the **Quai d'Orsay,** the centre of modern political and diplomatic Paris. The building to the R of the Chamber is the official residence of its President; still further R, the Ministère des Affaires Étrangères. The broad thoroughfare which opens obliquely south-eastward, L of the Chamber, is the Boulevard St. Germain, which we have crossed before in other parts of its semi-circle. It was Haussmannized in a wide curve through the quiet streets of the Faubourg, and the purlieus of the Quartier Latin, with ruthless regularity. Many of the tranquil aristocratic roads characteristic of the region lie R and L of it; their type should be casually noted as you pass them. Down the Rue de Lille stands the German Embassy; on the Boulevard itself, R, the Ministère de la Guerre, and further on, L, the Travaux Publics. Other ministries and embassies cluster thickly behind, about the diplomatic Rue de Grenelle and its neighbours. To the R, again, the Boulevard Raspail, another very modern street, not yet quite complete, runs southward through the heart of the Luxembourg district. Continue straight along the Boulevard St. Germain, till you reach the Place of the same name, with the church of **St. Germain-des-Prés** full in front of you. (It may also be reached directly by the Rue Bonaparte; but this other is a more characteristic and instructive approach to the Abbey Church which forms the centre of the quarter.) Observe how the new Boulevard skirts its side, giving a clever effect of its having always been there; the front of the church is round the corner in the Rue Bonaparte.

The exterior, with the houses still built against it in places, though picturesque, has little minute architectural detail. The massive tower has been so much renewed as to be practically modern; but the Romanesque arches near the top give it distinction and beauty. The mean and unworthy porch is of the 17th cent.; the inner portal, however (though its arch has been Gothicised), belongs to the Romanesque church and is not without interest. Observe the character of the pilasters and capitals, with grotesque animals. Statues of St. Germain, of Childebert and Ultrogothe (as at the other St. Germain) and of Clovis, etc., which once flanked the door, were destroyed at the Revolution. In the tympanum are the unusual subjects of the Eternal Father, blessing, and beneath Him a Romanesque relief of the Last Supper (*not*, as commonly, the Last Judgment).

The **interior** still preserves in most part its Romanesque arches and architecture; but the lower part of the nave is the oldest portion (early 12th cent.); the choir is about a century later. Most of the pillars have had their capitals so modernized and gilt as to be of relatively little interest, while the decorations, though good and effective, are in many cases of such a sort as effectually to conceal the real antiquity of the building. The church was used during the Great Revolution as a saltpetre factory, and was restored and re-decorated in polychrome a little too freely under the Second Empire. A few capitals, however, notably those of the Baptistery to the L as you enter retain their antique carving and are worthy of notice; while even the modern gilt figures on those of the aisle are Romanesque in character and quaint in conception. (You can examine some of the old ones which they replace in the garden at Cluny.)

Walk round the church. The architecture of the **ambulatory and choir**, though later, is in a much more satisfactory condition than that of the main body. The arches of the first story are mostly round, but pointed in the apse; those of the clerestory are entirely Gothic. The detail below is good Romanesque; study it. Observe the handsome triforium, between the two stories; and more especially the interesting capitals of the columns—relics of the original church of Childebert, built into the later fabric. The choir, on the whole, is a fine specimen of late 12th cent. work. The Lady Chapel, behind, is a modern addition.

After having thus walked round the aisles and the back of the choir to observe the architecture, return once more to the doorway by which you entered and proceed up **the nave**, in order to notice the admirable modern **frescoes by Flandrin** (Second Empire). These are disposed in pairs, each containing subjects, supposed to be parallel, from the Old and New Testaments. Note in these the constant survival of early traditions, revivified by Flandrin in accordance with the art of his own period. The subjects are as follows :—

Begin on the L. (1) The Annunciation (treated somewhat in the traditional manner, the relative positions of the Madonna and the Angel Gabriel being preserved); typified by the Almighty appearing to Moses in the Burning Bush, as His first Annunciation. (2) The Nativity, as the pledge of redemption; typified or rendered necessary by the Fall. (The New Testament scenes are of course the usual series; those from the Old Testament foreshadow them, for which reason they are placed in the opposite from the chronological order.) (3) The Adoration of the Magi (reminiscences of the conventional, entirely altered by Oriental costumes and attitudes of submission); typified by Balaam blessing Israel—a famous picture. (4) The Baptism in Jordan (positions conventional, with the three angels to the L as always); typified by the Passage of the Red Sea. (5) The Institution of the Eucharist, very original in treatment; typified by Melchisedec bringing forth bread and wine to Abraham. Now return by the R side, beginning at the transept:—(6) The Betrayal of Christ by Judas; typified by the Sale of Joseph. (7) The Crucifixion—a very noble picture; typified by the Offering of Isaac, full of pathos. (8) The Resurrection; typified by Jonah restored from the sea, the whale being with great tact omitted. (9) The Keys given to Peter; typified by the Dispersion of the Nations at Babel. (A little thought is sometimes required to connect these subjects, which are occasionally, as in the last pair, rather to be regarded as opposites than types—the one remedying the other. Thus, the counterpart to the Dispersal at Babel is Christ's command to preach the Gospel to all nations.)

Above this fine frieze of subject-pictures runs a course of single figures, grouped in pairs, on either side of the windows in the clerestory. They are Old Testament characters, from Adam and Eve onward, ending with John the Baptist, as the last of the prophets. But as all the characters have their names legibly inscribed beside them, I need not enumerate them; all, however, should be observed, especially Adam and Eve, Miriam, Deborah, and Judith. Hold your hat or a book to cover the light from the windows, if the glare is too great, and after a little while you will see them distinctly.

Now proceed again to the front of the choir. On either side are other mural paintings, also by Flandrin: L, The Entry of Christ into Jerusalem, very beautiful: R, . The

Bearing of the Cross. Round the choir, the Twelve Apostles: by the pointed arches of the apse, the symbols of the Evangelists—the angel, lion, bull, and eagle. Above all—an interesting link with the earlier history of the church—are the pious founders, Childebert and Ultrogothe; the original patron, St. Vincent, with his successor, St. Germain; and finally, Abbot Morard who rebuilt the church, substantially in its present form, after the Norman invasion. He is thus commemorated in the beautiful choir which represents the work of his successor, Abbot Hugues, in the next century.

Before leaving, observe, architecturally speaking, how a Romanesque church of this type leads up to the more complex arrangement, with chevet and chapels, in Notre-Dame and later Gothic churches. Note the simplicity and dignity of the choir. Note also the peculiar character of the vaulting, comparing it with the later type at Notre-Dame, and especially with the reversion to much the same form in Renaissance times at St. Étienne-du-Mont, and St. Eustache. In spite of its newness, much of the modern decorative work is extremely effective; indeed, as a specimen of almost complete internal decoration, this church, notwithstanding the cruel overlaying of its early Romanesque sculpture by gold and paint, is perhaps the most satisfactory of any in Paris, except the Sainte Chapelle. I strongly advise you to sit down for some time and inspect the capitals built into the aisle, and the beautiful Merovingian pillars of the triforium, with an opera-glass, at your leisure.

On quitting the church, walk round it for the view on every side, which is picturesque and characteristic. Behind it, in the Rue de l'Abbaye, stands an interesting portion of the 16th-century **Abbot's Palace**—the only remaining relic of the vast conventual buildings, once enclosed for defence by a wall and moat, and containing a large lay and clerical population, like a little city. The sumptuous carved and gilded figure of Childebert, the founder, in the Mediæval Sculpture Room at the Louvre, came from the doorway of the old Refectory—a magnificent work by Pierre de Montereau (the architect of the Sainte Chapelle)—now wholly demolished. After you have visited each church, you will often find it pleasant to look out for such isolated works, divorced at present from their surroundings, and placed at Cluny or elsewhere. They will always gain new meaning for you by being thus identified as belonging to such-and-such an original building. For instance, in the Christian Antiquities Room at the Louvre, you will find an interesting capital of a pillar belonging to the Merovingian church of St. Vincent.

Now return to the Boulevard St. Germain, which a little further on occupies the site of the old Abbey Prison, famous as the scene of the massacres in September, 1792. Take the Rue Bonaparte on the opposite side, and go straight on till you reach the **Place St. Sulpice**, with its huge church in front of you. The building replaces an earlier one to the same saint: under Louis XIV, when the Faubourg St. Germain was becoming the quarter of the nobles, it was rebuilt in a style of ugly magnificence, befitting the maker of Versailles and Marly.

St. Sulpice, a vast bare barn, is chiefly interesting, indeed, as a gigantic specimen of the coldly classical type of church built under Louis XIV, when Gothic was despised, and even the Renaissance richness of St. Eustache and St. Étienne was decried as barbaric. It is a painful monument of declining taste. The **exterior** is chilly. The *façade*, whose sole recommendation nowadays is its size and its massiveness, is a triumph of its kind; it consists of two stories, with arcades of Doric and Ionic pillars superimposed on one another, and crowned with a pair of octagonal towers, only one of which is completed. The scanty detail of the sculpture is of the familiar character of the decadent period. But Fergusson praises the general effect of the exterior.

The **interior** consists of a cruciform pseudo-classical nave, with aisles, two bare single transepts, and a choir ending in a circular apse,—all vast, gloomy, barren, and unimpressive. The pillars and pilasters have Corinthian capitals, and most of the sculpture betrays the evil influence of Bernini. The holy water stoups, by the second pillars, however, are more satisfactory: they consist of huge shells, presented by the Republic of Venice to François Ier, standing on bases by Pigalle,—an effective piece of decorative work in this unpleasing edifice. As a whole, this chilly interior stands in marked contrast to the polychromatic richness of St. Germain-des-Prés, and to the exquisite Gothic detail of Notre-Dame and St. Germain-l'Auxerrois. The roof and false cupola contrast very much to their disadvantage with the charming Renaissance vaulting of St. Étienne-du-Mont and St. Eustache. Accept this visit as penance done to the age of Louis XIV. Save historically, indeed, this barren church is almost devoid of interest. Like everything of its age, it aims at grandeur: it only succeeds in being gaunt and grandiose. The very size is thrown away for want of effective vistas and groups of pillars; it looks smaller than it is, and sadly lacks furnishing.

Several of the **chapels** around this disappointing church, however, contain many good modern pictures: most of them also bear the names of the saints to whom they are dedicated, which largely aids the recognition of the symbolism. I enumerate a few of them for their interest in this matter. **Right aisle** (1) St. Agnes. Jacob and the angel: Heliodorus expelled from the Temple: by Delacroix. (2) Chapel of Souls in Purgatory. Religion brings comfort to the dying; benefit of prayers for the dead: by Heim. (3) Chapel of St. Roch, the plague-saint. He prays for the plague-stricken: he dies in prison at Montpelier: by Abel de Pujol. (4) St. Maurice, the soldier saint. His legend: by Vinchon. **Left aisle.** The chapels here are chiefly dedicated to the newer humanitarian saints of Catholicism. (1) St. François Xavier. He resuscitates a dead man: miraculous cures at his burial: by Lafon. (2) St. François de Sales. He preaches in Savoy: he gives to Ste. J. F. Chantal the constitution of his Order of nuns: by Hesse. (3) St. Paul. His conversion; he preaches at Athens: by Drolling. (4) St. Vincent de Paul. He founds the hospital for foundlings, with the Sisters of Charity; he attends the death-bed of Louis XIII: by Guillemot. **Chapels of the choir:** L (1) St. John the Evangelist. His martyrdom: and his assumption. (2) San Carlo Borromeo. He ministers during the plague at Milan: he gives the sacrament to his uncle, Pius IV, on his death-bed. (3) Uninteresting. (4) St. Louis the King. He carries a dying man during the plague: he administers justice under the oak of Vincennes. **Lady Chapel,** a miracle of ugliness. Statue of the Virgin on clouds in a recess, by Pajon, lighted from above, and in execrable taste,—the worst feature in this insipid and often vulgar building. Bad statues and frescoes. The other choir chapels on the **R side** are dedicated to the older patron saints of Paris. (1) St. Denis. His preaching: his condemnation. (2) St. Martin. He divides his cloak with the beggar: he resuscitates a dead man. (3) Ste. Geneviève. She brings food from Troyes during the siege of Paris: miracles wrought by her relics. (4) Our Lady. Her Birth: her Presentation in the Temple, interesting as modern examples of the treatment of these traditional subjects. Over the door, N. or L side, her Death: S. or R side, her Assumption.

St. Sulpice has a reputation for good music.

The Fontaine St. Sulpice, in front of the church, is from Visconti's designs, and has appropriate statues of the four great French preachers—Bossuet, Fénélon, Massillon, and Fléchier. The pulpit here is still famous for its oratory.

From St. Sulpice, the Rue Férou, to the R of the *façade*, leads you straight to the Luxembourg Palace. The long low building almost directly opposite you as you emerge is the

** Musée du Luxembourg,

containing the works of modern French painters. This, of course, is one of the most important objects to be visited in Paris; but I do not give any detailed account of it here, because the pictures themselves are entirely modern, and chiefly by living painters and sculptors, the various examples being sent to the Louvre, or to provincial museums, within ten years of the death of the artist. A visit to this Museum is therefore indispensable to those who desire to form a just acquaintance with contemporary art. But nothing in the Gallery demands historical elucidation. The visitor should provide himself with the Official Catalogue, which will amply suffice for his needs in this Gallery. I need hardly say that a proper inspection of it *cannot* be combined in one day with the other objects mentioned in this Excursion. Devote to it at least one or two separate mornings.

Turning to the L, as we leave the end of the Rue Férou, the

first building on our R is the official residence of the President of the Senate; the second is Marie de Médicis's

Palace of the Luxembourg,

now employed as the seat of the Senate. Walk along its *façade*, the work of Jacques Debrosse, one of the ablest architects of the later classicizing Renaissance, in order to observe the modified style of the age of Henri IV and Louis XIII, which it still on the whole preserves, in spite of modern additions and alterations. Note the gradual falling-off from the exquisitely fanciful period of the earlier French Renaissance, which produced the best parts of the Louvre and St. Eustache; and the way this building lets us down gently to the bald classicism of Louis XIV and Perrault. If you know Florence, observe also the distinct reminiscences of the Pitti Palace. Continue your walk along the whole of the *façade*, as far as the corner by the Odéon Theatre, — the subventioned theatre of the students and the Quartier Latin. Then, turn into the **garden**, and note the rest of the building, whose *façade* towards this side, though restored under Louis Philippe, more nearly represents Debrosse's architecture than does that towards the main thoroughfare. You need not trouble about the interior: though it contains a few good modern paintings.

The **garden**, however, is well worth a visit on its own account, both for the sake of the typical manner in which it is laid out, and especially for the handsome **Fontaine de Médicis** by Debrosse, on the side next the Panthéon. The group of sculpture in the middle represents Polyphemus surprising Acis and Galatea. Go round to the back, to see the (modern) Fountain of Leda, — that favourite subject of Renaissance sculpture. The best way back from this Excursion is by the Rue de Seine, which leads you past the Marché St.-Germain.

Another building in this district to which, if possible, the reader should pay at least one visit, is the **École des Beaux-Arts** in the Rue Bonaparte. This collection is interesting, both because it contains a number of valuable fragments of French Renaissance work, especially architectural, and also because of its **Museum of Copies**, including transcripts (mostly very good) of the best pictures of various ages, many of which are useful to the student of art-history for comparison with originals in the Louvre and elsewhere. Everybody who has not been to Rome, Venice, and Florence, should certainly try to visit this Museum; and even those who have made firsthand acquaintance with the masterpieces of Italian art in their native homes will find that it sometimes affords them opportunities for comparison of works widely scattered in the originals, which can be better understood here in certain of their aspects than in isolation. The building is open to the public, free, from 12 to 4 on Sundays; on week-days, non-students are also admitted from 10 to 4 (except Mondays), on application to the Concierge (small fee). I strongly advise a Sunday visit, however, as you are then less hurried, and also as the door on the Quai Malaquais is open on that day. This building should, if possible, be made the object of a separate excursion. It takes a long time to inspect it thoroughly.

Pass through the Tuileries Gardens, or across the Place du Carrousel, and traverse the river by the Pont Royal or the Pont du Carrousel. The second turn to the R, after the last-named bridge, the Rue Bonaparte, will take you straight to the door of the École. The building occupies the site of the old Couvent des Petits-Augustins; the convent chapel and a few other remains of the original works are embedded in it. Enter the courtyard. Here, during the Great Revolution, the painter Alexandre Lenoir founded his Musée des Monuments for the accommodation of the tombs removed from St. Denis and other churches. To his indefatigable exertions almost alone we owe the preservation of these priceless Mediæval and Renaissance relics. Under the Restoration, most of the monuments were replaced in their original positions, and we shall visit several of them later at St. Denis. To the R of the entrance in this **First Court** is the beautiful **doorway of the Château d'Anet**—that gem of Early French Renaissance architecture, which was erected for Diane de Poitiers by Philibert Delorme and Jean Goujon, by order of Henri II, in 1548: many objects from the same building we have already seen elsewhere. The portal is now placed as the entrance to the old **Abbey Chapel**. The end of this court is formed by part of the **façade** from the **Château de Gaillon,** erected for the Cardinal d'Amboise, Minister of Louis XII, and one of the favourite residences of

François Ier. It presents mixed Renaissance and Gothic features, as did the sculpture of Michel Colombe from the same building, which we saw at the Louvre. Both these imposing works—the portal of Château d'Anet and this *façade*—should be compared with the Italian Renaissance doorway from Cremona and the Gothic one from Valencia, which we saw in the collection of sculpture at the Louvre. They are indispensable to a full comprehension of the French Renaissance. The Château de Gaillon was destroyed during the Revolution, and many of its finest monuments are now at the Louvre. If you have time, after seeing this Museum, go back and compare them.

The **Second Court,** beyond the *façade*, contains several fragments of buildings and sculpture, among which notice the capitals from the *old* church of Ste. Geneviève (Romanesque), and a fine stone basin of the 12th cent., brought from St. Denis.

Now, return to the First Court, and visit the former **Chapel.** It contains **plaster casts,** adequately described for casual visitors by the labels, as well as **copies of paintings.** These plaster casts, especially those of the pulpit from Pisa, by Nicolò Pisano, the first mediæval sculptor who tried to imitate the antique, will enable you to piece out your conception of Italian Renaissance sculpture, as formed at the Louvre. Do not despise these casts: they are excellent for comparison. Among the pictures, notice the copy of Mantegna's fresco of St. James conducted to Martyrdom, from the church of the Eremitani at Padua. The fresco itself is a work of Mantegna's first period, and I select this copy for notice because it will help you to fill in the idea you formed of that great painter from consideration of his originals at the Louvre. Notice, for example, the strenuous efforts at perspective and foreshortening; the introduction of decorated Renaissance architecture; the love of reliefs and ornament; the classical armour; and many other features which display the native bent of Mantegna, but not as yet in the maturity of his powers. Observe, again, the copy of Ghirlandajo's exquisite Adoration of the Magi, with its numerous portraits, disguised as the Three Kings, the Shepherds, and the spectators, to which I have already called attention when speaking of Luini's treatment of this subject in the Louvre.

I do not enlarge upon these mere copies, as the originals will occupy us at Florence or Munich ; but the student who has become interested in the evolution of art will find it a most valuable study to trace the connection, first, between these subjects and others like them in the Louvre, and, second, between these copies of works by various masters and the originals by the same artists preserved in that collection. Compare, and compare, and compare again ceaselessly.

The Inner Court, the **Cour du Mûrier,** leads to another hall, the **Salle de Melpomène,** entered on Sundays direct from the Quai Malaquais. This room also contains a large number of **copies** which are valuable for study to those who have not seen the originals, and which will often recall forgotten facts in new connections to those who *have* seen them. I would call special attention, from the point of view of this book, to the good copies of Raphael's and Perugino's **Marriage of the Virgin** : as the originals are respectively at Milan and Caen (two places sufficiently remote from one another), the composition of the two can be better compared here than under any other circumstances. As examples of development, I shall notice them briefly. Perugino's is, of course, the older work. It was painted for a chapel in the Cathedral at Perugia, where it still hung when Raphael painted his imitation of it. First look carefully at both works, and then read these remarks upon them. The Sposalizio or Marriage of the Virgin, one of the set subjects in the old series of the Life of Mary, and often used as an altar-piece, consists traditionally of the following features. In the centre, stands the High Priest, wearing his robes and ephod—or what the particular painter takes for such ; he joins the hands of Joseph and the Madonna. Joseph stands always on the L side of the picture, which Perugino has rightly assigned to him ; though Raphael, already revolutionary, has reversed this order. He holds in his hand a staff, which has budded into lily flowers—the tradition (embodied in the Protevangelion) being that the High Priest caused the various suitors for Mary's hand to place their staffs in the Holy of Holies, as had long before been done in the case of Aaron, intending that he whose staff budded should become the husband of the Holy Virgin. Joseph's put forth leaves and flowers; and so this staff, either flowering or otherwise, is the usual symbol by which you can recognise him in sacred art. Behind Joseph stand the other disappointed suitors, one or more of whom always breaks his staff in indignation. Behind Mary stand the attendant maidens—the Virgins of the Lord—together with Our Lady's mother, St. Anne, recognisable by her peculiar head-dress and wimple. (Compare Lionardo in the Salon Carré.) A temple always occupies the background. Perugino took the main elements of this scene from earlier painters. (You will find numerous examples in the churches and galleries at Florence and elsewhere.) But he transformed it in accordance with his peculiar genius and his views of art, substituting a round or octagonal temple of Renaissance architecture for the square Gothic building of earlier painters. Such round buildings were the conventional representation of the Temple at Jerusalem among Renaissance artists. The peculiar head-dress and the balanced position are also characteristic of Perugino. How closely Raphael followed his master on these points of composition you can see for yourself by comparing the two copies. But you can also see how thoroughly he transformed Perugino's spirit; retaining the form while altering the whole sentiment and feeling of the figures. You see in it Perugino's conception, but Raphael's treatment. I have called special attention to these two pictures because they admirably illustrate the value and importance of comparison in art. You cannot wholly understand the Raphael without having seen the Perugino; nor can you wholly understand the Perugino without having seen the Ghirlandajos and Fra Angelicos, and Taddeo Gaddis which preceded it. Go from one to the other of these two pictures and note the close resemblance even in the marble pavement, the grouping of each component cluster, and the accessories in the background. Nay, the more graceful attitude of the suitor who breaks his staff in the Raphael is borrowed from a minor figure in the background of the Perugino. It is only by thus comparing work with work that we can arrive at a full comprehension of early painting, and especially of the relations between painter and painter.

I will not call special attention to the various other copies in this Museum. I will merely point out, as casting light on subjects we have already considered, Verocchio's Baptism of Christ, Perugino's group from the same subject, Raphael's Entombment, Botticelli's Adoration of the Magi, and Madonnas by Filippo Lippi, Giovanni Bellini, Correggio, and Mantegna. Many of these can be compared here and nowhere else. For those who are making a long stay in Paris, a judicious use of this collection, in conjunction with the Louvre, will cast unexpected light in many cases on works in that Gallery which it has been impossible here to describe in full detail.

The **Amphithéâtre,** approached from the Second Court, contains in its **Vestibule** a number of **plaster casts,** also valuable for purposes of comparison. The transitional archaic period of Greek sculpture, for instance, ill represented at the Louvre, is here well exemplified by casts from the statues in the pediment of the Temple of Athene at Ægina, now in the Pinakothek at Munich. Compare these with the reliefs from Thasos in the Salle de Phidias. Similarly, casts of the Children of Niobe, belonging to the same school as the Venus of Milo, are useful for comparison with that famous statue. The Amphitheatre itself, behind the Vestibule, contains Paul Delaroche's famous **Hémicycle,** one of that great painter's most celebrated works. Do not think, because I do not specify, that the other objects in this Museum are unworthy of notice. Observe them for yourself, and return afterwards to the Louvre time after time, comparing the types you have seen here with originals of the same artists and variants of the same subject in that collection.

VI

ST. DENIS

ABOUT six miles north of the original Paris stands the great **Basilica of St. Denis**—the only church in Paris, and I think in France, called by that ancient name, which carries us back at once to the days of the Roman Empire, and in itself bears evidence to the antiquity of the spot as a place of worship. Around it, a squalid modern industrial town has slowly grown up; but the nucleus of the whole place, as the name itself shows, is the body and shrine of the martyred bishop, St. Denis. Among the numerous variants of his legend, the most accepted is that which makes the apostle of Paris have carried his head to this spot from Montmartre. (Others say he was beheaded in Paris and walked to Montmartre, his body being afterwards translated to the Abbey; while there are who see in his legend a survival of the Dionysiac festival and sacrifice of the vine-growers round Paris—Denis=Dionysius=Dionysus.) However that may be, a chapel was erected in 275 above the grave of St. Denis, on the spot now occupied by the great Basilica; and later, Ste. Geneviève was instrumental in restoring it. Dagobert I, one of the few Frankish kings who lived much in Paris, built a "basilica" in place of the chapel (630), and instituted by its side a Benedictine Abbey. The church and monastery which possessed the actual body of the first bishop and great martyr of Paris formed naturally the holiest site in the neighbourhood of the city; and even before Paris became the capital of a kingdom, the abbots were persons of great importance in the Frankish state. The desire to repose close to the grave of a saint was habitual in early times, and even (with the obvious alteration of words) ante-dated Christianity—every wealthy Egyptian desiring in the same way to "sleep with

Osiris." Dagobert himself was buried in the church he founded, beside the holy martyr; and in later times this very sacred spot became for the same reason the recognised burial-place of the French kings. Dagobert's fane was actually consecrated by the Redeemer Himself, who descended for the purpose by night, with a great multitude of saints and angels.

The existing Basilica, though of far later date, is the oldest church of any importance in the neighbourhood of Paris. It was begun by Suger, abbot of the monastery, and sagacious minister of Louis VI and VII, in 1121. As yet, Paris itself had no great church, Notre-Dame having been commenced nearly 50 years later. The earliest part of Suger's building is in the Romanesque style; it still retains the round Roman arch and many other Roman constructive features. During the course of the 50 years occupied in building the Basilica, however, the Gothic style was developed; the existing church therefore exhibits both Romanesque and Gothic work, with transitional features between the two, which add to its interest. Architecturally, then, bear in mind, it is in part **Romanesque, passing into Gothic.** The interior is mostly pure Early Gothic.

The neighbourhood to Paris, the supremacy of the great saint, and the fact that St. Denis was especially the **Royal Abbey,** all combined to give it great importance. Under Suger's influence, Louis VI adopted the **oriflamme** or standard of St. Denis as the royal banner of France. The Merovingian and Carlovingian kings, to be sure—Germans rather than French—had naturally been buried elsewhere, as at Aix-la-Chapelle, Rheims, and Soissons (though even of them a few were interred beside the great bishop martyr). But as soon as the **Parisian dynasty** of the Capets came to the throne, they were almost without exception buried at St. Denis. Hence the abbey came to be regarded at last mainly as the **mausoleum of French royalty,** and is still too often so regarded by tourists. But though the exquisite Renaissance tombs of the House of Valois would well deserve a visit on their own account, they are, at St. Denis, but accessories to the great Basilica. Besides the actual tombs, too, many monuments were erected here, in the 13th cent. (by St. Louis) and afterwards, to earlier kings buried elsewhere, some relic of whom, however, the abbey possessed and thus honoured. Hence several of the existing tombs are of far later date than the kings they commemorate; those of the Valois almost alone are truly contemporary.

At the Revolution, the Basilica suffered irreparable losses. The very sacred reliquary containing the severed head of St. Denis was destroyed, and the remains of the martyr and his companions desecrated. The royal bones and bodies were also disinterred and flung into trenches indiscriminately. The tombs of the kings were condemned to destruction, and many (chiefly in metal) were destroyed or melted down, but not a few were saved with difficulty by the exertions of antiquaries, and were placed in the Museum of Monuments at Paris (now the École des Beaux-Arts), of which Alexandre Lenoir was curator. Here, they were greatly hacked about and mutilated, in order to fit them to their new situations. At the Restoration, however, they were sent back to St. Denis, together with many other monuments which had no real place there; but, being housed in the crypt, they were further clipped to suit their fresh surroundings. Finally, when the Basilica was restored under Viollet-le-Duc, the tombs were replaced as nearly as possible in their old positions; but several intruders from elsewhere are still interspersed among them. Louis XVIII brought back the mingled bones of his ancestors from the common trench and interred them in the crypt.

Remember, then, these things about St. Denis: (1) It is (or was), first and above all things, **the shrine of St. Denis and his fellow-martyrs.** (2) It contains the remnant of **the tombs of the French kings.** (3) It is **older** in part than almost any other building we have yet examined.

As regards the **tombs,** again, bear in mind these facts. All the oldest have perished; there are none here that go back much further than the age of St. Louis, though they often represent personages of earlier periods or dynasties. The best are those of the Renaissance period. These are greatly influenced by the magnificent tomb of Giangaleazzo Visconti at the Certosa di Pavia, near Milan. Especially is this the case with the noble monument of Louis XII, which closely imitates the Italian work. Now, you must remember that Charles VIII and Louis XII fought much in Italy, and were masters of Milan;

hence this tomb was familiar to them; and their Italian experiences had much to do with the French Renaissance. The Cardinal d'Amboise, Louis's minister, built the Château de Gaillon, and much of the artistic impulse of the time was due to these two. Henceforth recollect that though François Ier is the Prince of the Renaissance, Louis XII and his minister were no mean forerunners.

The Basilica is open daily; the royal tombs are shown to parties every half-hour; but the attendants hurry visitors through with perfunctory haste, and no adequate time is given to examine the monuments. Therefore, **do not go to St. Denis till after** you have seen the **Renaissance Sculpture** at the Louvre, which will have familiarised you with the style, and will enable you better to grasp their chief points quickly. Also, go **in the morning, on a bright day**: in the late afternoon or on dark days you see hardly anything.]

Start from the Gare du Nord. About four trains run every hour. There is also a tramway which starts from the Opéra, the Madeleine, or the Place du Châtelet, but the transit is long, and the weary road runs endlessly through squalid suburbs, so that the railway is far preferable. Start early. Take your opera-glasses.

From the St. Denis station, take the road directly to the R as far as the modern Parish Church, when a straight street in front of you (a little to the L) leads directly to the Basilica. On the L of the Place in front of the great church is the Hôtel de Ville, on which it is interesting to notice, high up on the front, the ancient royal war-cry of "Montjoye St. Denis!"

Turn to the **Basilica.** The **façade**, of the age of Abbot Suger, is very irregular. It consists of two lateral towers, and a central portion, answering to the Nave. Only the south tower is now complete; the other, once crowned by a spire, was struck by lightning in 1837. Observe the inferiority in unity of design to the fine *façade* of Notre-Dame, the stories of the towers not answering in level to those of the central portion. We have here the same general features of two western towers and three recessed portals; but Notre-Dame has improved upon them with Gothic feeling. The lower arches are round and Romanesque. The upper ones show in many cases an incipient Gothic tendency. The **rose window** has been converted into a clock. On either side of it, in medallions, are the symbols of the four Evangelists. Observe the fine pillars and Romanesque arcade of the one complete tower. Also, the reliefs of kings of Israel and Judah in the blind arcade which caps the third story in both towers. The coarse and ugly battlements which spoil the front are part of the defensive wall of the Abbey, erected during the English wars in the 14th century. Behind them, a little way off, you can see the high and pointed roof of the nave, crowned by the statue of the patron, St. Denis.

Now, enter the enclosure and examine the **three round-arched portals**. The *Central Doorway* has for its subject the usual scene of the Last Judgment. The architecture of the framework is still in the main that of the 13th cent. The relief in the tympanum has been much restored, but still retains its Romanesque character. In the centre is Christ, enthroned, with angels. On His R hand, the blessed, with the Angel of the Last Trump as elsewhere. On His L, the condemned, with the Angel bearing the sword, and thrusting the wicked into Hell: all conventional features. The Latin inscriptions mean, "Come, ye blessed of My Father"; and "Depart from Me, ye wicked." Beneath is the General Resurrection, souls rising (mostly naked) from the tomb. To R and L of the doorway, below, are the frequent subjects of the Wise and Foolish Virgins. Above, on the archway, figures of saints and patriarchs, amongst whom is conspicuous King David. Notice in the very centre or key of the archway, Christ receiving souls from angels. To His R, Abraham with three blessed souls in his bosom (as at St. Germain l'Auxerrois). To His L, devils seizing the condemned, whom they thrust into hell, while angels struggle for them. Higher still, on the arch, angels swinging a censer, and an angel displaying a medallion of the lamb. This door formed the model on which those of Notre-Dame, the Sainte Chapelle, St. Germain l'Auxerrois, and many others in Paris of later date, were originally based. The actual doors have naïve bronze reliefs of the Passion, Resurrection, and Ascension. Notice the quaint character of these reliefs, and of the delicate decorative design which surrounds them,—broken, in the case of the Supper at Emmaus, by the figure of a monk, probably Abbot Suger, grasping a pillar. The Resurrection, with its sleeping Roman soldiers, and the Kiss of Judas, with Peter sheathing his sword and Christ healing the ear of Malchus, are also very typical. Do not fail to notice, either, the beautiful decoration of the pilasters and their capitals. All this is delicate and characteristic Romanesque tracery.

The other doors commemorate the **History of St. Denis.** On the *South Door* is a much-restored and practically modern relief of St. Denis in prison with Christ bringing him the last sacrament; it has been largely made up by the aid of the old French painting of the same subject in the Louvre. In front are figures symbolical of his martyrdom—the executioner, etc. On the sides, reliefs of the Months. On the *North Door*, St. Denis condemned and on his way to Montmartre, with his two companions, Rusticus and Eleutherius, chained; they are accompanied in the sky by the Eternal Father and the heavenly host. On the archway, interesting reliefs of the three martyrs, with an angel supporting the châsse containing their relics. On the sides, the signs of the Zodiac.

Walk round the **North Side** to observe the decorated flamboyant architecture of the chapels of the North Aisle (much later) with the flying buttresses above them. Also, the North Transept, with its rose window, and the peculiar **radiating chapels** around the **apse,** which form a characteristic feature of the Romanesque style. Observe these as well as you can from the extreme end of the railing. Return to Transept. The sculpture over the North Portal represents the Decapitation of St. Denis. On the centre pier, a Madonna and Child. R and L, Kings of Judah.

The South Side is inaccessible. It is enclosed by buildings on the site of the old monastery (not ancient—age of Louis XIV), now used as a place of education for daughters of Chevaliers de la Légion d'Honneur.

The **interior** is most beautiful. The first portion of the church which we enter is a **vestibule** or *Galilee* under the side towers and end of the Nave. Compare Durham. It is of the age of Abbot Suger, but already exhibits pointed arches in the upper part. The architecture is solid and massive, but somewhat gloomy.

Descend a few steps into the **Nave**, which is surrounded by single aisles, whose vaulting should be noticed. The architecture of this part, now pure Early Gothic, is extremely lovely. The triforium is delicate and graceful. The windows in the clerestory above it, representing kings and queens, are almost all modern. Notice the great height of the Nave, and the unusual extent to which the triforium and clerestory project above the noble vaulting of the aisles. Note that the triforium itself opens directly to the air, and is supplied with stained-glass windows, seen through its arches. Sit awhile in this light and lofty Nave, in order to take in the beautiful view up the church towards the choir and *chevet*.

Then walk up to the Barrier near the Transepts, where sit again, in order to observe the **Choir** and **Transepts** with the staircase which leads to the raised Ambulatory. Observe that the transepts are simple. The ugly stained glass in the windows of their clerestory contains illustrations of the reign of Louis Philippe, with extremely unpicturesque costumes of the period. The trousers are unspeakable. The architecture of the Nave and Choir, with its light and airy arches and pillars, is of the later 13th century.

The reason for this is that Suger's building was thoroughly restored from 1230 onwards, in the pure pointed style of that best period. The upper part of the Choir, and the whole of the Nave and Transepts was then rebuilt—which accounts for the gracefulness and airiness of its architecture when contrasted with the dark and heavy vestibule of the age of Suger.

Note from this point the arrangement of the Choir, which, to those who do not know Italy, will be quite unfamiliar. As at San Zeno in Verona, San Miniato in Florence, and many other Romanesque churches, **the Choir is raised** by some steps above the Nave and Transepts; while **the Crypt** is slightly depressed beneath them. In the Crypt, in such cases, are the actual bodies of the saints buried there; while the Altar stands directly over their tombs in the Choir above it.

Look every way from this point at the tombs within sight, at the Choir and Transepts, and at the steps of the Ambulatory. Do not be in a hurry to enter. On the contrary, sit awhile longer in the body of the Nave, **outside** the barrier, and read what follows.

[The custodians hurry you so rapidly through the reserved part of the church that it will be well **before entering the enclosure** to glance through the succeeding notes, explanatory of what you are about to see. The remarks to be read *as you go round the building* I insert separately, in the briefest possible words, as aids to memory.

The tomb of **Louis XII** (d. 1515) and his wife, Anne de Bretagne (d. 1514), is the earliest of the great Renaissance tombs in France, and the first in order in this Basilica. Long believed to be of Italian workmanship, it is now known to be the production of Jean Juste of Tours, unknown otherwise, but supposed to be a Florentine. It is imitated from the Giangaleazzo Visconti, already mentioned, in the Certosa di Pavia. This tomb, the first you see, struck the keynote for such works of the Renaissance in France. It is a good and apparently French imitation of the Italian original, and it fitly marks Louis XII's place in the artistic movement. Remember his statue by Lorenzo da Mugiano in the Louvre, and his connection with Cardinal d'Amboise and the Château de Gaillon.

The next important monument is that of **Dagobert I** (d. 638), the founder of the Abbey, probably erected in his honour, as a sort of shrine, by St. Louis in the 13th cent. In order to understand this tomb (which you are only allowed to see across the whole breadth of the choir), it is necessary to know the **legend** to which the mediæval sculptures on the canopy refer. When Dagobert died, demons tried to steal his soul; but he was rescued by St. Denis, to whom he had built this abbey, assisted by St. Maurice and St. Martin of Tours—a significant story, pointing the moral of how good a thing it is to found a monastery. The narrative is told in three stages, one above the other. (1) An anchorite, sleeping, is shown by St. Denis in a dream that the king's soul is in danger; to the R, Dagobert stands in a little boat (like the boat of Charon); demons seize him and take off his crown. (2) The three saints come to the king's rescue, attended by two angels, one swinging a censer, the other holding a vase of holy water; St.

Martin and St. Denis see the tortured soul; the soldier St. Maurice, sword in hand, attacks the demons. (3) The three saints, attended by the angels, hold a sheet, on which the soul of Dagobert stands, praying. The Hand of God appears in a glory above, to lift him into heaven. These are on the canopy; beneath, on the tomb itself, lies a modern restored recumbent statue of Dagobert; there are also erect figures of his son Sigebert (restored), and his queen, Nantilde (original).

The tomb of **Henri II** (d. 1559) and his queen, **Catherine de Médicis** (d. 1589)—the third of any importance—was executed by the great sculptor, Germain Pilon, during the lifetime of the latter. (It was he, too, you will remember, who made the exquisite group of figures, now in the Louvre, to support the urn which was to contain their hearts.) As in many contemporary tombs, the king and queen are represented alive and kneeling, in bronze, above, and nude and dead in marble on the tomb below. (We saw a similar tomb at the Louvre.) A **second monument,** close by, to the same king and queen, has recumbent marble figures on a bronze couch,—Catherine is said in her devouter old age to have disapproved of the nudity of the figures on the first tomb—but as it was usual to distribute relics of French kings to various abbeys, such duplicate monuments were once common.

The tomb of **Frédégonde** (d. 597) from St. Germain-des-Prés, is a curious mosaic figure of marble and copper, almost unique in character. It is **not** of the Queen's own age, but was added to her shrine in the 12th century. Most of these early kings and queens, founders and benefactors of monasteries, were either actually canonized or were treated as saints by the monks whom they had benefited: and tombs in their honour were repaired or reedified after the Norman invasion and other misfortunes.

Two monuments of the **children of St. Louis,** from other abbeys, carried first to Lenoir's Museum, are now in this Basilica. They are of enamelled copper, with **repoussé** figures, executed at Limoges.

The most costly, though not to my mind the most beautiful, of the Renaissance tombs is that of **François I**er (d. 1547). On the summit are kneeling figures of the King, his wife Claude, and their three children. The reliefs on the pedestal represent the battles of Marignano and Cerisole. This tomb, like that of Louis XII, is ultimately based on the Visconti monument in the Certosa, but it exhibits a much later and more refined development of French Renaissance sculpture than its predecessor. It is by Germain Pilon, Philibert Delorme, and (perhaps) Jean Goujon. The architectural plan is noble and severe: but it lacks the more naïve beauty of Jean Juste's workmanship.

It was the curious custom to treat the bodies of French Kings (who, as royal, were almost sacred) much as the relics of the Saints were treated. Hence the head and heart were often preserved separately and in different places from the body to which they belonged. François Ier himself was interred here: but an **urn** to hold his heart was placed in the Abbaye des Hautes Bruyères, near Rambouillet. This urn is a fine Renaissance work by Pierre Bontemps. Taken to Lenoir's Musée des Monuments at the Revolution, it was afterwards placed beside the king's tomb in this Basilica.

Look out in the Apse for the Altar of St. Denis, and his fellow-martyrs. Near it used once to hang the Oriflamme, that very sacred banner which was only removed when a King of France took the field in person. It was last used at Agincourt. A reproduction now represents it.

The other monuments can be best observed by the brief notes given as we pass them. The arrangements for seeing them are quite as bad as those in our own cathedrals, and it is impossible to get near enough to examine them properly. Therefore, **take your bearings from the Nave** *before* you enter, and try to understand the architecture of the choir as far as possible before you pass the barriers.

Disregard the remarks made by the guide (who expects a tip), and read these brief notes for yourself as you pass the objects.]

Enter the enclosure.

North Aisle: L, several good mediæval recumbent tombs, mostly from other abbeys, named on placards. Read them.

Then, **Tombs of the Family of St. Louis,** recumbent, also named: 13th and 14th cents.

Tomb of Louis XII, and his wife Anne de Bretagne, by Jean Juste of Tours. After the Certosa monument. Beneath, Twelve Apostles; four allegorical figures of Virtues: king and queen, in centre, recumbent; above, on canopy, king and queen kneeling. On base, reliefs of his Italian victories.

R, column commemorating Henri III, by Barthélemy Prieur.

Stand by **steps** leading to **raised Ambulatory,** only point of view for ** **Tomb of Dagobert,** on opposite side of choir, 13th cent. Legend of his soul, see above. Erect statues of Sigebert, his son, and Nantilde, his queen. Insist on time to view it with opera-glass.

L, **Tomb of Henry II** and Catherine de Médicis. King and queen recumbent, in marble, below; kneeling, in bronze, above. At corners, the four cardinal virtues, bronze. Also after Certosa.

Ascend steps to Ambulatory.

Below, monuments of the Valois family.

Above, L, second monument of Henri II and Catherine de Médicis, recumbent marble on bronze mattress. Observe monograms of H and D, as on Louvre.

Proceed round Ambulatory. **Chapels** to the L have stained-glass windows of 12th and 13th cents. Interesting subjects, which note in passing. ** Beautiful **view across the church** as you pass the transepts.

In the centre of the **apse** of the Choir (above the tombs in Crypt), is the Altar of St. Denis, with his fellow-martyrs, St. Rusticus and St. Eleutherius—modern imitation of the original shrine, broken at the Revolution. During the *neuvaine* (nine days after St. Denis' day—Oct. 9) the Reliquaries are exposed in the Nave, near the barrier. On one side of the Altar is a reproduction of the Oriflamme.

Beyond this Altar, continue along the South Side of the Ambulatory, to the **Sacristy.** Modern paintings, here, relating to the History of the Abbey. Labels beneath describe their subjects.

Adjoining it is the **Treasury,** containing only uninteresting modern church utensils.

Beyond the Sacristy, **Tomb of Frédégonde,** from St. Germain-des-Prés. Hands, feet, and face probably once painted.

Descend steps from ambulatory.
Descend to Crypt.

This, the oldest portion of the existing building, was erected by Suger, to contain the Tombs of the Three Martyrs, buried under their altar. Its architecture is the most interesting of all in the Basilica. Notice the quaint Romanesque capitals of the columns. In the centre, bones of the Royal Family, within the grating. Neglect them, and observe the arches.

In the **Crypt Chapels**, uninteresting modern statues (Marie Antoinette, Louis XVI, colossal figures for the Monument of the Duc de Berry, etc.). Neglect these also, and observe rather the architecture and **good fragments of glass** in windows, particularly a very naïve Roasting of St. Lawrence.

Return to church.
Monument of Du Guesclin, 1380.
Louis de Sancerre, 1402.
Renée de Longueville, from the Church of the Célestins.

Blanche and Jean, children of St. Louis, enamelled copper, Limoges; from other abbeys.

**François Ier, his wife, Claude, and their three children, above. On pedestal, Scenes from his battles; High Renaissance work: Philibert Delorme, Germain Pilon, and Jean Goujon. More stately, but less interesting than Louis XII.

**Urn, to contain heart of François Ier, from the nunnery of Hautes Bruyères.

Louis d'Orléans and Valentine of Milan, from the Church of the Célestins.

Charles d'Étampes; 1336, with 24 small figures of saints.

Leave the enclosure and return to the church. I advise you then to read this all over again, and finally, go round a second time, to complete the picture.

The Abbey and Church are closely bound up at every turn with French history. In Dagobert's building, in 754, Pope Stephen II, flying from the Lombards, consecrated Charlemagne and his brother Carloman. In the existing Basilica, St. Louis took down the Oriflamme to set forth on his Crusade; and Joan of Arc hung up her armour as a votive offering after the siege of Orleans. But indeed, St. Denis played an important part in all great ceremonials down to the Revolution, and its name occurs on every page of old French history.

On your return to Paris, you may find this a convenient moment to visit **St. Vincent de Paul,** which lies two minutes away from the Gare de Nord.

After visiting St. Denis the reader will probably find it desirable to examine certain objects from the **Treasury of the Basilica** now preserved in the **Louvre.** They are mostly contained in the Galerie d'Apollon, in the glass case nearest the window which looks out upon the Seine. (Position of cases liable to alteration: if not here, look out for it elsewhere in the same room.) The most important of these objects is an antique Egyptian vase in porphyry, which Abbot Suger had mounted in the 12th cent. in a silver-gilt frame, as an eagle. It contains an inscription composed by the Abbot in Latin hexameters, and implying that it was to be used for the service of the altar. Near it is an antique Roman sardonyx vase, also mounted as a jug by Suger in the 12th cent., and from the same Treasury: its inscription says, "I, Suger, offer this vase to the Lord." Also, another in rock-crystal, which has been similarly treated: it bears the name of Alienor d'Aquitaine: she gave it to Louis VII, who passed it on to Suger: a 12th cent. inscription on the base records these facts, as well as its dedication to Sts. Rusticus and Eleutherius. The same case contains a beautiful Carlovingian serpentine paten, which formed part of the treasure of Dagobert's Abbey. Observe, close by, the beautiful silver-gilt Madonna, characteristic French work of the 14th cent., offered by Queen Jeanne d'Evreux to the Abbey of St. Denis, and bearing an easily-deciphered inscription in old French. Note that the Madonna in this royal offering carries in her hand the fleur-de-lis of France. Compare this work mentally with the other early French Madonnas we have already observed in the Mediæval Sculpture Room.

Among other objects in this same case observe the curious double cross, with cover and lid to contain it; where the inscription above the head of the inner cross indicates the natural origin of the doubling. Close inspection of this object will explain to you many little points in others. Several similar Crucifixions, with Madonna and St. John and attendant angels, are in the same room: compare them with it. To the R is a good relief of the Maries at the Sepulchre; a double crucifix with St. John and the Madonna; and a reliquary fashioned to contain the arm of St. Louis of Toulouse. Most of these objects are sufficiently explained by the labels: the antique inscriptions, sometimes in Greek, are easily legible. (Beautiful view out of window to L.)

The examination of this case will form a point of departure for the visitor who cares to examine the **minor art-works** in the Galerie d'Apollon and other rooms of the Louvre. I have left them till now, for the sake of the peg on which to hang them. I will therefore note here, in this connection, one or two other things which may assist the reader in the examination of the remainder, leaving him, as usual, to fill in the details of the scheme by personal observation and comparison of objects.

Walk down the centre of the Galerie d'Apollon, on the side towards the windows, passing the tawdry crown jewels, and the many exquisite Classical or Renaissance works in the cabinet beyond it, all of which you can afterwards examine at your leisure. (Some of the antique busts in precious stones come from Abbey Treasuries, where they were preserved and sanctified during the Middle Ages.) But in the last case save one, observe, near the centre, a very quaint little figure of St. Lawrence, lying comfortably on his gridiron, and holding in his hands a tiny reliquary, almost as big as himself—a finger with a nail on it, intended for the reception of a bone of the Saint's own little finger. This odd little reliquary, French 14th cent., when compared with that for the arm of St. Louis of Toulouse, will help you to understand many similar reliquaries, both here and elsewhere. The martyr is put there as a mode of signifying the fact—"This is a bone of St. Lawrence." Above it, note again five charming crosiers, containing respectively representations of the Madonna enthroned, the Annunciation, the Coronation of the Virgin, again the Annunciation, and a decorative design of great beauty. Note their date and place of origin on the labels. When once your attention has been called to the occurrence of such definite scenes in similar objects, you will be able to recognise them at once for yourself in many like situations. In the Annunciation to the L, observe once more the very odd way in which the usual lily is carefully obtruded between the angel Gabriel and Our Lady. Some obvious barrier between the two was demanded by orthodoxy: here, the decorative device by which the difficulty has been surmounted is clever and effective. Between this crosier and that of the Coronation, look again at a queer little reliquary, held by the Madonna and Child, with a glass front for the exhibition of the relic. Another Madonna, close by to the L, similarly holds on her lap a charming little reliquary basin. The same case contains several coffers and reliquaries in *champlevé* enamel, the most interesting of which is the Coffer of St. Louis, with decorative designs showing Romanesque tendencies. At the far end of the case, two charming silver-gilt angels, 14th cent., also bearing reliquaries. Examine in detail all the objects in this most interesting case. They will help, I hope, to throw light upon others which you will see elsewhere.

I do not intend to go at equal length through all the cases in this interesting room; but your visit to St. Denis ought now to have put you in a fit frame of mind for comprehending the meaning of most of these works by the light of the hints already given. I will only therefore call special attention to the beautiful decorative box, containing a book of the Gospels, in French enamel-work and jewellery of the 11th cent., in the last window on the right, before you reach the Rotonde d'Apollon. This valuable book-cover is also from the Abbey Treasury of St. Denis. It exhibits the usual Crucifixion, with the Madonna and St. John, and the adoring angels, together with figures of the symbols of the Evangelists, whose names are here conveniently attached to them. The next case, to the R of this one, also contains *champlevé* enamels of the 12th and 13th cents., all of which should similarly be examined. Note among them, to the extreme R in the case, a very quaint quatrefoil with St. Francis receiving the Stigmata; a subject with which you will already be familiar from Giotto's treatment, and whose adaptation here to a decorative purpose is curious and enlightening. Next to it, L, a Death of the Virgin.

Further on, two delicious little plaques—one, of Abraham and Melchisedech, with St. Luke—(Abraham, as soldier, being attired in the knightly costume of the Bayeux Tapestry); and the other of the Offering of Isaac, with St. Mark; two of a series of the Evangelists with Old Testament subjects. Above these, the Emperor Heraclius killing Chosroes, with cherubim. Still higher, a most exquisite Adoration of the Magi. Also Christ in Glory, in a mandorla, with the symbols of the Evangelists; and two closely similar Crucifixions, with a Madonna and St. John, and adoring angels. Compare these with the similar subject in the first case we visited. This frame also contains three charming saints in Byzantine style, a good St. Matthew, and a little King David holding a psalter. Do not leave one of the objects in this window unidentified and unexamined.

I notice all these decorative treatments here merely in order to suggest to the reader the way in which the knowledge he has gained of the fabric of St. Denis may be utilised to examine works of art from the great Abbey both here and at Cluny. You will find it useful to visit both collections on your return from such a church, in order to mentally replace in their proper surroundings works now divorced from it. Some other good objects from the same Treasury may also be seen at the Bibliothèque Nationale.

VII

THE OUTER RING, ETC.

PARIS, **outside the great Boulevards** comprises by far the larger part of the existing city. Nevertheless, it contains comparatively few objects of historical or artistic importance, being almost entirely modern and merely residential. Walks and drives in this part of Paris are pleasing, of course, as exhibiting the life of the great town, and they embrace many points of passing interest, such as the Trocadéro, the Champs Élysées, the Champ-de-Mars, the Place de l'Étoile, the Arc de Triomphe, the Parc Monceau, the church of the Sacré-Cœur on the height of Montmartre, etc., etc. Most of these the visitor will find out for himself. They do not need any explanation or elucidation.

Among the very few objects of historical interest in this district, I would call special attention to the **Maison de François I**^{er}**,** on the Cours-la-Reine, at the first corner after you pass the Palais de l'Industrie. This beautiful little gem of domestic Renaissance architecture was erected for François Ier at Moret, near Fontainebleau, in 1527, probably as a gift for Diane de Poitiers, the mistress of Henri II, though it is also asserted that the king built it for his sister, Queen Margaret of Navarre. It was taken down in 1826, and rebuilt on the present site. The style recalls that of the Renaissance palaces of Venice. The delicate and beautiful decorative work of the pilasters, etc., and the dainty portrait medallions deserve inspection. Do not miss this charming little building, which should be compared with Jean Goujon's portion of the Louvre, and with the Renaissance remains at the École des Beaux-Arts and elsewhere.

A collection to which a few hours may be devoted, in the same connection, by those who have time, is the **Musée Carnavalet,** which lies, however, *within* the Boulevards. The building is a fine Renaissance mansion, once the residence of Madame de Sévigné. Many of the objects preserved here have a purely sentimental and to say the truth somewhat childish interest, consisting as they do of relics of the Great Revolution or other historical events, which derive whatever value they happen to possess from their sentimental connection only. But some of the objects have real artistic and historical importance ; so have the decorations by Jean Goujon. When you have seen everything else enumerated here, you may give with advantage a Thursday morning to this somewhat scratch collection. The most important objects are those in the garden.

For the Champs Élysées, the Arc de Triomphe, and the other buildings or promenades of wealthy, modern, western Paris, the guidance of Baedeker is amply sufficient.

The buildings already enumerated and the objects noted in them form the most important sights in Paris, and are as many as the tourist is likely to find time for visiting during a stay of some weeks. If, however, he can add a few days to his sojourn, I give briefly some hints as to a list of other objects worthy his notice—taking it for granted, of course, that he will find his way to the Champs Élysées, the Bois de Boulogne, the theatres, etc., by the light of nature, not unaided by Baedeker. Amid the mass of information tendered in the ordinary Guides, the visitor scarcely knows how to distinguish the necessary from the optional. This short list may help him in his selection.

In the old region on the South Side (between the river and Cluny) are two churches worth inspection by the antiquarian : (1) **St. Julien-le-Pauvre**, the former chapel of the old Hôtel Dieu, which here occupied both banks, spreading to the spot now covered by the statue of Charlemagne ; transitional ; 12th cent.; and (2) **St. Séverin**, dedicated to two local Gallic saints, of the same name ; good flamboyant Gothic ; its interesting portal commemorates St. Martin, part of whose famous cloak was kept in a chapel here ; the *façade* was brought from St. Pierre-aux-Bœufs, on the Île de la Cité, demolished in 1837; good modern reliefs on altar represent episodes in the lives of the two saints—St. Séverin the Abbot healing Clovis, and St. Séverin the Hermit ordaining St. Cloud. Altogether, a church to be visited and understood, rich in historic interest.

Among churches of the later period, the **domes** and their development are worthy of study, as illustrating the ideal of the 17th and 18th cents. The earliest was **St. Paul et St. Louis** (originally Jesuit), 1627, with a massive and gaudy Louis XIV doorway; interior, florid and tawdry, after the Jesuit fashion. Next comes the **Sorbonne**, 1635, interesting from its original connection with St. Louis (his confessor, Robert de Sorbon, founded the hostel, of which this is the far later church, for poor theological students); it is the first important dome, and contains an overrated monument to Richelieu by Lebrun, executed by Girardon. If you have plenty of time, you may visit it. Then the **Invalides**, 1705, now containing the tomb of Napoleon. Lastly, the **Panthéon**, already described. If visited in this order, they form an instructive series. Note the gradual increase in classicism, which culminates in the **Madeleine.** The earlier domes resemble those of the Rome of Bernini: the later grow more and more Grecian in their surroundings. The **Institut** (included here for its dome) and **Val-de-Grâce** are sufficiently inspected with a glance in passing.

The churches of the innermost Paris are mostly dedicated to local saints; those of the outer ring of Louis XIV to a somewhat wider circle of Catholic interest; among them, **St. Roch**, the famous plague-saint, deserves a visit; it is rococo and vulgar, but representative. The churches in the outer ring are of still broader dedication, often to newer saints of humanitarian or doctrinal importance. Among these quite modern buildings, **St. Vincent-de-Paul** ranks first, on account of its magnificent frieze by Flandrin, running round the nave, and representing a procession of saints and martyrs, suggested by the mosaics in Sant' Apollinare Nuovo at Ravenna; this the visitor should on no account omit; it lies near the Gare du Nord, and is a good example of the basilica style, successfully adapted to modern needs. Baedeker will here efficiently serve you. But, though artistically fine, Flandrin's frescoes are not nearly so effective as the original mosaics in Theodoric's basilica. The other great modern churches—St. Augustin, St. Ambroise, La Trinité, Notre-Dame-de-Lorette, Ste. Clotilde, etc.—need only be visited by those who have plenty of time, and who take an intelligent interest in contemporary Catholicism. But, if you can manage it, you should certainly mount the hill of **Montmartre**, the most sacred site in Paris, both for the sake of the splendid view, for the memories of St. Denis (the common legend says, beheaded here; a variant asserts, buried for the first time before his translation to the Abbey of St. Denis), and for the interesting modern Byzantine-Romanesque pile of the **Sacré-Cœur** which now approaches completion. Close by is the quaint old church of St. Pierre-de-Montmartre, and behind it a curious belated Calvary.

Those whom this book may have interested in church-lore will find very full details on all these subjects in Miss Beale's "Churches of Paris." Another useful book is Lonergan's "Historic Churches of Paris." With the key I have striven to give, and the aid of these works, the visitor should be able to unlock for himself the secrets of all the churches.

Two pretty little parks which deserve a passing visit are the **Parc Monceau**, near the Ternes, and still more, the **Buttes Chaumont**, in the heart of the poor district of La Villette and Belleville, showing well what can be done by gardening for the beautification of such squalid quarters. The **Jardin d'Acclimatation** in the Bois de Boulogne, and the **Jardin des Plantes**, at the extreme east end of the South Side are both interesting, especially to the zoologist and botanist. The last-named is best reached by a pleasant trip on one of the river steamers.

Of collections, not here noted, the most important is the **Musée Guimet** of Oriental art, near the Trocadéro. It should be visited (if time permits) by all who are interested in Chinese, Japanese, and Indian products. The **Trocadéro** itself contains a good collection of casts, valuable for the study of comparative plastic development; but they can only be used to effect by persons who can afford several days at least to study them (in other words, residents). The Ethnographical Museum in the same building is good, but need only detain those who have special knowledge in the subject.

To know **what to avoid** is almost as important as to know what to visit. Under this category, I may say that no intelligent person need trouble himself about Père-Lachaise and the other cemeteries; the Catacombs; the various Halles or Markets; the interiors of the Conservatoire des Arts et Métiers (except so far as above indicated), the Bourse, the Banque de France, the Bibliothèque Nationale (unless, of course, he is a student and wishes to read there), the Archives, the Imprimerie Nationale, the various Courts and Public Offices, the Gobelins Manufactory, the Sèvres porcelain works, the Institut, the Mint, the Invalides, the Chamber of Deputies, the buildings in the Champ-de-Mars (except while the Salon there is open), the Observatory, and so forth. In Paris proper, I think I have enumerated above almost everything that calls for special notice from any save specialists.

Three **Excursions from Paris** are absolutely indispensable for any one who wishes to gain a clear idea of the France of the Renaissance and the succeeding epoch.

The first, and by far the most important of these, is that to **Fontainebleau**, a visit to which is necessary in order to enable you properly to fill in the mental picture of the change wrought by François Ier and his successors in French art and architecture. It is an inevitable complement to your visits to the Louvre. This excursion, however, should only be made after the visitor has thoroughly seen and digested the Renaissance collections in the Louvre, and the École des Beaux-Arts, as well as the Tombs of the Kings at St. Denis. Baedeker is an amply sufficient guide for this the most interesting and instructive excursion that can be made from Paris. One day suffices for a visit to the Château and a glimpse of the Forest; though a week can be pleasantly spent in this charming region. After your return, you will do well to visit the Renaissance Sculpture at the Louvre again. Many of the works will gain fresh meaning for you after inspection of the surroundings for which they were designed, and the architecture which formed their natural setting.

The second excursion, also valuable from the point of view of the study of the Renaissance, is that to **St. Germain,** where the Château itself, and the exquisite view from the Terrace, are almost equally delightful. Those interested in **prehistoric archæology,** too, should not miss seeing the very valuable collection in the Museum installed in the Château, probably the finest of its sort in the world, and rich in drawings and other remains of the cave-men of the Dordogne.

The third excursion, in every respect less pleasing and instructive, is that to **Versailles.** This must be taken rather as a duty than as a pleasure. Leave it for some enticing day in summer. Neither as regards art or nature can the great cumbrous palace and artificial domain of Louis XIV be compared in beauty to the other two. The building is a cold, formal, unimposing pile, filled with historic pictures of the dullest age, or modern works of often painful mediocrity, whose very mass and monotony makes most of them uninteresting. The grounds and trees have been drilled into ranks with military severity. The very fountains are aggressive. Nevertheless, a visit to the palace and gardens is absolutely necessary in order to enable the visitor to understand the France of the 17th and 18th centuries, with its formal art and its artificial nature. You will there begin more fully to understand the powdered world of the du Barrys and the Pompadours, the alleys and clipped trees of Le Nôtre's gardens, the atmosphere that surrounds the affected pictures of Boucher, Vanloo, and Watteau. Take it in this spirit, and face it manfully. Here, again, the indications in Baedeker are amply sufficient by way of guidance.

When you have seen these three, you need not trouble yourself further with excursions from Paris, unless indeed you have ample time at your disposal and desire country jaunts for the sake of mere outing. But these three you omit at your historical peril.

In conclusion, I would say in all humility, I am only too conscious that I have but scratched in this book the surface of

Paris. Adequately to fill in the outline so sketched, for so great and beautiful a city, so rich in historical and artistic interest, would require a big book—and big books are not easy to carry about with one, sight-seeing. Moreover, I reflect by way of comfort, it is not good for us to be told everything; something must be left for the individual intelligence to have the pleasure of discovering. All I have endeavoured to do here is to *suggest a method*; if I have succeeded in making you take an interest in Mediæval and Renaissance Paris, if I have stimulated in you a desire to learn more about it, I have succeeded in my object. However imperfect this work may be—and nobody can be more conscious of its imperfections than its author—it will be justified if it arouses curiosity and intelligent inspection of works of art or antiquity, in place of mere listless and casual perambulation.

It is common in England to hear superior people sneer at Paris as modern and meretricious. I often wonder whether these people have ever really seen Paris at all—that beautiful, wonderful, deeply interesting Paris, some glimpse of which I have endeavoured to give in this little volume. To such I would say, when you are next at your favourite hotel in the Avenue de l'Opéra, take a few short walks to St. Germain-des-Prés, the Place des Vosges, St. Étienne-du-Mont, St. Eustache, and Cluny, and see whether you will not modify your opinion.

THE END.

INDEX

Ancient Sculpture, 154-168.
Antinous, 163.
Archæology, Prehistoric, 251.
Armour, 46.
Assyrian Antiquities, 189.

Boucher, 111.
Boulevards, The, 197, 198, 208, 209.
Burgundian Art, 175, 177.

Canova, 188.
Carnavalet Museum, 247.
Carpaccio, 148, 149.
Carrousel, Place de, 69.
Caryatides, 167.
Cellini, 174.
Childebert, 65, 178, 213.
Christian Sculpture, Early, 193-196.
Cimabue, 74.
Classical Sculpture, 153-168.
Claude of Lorraine, 108, 110.
Cluniac Priory, 211.
Cluny, The Museum, 37-55.
Colombe, Michel, 179, 225.
Copies, Museum of, 225-229.
Correggio, 85.

Dagobert, Tomb of, 237.
David, 112, 114.
Debrosse, Jacques, 215, 224.
Delacroix, 114.
Delaroche, Paul, 109, 114, 229.
Della Robbia, 48, 170, 171.
Diana of Gabii, The, 162.
Dieulafoy Collection of Persian Antiquities, 190, 191.
Donatello, 169, 170.
Drawings, Collection of, 192.
Dutch School of Painting, The, 104, 105, 114.

Ebony carvings, 53.
École des Beaux-Arts, The, 224-229.
Egyptian Antiquities, 189.

Enamels, 49, 50, 244.
English School of Painting, The, 107.
Etruscan Antiquities, 192.

Faubourg St. Germain, The, 35, 213-229.
Flandrin, Frescoes by, 218-220, 248.
Flemish School of Painting, The, 100-106.
Fontainebleau, 250.
Fontaine des Innocents, 203.
Fontaine St. Sulpice, 223.
Fra Angelico, 78, 150.
Fragonard, 111, 113.
Francois I., Tomb of, 238.
Frédégonde, Tomb of, 238.
French School of Painting, The Early, 99, 100, 108-114.
French School of Painting, The Modern, 107, 114, 115, 223.
French Sculpture, 174-188.
Frescoes, 83, 144, 219.

German School of Painting, The, 106, 107.
German Sculpture, 181.
Ghirlandajo, 81, 151-153.
Giotto, 74.
Goldsmith's Work, 53, 193.
Goujon, Jean, 67, 70, 167, 182-187, 203, 225, 247.
Greek Sculpture, 155-163.
Greuze, 111, 113.
Guimet Museum, 249.

Hermaphrodite, 158, 168.
Holbein, 106, 107.
Hotel de Ville, The, 200.

Île de la Cité, The, 12, 13, 16-30.
Ingres, 84, 114.
Italian Pictures, 74-99.
—— Sculpture, 169-174.
Ivories, 52, 53, 192.

INDEX

Labarum, The, 194.
Lebrun, Madame, 110, 112.
Le Sueur, 109.
Limoges Enamels, 50.
Lionardo, 87, 89, 92.
Louvre, The, 15, 62-196, 242-245.
Luini, 83, 145-148.
Luxembourg Museum, 223.
—— Palace, 215, 224.

Madeleine, The, 209.
Madonnas, 131-143.
Maison de Francois I, 246.
Majolica, 170.
Mantegna, 80, 85, 116-124.
Massone, 124-126.
Médicis, Marie de, 102-104.
Memling, Hans, 84, 85, 101.
Michael Angelo, 172.
Millet, 115.
Mino da Fiesole, 173, 174.
Mithra of the Capitol, The, 166, 167.
Moabite Stone, The, 189.
Mohammedan Potteries, 50.
Montmartre, 249.
Murillo, 89, 98.

Nike of Samothrace, The, 73.
Notre Dame, 22-30.

Opera House, The, 210.

Paintings in the Louvre, 27-153.
Palais Bourbon, The, 216.
—— de Justice, The, 16-18.
—— Royal, The, 199.
Panthéon, The, 56-58.
Persian Antiquities, 191.
—— Pottery, 51.
Perugino, 75.
Phœnician Antiquities, 189.
Pilon, Germain, 18, 44, 183-186, 238, 239.
Place des Victoires, 207.
—— des Vosges, 212.
Pottery, 46-48, 192.
Poussin, N., 108, 110.
Predella, 117.
Primitifs, Salle des, 73-83.
Puvis de Chavannes, 58.

Quai d'Orsay, The, 217.
Quentin Matsys, 101.

Raphael, 85, 88, 95, 126-130, 227.
Reliquaries, 193, 242-245.

Renaissance Paris, 62-71.
—— Sculpture, 168-187.
Rhodian Pottery, 50, 51.
Rive Droite, The, 197-212.
Rive Gauche, The, 34-61.
Roman Paris, 12, 35, 55.
Roman Sculpture, 163-167.
Romanesque Architecture, 215.
Rubens, 102-104, 106.

Sainte Chapelle, The, 19-22.
St. Denis, 13, 14.
—— Abbey of, 230-245.
St. Etienne-du-Mont, 56, 58-60.
St. Eustache, 203-207.
St. Geneviève, 13, 14, 15, 55.
St. Germain, 251.
St. Germain-des-Prés, 213-215, 217-221.
St. Germain l'Auxerrois, 64-66.
St. Gervais, 201-203.
St. Merri, 202.
St. Sulpice, 221-223.
St. Vincent, 213.
St. Vincent de Paul, 248.
Salon Carré, The, 84-90.
Salle Duchâtel, The, 83, 84.
Salle de Pheidias, The, 157.
Sarcophagi, 158, 159, 194.
Sculpture at Cluny, 38-54.
—— in the Louvre, 72, 73, 153-188.
Sorbonne, The, 248.
Spanish School of Painting, The, 97, 98.
Spanish Carving, 40.
Sposalizio, 227.

Tanagra Figures, 192.
Tapestry, 40, 42, 44, 48.
Thermes, The, 12, 35, 55.
Titian, 92, 93.
Trocadéro, The, 249.
Troyon, 115.
Tuileries, The, 199.

Van Dyck, 105.
Van Eyck, 87.
Vases, Greek, 192.
Vendôme Column, The, 210.
Venus of Arles, The, 161.
Venus of Milo, The, 159, 160.
Veronese, 86, 90.
Versailles, 251.

Watteau, 111, 113.

www.ingramcontent.com/pod-product-compliance
Lightning Source LLC
Chambersburg PA
CBHW021408230426
43666CB00006B/676